Being Alive

Anne Alvarez is an enormously influential psychoanalytic psychotherapist whose work on autism and severe personality disorders in children has been important internationally. Her book *Live Company* has been a source of inspiration over the years both for colleagues and generations of students. Her work is celebrated here by a group of distinguished psychoanalytic practitioners from around the world.

Being Alive brings together assessment of Alvarez's work and evaluation of how her seminal ideas have influenced contemporary thinking and practice. Working from her experience with autistic, borderline and deprived children, she has been a bridge between schools of thought and academic disciplines. These chapters illustrate with both theoretical debate and clinical examples how each individual has been able to build on or connect up with her ideas to enrich their own work. It includes chapters linking different lines of thinking within psychoanalysis, demonstrating too how converging ideas from other disciplines such as neurobiology have borne out Alvarez's changes of technique in the consulting room. We live in exciting times, as is seen more and more in terms of cutting-edge research on the brain and in the way such research develops how the psychological affects the physical and how difficulties encountered early in life are addressed in an approach, advocated by Alvarez, which combines both a psychoanalytic and a developmental view.

This book will be of great interest to child and adolescent psychotherapists in training and practice, and also to clinical psychologists, psychoanalysts and psychiatrists working with autistic/severely disturbed children.

Judith Edwards is a consultant child and adolescent psychotherapist at the Tavistock Clinic, and until 1999 was joint editor of the *Journal of Child Psychotherapy*.

Photograph by Al Alvarez

Being Alive

Building on the work of Anne Alvarez

Collected and edited by
Judith Edwards

First published 2001 by Brunner-Routledge
27 Church Road, Hove, East Sussex BN3 2FA

Simultaneously published in the USA and Canada
by Taylor & Francis Inc
29, West 35th Street, New York, N.Y. 10001

Brunner-Routledge is an imprint of the Taylor & Francis Group

© 2001 Judith Edwards

Typeset in Times by DP Photosetting, Aylesbury, Bucks
Printed and bound in Great Britain by TJ International, Padstow, Cornwall

British Library Cataloguing in Publication Data
A catalogue record for this book is available from the British Library

Library of Congress Cataloging in Publication Data
Being alive : building on the work of Anne Alvarez / [edited by] Judith Edwards.
    p. cm.
    "List of publications by Anne Alvarez": p.
    Includes bibliographical references (p.) and index.
    ISBN 1-58391-130-8 – ISBN 1-58391-131-6 (pbk.)
    1. Child analysis.   2. Developmental psychology.   3. Alvarez, Anne, 1936–.
4. Alvarez, Anne, 1936—Bibliography.   5. Autistic children.   6. Borderline personality
disorder in children.   I. Alvarez, Anne, 1936–.   II. Edwards, Judith, 1944–.

RJ504.2 .B44 2001
618.92′8917—dc21
                                                  2001035707

And yet the books will be there on the shelves, separate beings
That appeared once, still wet
As shining chestnuts under a tree in autumn...

So much more durable
Than we are, whose frail warmth
Cools down with memory, disperses, perishes...
Yet the books will be there on the shelves, well born,
Derived from people, but also from radiance, heights...

Czeslaw Milosz, *Collected Works*
(Reproduced by kind permission of Penguin Books)

Contents

PART II
Mainly clinical

Notes on contributors

Neil Altman (USA) is co-chairperson of the Relational Orientation Post-doctoral Program in Psychotherapy and Psychoanalysis at New York University, and co-editor of *Psychoanalytic Dialogues: A Journal of Relational Perspectives*. He is faculty and supervisor in the child analytic training program at the National Institute for Psychotherapies, and supervisor in the child analytic training program at the William Alanson White Institute.

Peter Blake (Australia) is a senior clinical psychologist and a Tavistock-trained child psychotherapist. Over the last thirty years he has worked in child and family teams in community health centres in England and Australia. He is the Foundation President of the Child Psychoanalytic Foundation, which is a charity based in Sydney, Australia. He is course director of the Sydney Observation Course and the Sydney child psychotherapy training, which is linked to the Tavistock Clinic. He is editor of the *Child Psychoanalytic Gazette,* has lectured in a number of Australian universities and is currently an honorary lecturer at the University of Wollongong. He is now in private practice in Sydney.

Judith Edwards (Great Britain) is a Consultant Child and Adolescent Psychotherapist who has recently completed a four-year term as joint editor of the *Journal of Child Psychotherapy*. She is an academic tutor on the child psychotherapy training at the Tavistock Clinic, and she also teaches child development research both at the Clinic and in Bristol. Her current clinical base is at a family consultation centre. Recent publications, apart from those in academic journals, include chapters on autism and on international developments in the *Handbook of Child Psychotherapy: Psychoanalytic Approaches* (eds Horne and Lanyado, Routledge 1999) and in *Autism and Personality* (Alvarez and Reid, Routledge 1999).

Elsa First is an associate in Clinical psychiatry and core faculty member of the Columbia University Psychoanalytic Center's Parent/Infant Psychotherapy Program, and is an Adjunct Clinical Associate Professor of

Psychology and a supervisor in the New York University Post-Doctoral Program in Psychoanalysis and Psychotherapy. She trained in child psychoanalysis at the Anna Freund Centre, and is a training and supervising analyst in the New York Freudian Society, and a member of the IPA. As a psychoanalyst and psychotherapist in private practice she works with children, adolescents and adults, and with infants and parents. Publications include "The Leaving Game or: I'll Play You and You Play Me: The Emergence of the Capacity for Dramatic Role Play in Two-Year-Olds" in *Children At Play: Clinical and Developmental Approaches to Symbolic Play*. A. Slade and D. Wolf, Eds. New York: Oxford University Press, 1994. Current interests include the teaching of infant observation and study of the intergenerational transmission of trauma.

Peter Fonagy (Great Britain) is Freud Memorial Professor of Psychoanalysis and Director of the Sub-Department of Clinical Health Psychology at University College London, and also Director of Research at the Anna Freud Centre, London. He is Director of the Menninger Clinical Outcomes Research and Effectiveness Centre and the Child and Family Centre, both at the Menninger Foundation, Kansas. He is a clinical psychologist and a training and supervising analyst at the British Psychoanalytical Society in child and adult analysis, and his psychoanalytic interests centre round issues of borderline psychopathology and early attachment relationships. He is on the editorial board of a number of major journals, and is widely published himself, being particularly interested in outcome research and the impact on personality development of the early parent–child relationship.

Maria Teresa Gallo (Italy) is a consultant professor at the University of Turin, in the Faculty of Medicine and Surgery (School of Specialisation in Child Neuropsychiatry) where she teaches on a course on the issues involved when working with abused and maltreated children. She also works with the Turin Law Courts in investigative work with abused children. She is a psychoanalytic child psychotherapist also running seminars on Infant Observation and Young Child Observation at the ASARNIA (Turin) and ASNEA (Milan) schools of child psychoanalytic psychotherapy. She taught child development research as part of a Masters course at the University of East London, and also on the MA Psychoanalytic Observational Studies franchise to AIPPI in Milan. Her area of special scientific interest is work with under-five children and also older children who have been severely abused and deprived.

Victoria Hamilton (USA) studied art and philosophy before undertaking clinical training at the Tavistock Clinic and postgraduate study at the Psychoanalysis Unit of the University of London. Dr Hamilton is now a supervisor and training analyst at the Institute of Contemporary Psychoanalysis in Los Angeles where she practises with both adults and children. She is the author of *Narcissus and Oedipus* (1982) and *The Analyst's Preconscious* (1996).

Didier Houzel (France) is Professor of Child and Adolescent Psychiatry at the University of Caen (Normandy, France). He is a full member of the International Psychoanalytic Association and member of the Association Psychanalytique de France. His work focuses mainly on the psychoanalytic treatment of autistic and psychotic children, and he was supervised in this field by Donald Meltzer and Frances Tustin. He is joint editor, with Claudine Geissman, of the *Journal de la psychanalyse de l'enfant*.

Trudy Klauber (Great Britain) is a Consultant Child and Adolescent Psychotherapist at the Tavistock Clinic, where she is Organising Tutor of the MA in Psychoanalytic Observational Studies. She lectures and teaches in Europe and the USA, and is particularly interested in the significance of trauma in work with extremely disturbed children and with parents. She has recently been guest editor of *The International Journal of Infant Observation* and has contributed chapters to several books, including *Autism and Personality* (eds Alvarez and Reid, Routledge 1999). She is at present working on a book on Asperger's Syndrome as co-editor with Maria Rhode.

Bianca Lechevalier-Haïm (France) is an adult and child psychoanalyst, training analyst of the Paris Psychoanalytical Society (SPP) and medical director of the University Child Guidance Clinic in Caen, France. She is Assistant Lecturer in Clinical Psychology at the University of Caen, and since 1965 she has been treating autistic children psychoanalytically. She has published work on childhood autism, on counter-transference, and on the consequences for future generations of the Shoah. In collaboration with her husband, a neurologist, she has published *Le Corps et Le Sens: Dialogue entre une psychoanalyste et un neurologue* [*Body and Meaning: Dialogue between a psychoanalyst and a neurologist*], (Lausanne, Delachaux et Niestle).

Suzanne Maiello (Italy) is in psychoanalytic practice with children and adults in Rome. She is a founder member and past president of AIPPI (Italian Association of Psychoanalytic Child Psychotherapy), and past organising tutor of AIPPI Tavistock-model training courses in Italy. Recipient of the first Frances Tustin Memorial Prize in 1997 at the Psychoanalytic Center of California in Los Angeles, she is the author of publications in European and American psychoanalytical books and journals. Her special field of interest is that of primitive mental states (prenatal proto-mental activity, prenatal auditory memory and the constitution of an early "sound-object"), prenatal or perinatal trauma and its relation to psychopathology.

Gabriella Pansini (Italy) was born in southern Italy and graduated from the University of Lecce in modern literature in 1967, then taking a subsequent psychology degree with a diploma of specialisation in clinical psychology, being taught by Jean Piaget. After living in Geneva and Santiago in Chile she returned to Turin in 1982, subsequently training as a child and adolescent psychotherapist with Anne Alvarez as her tutor and teacher.

Maria Rhode (Great Britain) is Consultant Child Psychotherapist in the Children and Families Department of the Tavistock Clinic, and a tutor on child psychotherapy training. She has contributed papers and book chapters on autism and infant observation, and is co-editor (with A. Dubinsky, H. Dubinsky and Rustin) of *Psychotic States in Children* (London, Duckworth, 1997). She is currently co-editing a book with Trudy Klauber on interdisciplinary approaches to Asperger's Syndrome.

Anne-Marie Sandler (Great Britain) was born in Geneva, studied with Jean Piaget, and was for a time his assistant. She came to England and trained in child analysis with Anna Freud, going on to complete the adult training in the British Psychoanalytical Society, where she is a training and supervising analyst. She has been President of the British Society and of the European Psychoanalytical Federation, and Vice-President of the International Psychoanalytical Association. She was formerly Director of the Anna Freud Centre. Many of her published papers were written in collaboration with her late husband, Joseph Sandler. They also collaborated on a book, *Internal Objects Revisited* (1998).

Allan N. Schore (USA) is Assistant Clinical Professor of Psychiatry and Biobehavioural Sciences, University of California at Los Angeles Medical School, and is on the teaching faculties of the Institute of Contemporary Psychoanalysis and the Southern California Psychoanalytic Institutes. He is the author of *Affect Regulation and the Origin of the Self: The Neurobiology of Emotional Development*, as well as numerous articles and chapters in various disciplines. He is on the editorial board of *Neuro-Psychoanalysis*, Special Editor of the *Infant Mental Health Journal*, and has written the Foreword to the reissue of John Bowlby's volume *Attachment*.

Foreword

Victoria Hamilton

This piece first appeared as an extensive review article in the *Journal of Child Psychotherapy* (1994, Vol. 20 No. 1). *Live Company* (London, Routledge, 1992) represents the culmination of long experience of working with the most disturbed children and of thinking about modifications and extensions of, and new thinking about, existing psychoanalytic theory to address their condition. All the ideas taken up in subsequent chapters of this book are elaborated here, and it seems there could be no more fitting way to begin this collection, which honours the work of Anne Alvarez and her contribution to the thinking and practice of psychoanalytic psychotherapy.

Live Company is a beautifully written, carefully documented exposition of 30 years' intensive psychoanalytic work by a highly accomplished child psychotherapist. In a modest way, sparing the reader none of the horror, disbelief and boredom of this work, Alvarez describes her heroic efforts to reclaim "greennesse" in the "shrivelled hearts" of hopeless children, children who to all intents and purposes had become dead to the world. Some are autistic, others live on the tenuous border between sanity and madness; some have grown up in nice, caring households, others have suffered gross injustices and indignities through abuse and deprivation.There are 16 chapters, which take us through the ups and downs of treatment, charting the progress and regress of her patients, as well as the pathways and blind alleys of Alvarez's personal analytic development. With unusual candour Alvarez tells us about the psychoanalytic concepts which have helped, as well as those which may have hindered, her understanding. Where the language of psychoanalysis falls short, Alvarez turns to literature and to developmental psychology. For the psychoanalytic reader who enjoys the wider culture, the book is unusually imaginative as well as informative. From the first chapter, the long fall, to the final chapter on the use of counter transference in relation to the rites and rituals of autism, we follow Alvarez's work with Robbie, an autistic boy who started treatment at age four and is now an adult of 30. Robbie, like many of the children described, experienced the beginning of life as a long fall into nothingness. From this vegetative wasteland, Alvarez reclaims his attention, helping Robbie to become vertebrate so that he can use his atrophied muscles and bones to stand up and support a body capable of housing a mind. For without a home in the body the mind has no place in which to grow, and without the mind there is no place in which thoughts can be thought. Richard Wollheim, expanding on Freud's statement that the ego is first of all a bodily ego, observes that "it is not merely that we are at home in our body: we are at home in our mind somewhat as in a body".

The mindless children described by Alvarez haunt this world in bodies which feel like sieves, full of holes where nothing holds. Like ghosts, they pass heedlessly through time and space. In place of another human being, for instance, Robbie related to a net with a hole in it. Alvarez's quest was to "become dense enough, substantial enough, condensed enough to provide him with something, or someone who could concentrate his mind". Having fallen into nowhere, where there is nobody, "it is as though there is nothing left on which to leave a trace, no imagined listener". Quoting Kundera, Alvarez describes the hollow feelings in the body, the emptiness in the eyes, which come "from the unbearable absence of weight". Robbie first said "Hello" to Alvarez when he was thirteen, on the last session before a break; he looked at her as if he recognised an old friend he had not seen for ten years. As he looked across at her, his dead gaze was gone. A little while later, on return from a break, Robbie was able to say that he had arrived "A bit too early", no one was ready to receive him; this comment reveals some sense of time.

The focus on it or body *experience* reminds me of the work of Marion Milner, one of the few child and adult analysts who has written extensively on the 'concentration of the body' and of the lively as opposed to deadly associations between weight, falling and blackness. Milner's technique seems closer to that of Alvarez than some of the Bionian authors cited whose focus could be described as purely mental. Bion, like Freud, was concerned with the development of thinking and with the precursors of mental life. Based on their understanding of the non-symbolic, concrete nature of psychotic thinking, both Freudian and Kleinian psychoanalysts have tended to conceptualise mental processes as separate from bodily experience. Here, perhaps, there is a difference between child and adult analysts in that child analysts cannot get away from bodies. It is notable that, with the exception of Bion, the psychoanalytic authors most frequently quoted by Alvarez are child analysts – Joseph, Meltzer, O'Shaughnessy, Tustin and Winnicott.

Alvarez seems reticent to acknowledge the originality of her contribution to the psychoanalytic understanding of human development and disturbance, declaring a mere extension of established psychoanalytic concepts when, in many cases, a complete reversal of perspective is demanded. In the spirit of the ethologist Niko Tinbergen, Alvarez starts off by reminding us that sanity is fragile and that madness, once known, can exert a lethal seductive power. Tinbergen (1952) describes survival as a "multi-dimensional tightrope act", noting that it does not occur to the healthy and happy person that there are infinitely more ways in which he could have failed than the narrow road to success. *Live Company* is packed full of new insights and turns of thought, making it hard to select those which might have had most impact on our thinking. I shall focus on four areas: neutrality and reclamation, learning, theory of defence and identification.

Neutrality and reclamation

Alvarez stresses the therapist's capacity to be active to the extent of expressing alarm, gravity and delight in place of neutrality, adaptation and containment. Here is one of Alvarez's most original contributions: the concept of "reclamation". This concept not only introduces notions of the therapist's vitality and activity, it also articulates an essential counterpart (countertransference role) to the autistic individual's inability to reach out and grasp. When a normal baby reaches out and grasps, he expresses urges towards other people and objects. As Frances Tustin has observed, autistic children rarely suck their thumbs: bringing the thumb to the mouth involves crossing space which takes time. Autistic children have no concept of space or time. The therapist who reclaims must first claim the subject's attention; through her sense of urgency, the therapist hopes to resuscitate an urge toward something live in place of the familiar spineless abandonment to nothingness. She must alert the child to the gravity of the situation. Alvarez notes the important moments in therapy when an autistic child starts to use handles: "it seems that they have finally got both an object they can conceive of as graspable and holdable and a self that feels able to reach and grasp (p. 124).

Alvarez talks about "autistic laziness" and the atrophy and flabbiness of limbs which result from years of disuse. Robbie's hands had hardly any knuckles. Unlike ordinary children, Robbie had no concept of "trying" (p. 40). This of course was a great impediment to learning. In his late twenties, Robbie expressed great sadness and regret over the childhood he had missed – "I want to grow down, begin again . . . I want to play with bricks and build a house. I want to collect chestnuts and conkers, and have a doll . . . I want to go to the adventure playground and climb things. Climb them to the top. I want to kick a ball" (pp. 48–9). Alvarez tells us of the momentous achievement when Sally, a ten-year-old autistic girl, exclaimed, "One can jump up. I have got arms. Luckily I do." Later in the session, following some pretend play, Sally commented, "But what is real is I have arms" (p. 134) . Alvarez observes that Sally had discovered she had arms which could hold on to the therapist's attention.

The concept of reclamation as a vital, countertransference response to wasting (of time, body and mind) expands the psychoanalytic theory of countertransference. At the end of the book, looking back on her career,

Alvarez judges her early responses to have been too passive and too per-missive. She allowed the psychotic children to perseverate to no good end. Thirty years ago (when Alvarez trained), in contrast to the views on coun-tertransference of Michael Balint, Paula Heimann and Donald Winnicott, most Kleinians followed Melanie Klein in her negative view of counter-transference phenomena. Alvarez tells us how contemporary Kleinian approaches to countertransference, notably those of Betty Joseph and Frances Tustin, freed her to listen to her feelings of profound boredom, distaste and horror as *appropriate* responses to the children's lack of any sense of boredom and urgency.

Learning

Alvarez reverses the traditional psychoanalytic approach to learning. Since Freud's first observations of the play of an eighteen-month-old boy with a cotton reel, the psychoanalytic theory of learning has emphasised experiences of loss and separateness. Alvarez, like Bowlby and the attachment theorists, reminds us that as much can be learned about a child's internal world from experiences of reunion and proximity as from separation and absence. Indeed, Bowlby observed that reunion behaviours hold the key to under-standing of patterns of attachment. How the child greets his mother tells us about the figure the child has held within during the separation. Alvarez uses Frances Tustin's term "rhythm of safety" to capture the "lifelong rhythm of gain, loss, gain, loss, reunion, parting, reunion, parting which is what human relationships and human life are about" (p. 129). Stressing the importance of a secure base or "background of safety" (Sandler, 1959), Alvarez opens our minds to envisage a child who is "freed" rather than "driven" to learn. Alvarez points out the obvious: most children have a love of hide and seek. The joy they express both at finding and being found is related to the pleasure they feel at discovering a person who wants them and wants to find them. For children emerging from nowhere, interpretations of "foundness" are as important as those of "lostness".

Defences

Alongside the mechanisms of defence which permit adaptation to reality, Alvarez places experiences of *overcoming* states of fear, isolation and per-secution. By focusing on the importance of "overcoming" – the active counterpart to the therapist's reclaiming – Alvarez challenges us to recon-sider the concept of defence. Overcoming, like reclaiming, emphasises the role of will in health and therapy. It makes us consider what lies on the other side of defence, in the future, as much as the past situations defended against. How does a hollow man experience substance? Here, Alvarez lifts us out of our customary psychoanalytic morality and asks us to imagine the very first glimmers, twinges, sensations of becoming alive. This imaginative exercise, based on Alvarez's "supervision of her own autistic laziness of mind", opens up interesting perspectives on manic-depressive, narcissistic and idealising defences, as well as on reparation and forgetting. All these concepts have accrued moralistic meanings: for instance, in Klein's view, depressive states are good, whereas manic ones are bad. Klein also described good and bad reparations, and analysts of all orientations uphold the virtues of remembering over those of forgetting. Alvarez's novel approaches to defence are described in the following three subsections.

Manic-depressive states, narcissism and idealisation

Instead of glorifying at the depressive pole of manic depressive states, the reader is asked to consider the therapeutic and developmental value of states of excitement, idealisation and even triumph. Alvarez alerts us to the dangers of the over use of Klein's concept of "depressive position" as a prescription for living. The depressive position suggests "sobriety, freedom from the illusion and grandiosity (p. 129). But, for patients who have sunk into deep despair and who may be beginning to move towards hope and lightheartedness, states of illusion and grandiosity may be crucial. Take the term "omnipotence": clearly, the qualifier "omnipotent" has derogatory connotations and can be extremely deflating to someone who is struggling with feelings of uselessness and hopelessness. Alvarez makes us think: well, how does a very weak person overcome apathy? Surely, he has to imagine himself as potent in order to initiate action. Lacking any experience of potency, he will most likely imagine himself as omnipotent; that is, much more potent than he actually is. Relief, joy and hope may seem to the observer to amount to little more than "manic denial", but to the experiencing subject such states feel critical to overcoming or overturning the familiar pull towards death and despair. How often have therapists looked at bursts of happiness and glimpses of ecstasy as idealised states, defensive against depression. By interpreting the underlying depression which the elation "masks", the therapist may miss a vital turning point – vital in the sense of a brief glimmer of hope which might offer the alerted therapist a golden opportunity for reclamation. Thus, instead of looking for what the mask hides, Alvarez suggests that masks are not just disguises but "experiments with, attempts to try on, a new identity" (p. 179). Identifications can be "borrowed", not just stolen (p. 178). Alvarez (p. 183) quotes Goethe:

> So let me be seen, until I am
> Strip not my white robe from me.

Alvarez points out that an interpretation of defensive idealisation implies "a wish for a state which is unattainable", instead of the fact that the patient has just had or found in the present a surprisingly good experience. Alvarez makes us think of the tense in which we formulate an interpretation. Interpretations which emphasise the past or the future can move the patient away from present experience and may even make the patient feel kicked out of the new home in his therapist's mind that he has only just found (p. 124). Alvarez gives two moving clinical examples of two twelve-year-old boys, Ricky and Andrew, both of whom drew large, spacious and grand cars following upon breaks and disruptions of the sessions. Ricky drew an enormous car with "everything you could wish for in it, a swimming pool, television, a telephone so you could phone someone. Also a bath, a fridge, food and a bed. Imagine having something like that all to yourself" (p. 122). Andrew first drew, as if from the back seat, a comfortable, spacious car with a sun roof, lights and steering wheel; he then drew a Rolls-Royce, drawn this time as if from the outside. Ricky's therapist interpreted the defensive aspect of his drawing of the ideal car, whereupon Ricky seemed to deflate and to turn away to thoughts of a boyfriend who had been kicked out by his aunt. He remained deflated for the rest of the session. In contrast, Andrew's therapist commented on Andrew's state of well being over being understood by her, adding that he was "feeling great like a Rolls Royce".

Alvarez' command of language, of grammar, cannot be separated from her therapeutic skills. It is not as if language can be prised apart from reality so that we can dismiss the way a therapist writes as mere style or literary device. Alvarez is alert to a patient's use of parts of speech, noting, for example, the crucial developmental step in Robbie's sense of self when he began to use verbs. Many therapists write in the passive voice, as if downplaying their own activities. Alvarez's concept of reclamation reflects her concentration on signs of alertness, vitality and activity. As well as noting the ways in which a therapist can deny present experience, Alvarez discusses the psychological development embedded in a person's use of the future and subjunctive tense. Most disturbed children, psychotic, borderline or deprived, lack any sense of the future and, therefore, of hope – of what will or may be. Grandiose boastful fantasies, even lies, can contain dreams of future powers; depending on the therapist's interpretations, these gross "illusions' can be transformed into thoughts such as "I wish" or "I hope that I can". In relation to Andrew's drawing of the Rolls-Royce discussed above, Alvarez notes the difference between two wordings, one in which the therapist interprets "You feel I *should* have" ... and "You wish I *would* have..." The second formulation suggests the need instead of a demand and is therefore less deflating and moralistic.

Reparation: good and bad

Alvarez's vigilant attention to signs of life leads to new thoughts on Melanie Klein's concept of reparation. As with idealisation, splitting and protective identification, there is a good – and bad – dimension to many of Klein's concepts. Klein distinguished between true and false reparation. True reparation was based on love and respect for the "object" close (in the depressive position), whereas false reparation was motivated by manic and obsessive defences (in the paranoid-schizoid position). Alvarez, however, finds that wishes "to be pleasing" or "to give pleasure", even when motivated by paranoid fears of persecution, carry great meaning for deprived and borderline children. From such "narcissistic" wishes to give pleasure, genuine care for the object can develop. Alvarez emphasises the importance of the conditions of the *object* for the child's belief reparability. How receptive is the object to the child's reparative impulses? She notes the important finding from infancy research in which the baby's smile can effect a cure for the mother's depression. What happens when the child's or patient's attempts to please misfire and produce an avoidance response in the mother or therapist?

Alvarez discusses Klein's use of the defence "devaluation" – for instance, when a child disparages or expresses contempt for the therapist. Deprived and chronically depressed children may not devalue something once prized, since they lack the capacity to value or feel valued in the first place. Alvarez illustrates this point by describing a very deprived little boy who, identified with an ugly slimy slug, drawled and dribbled and dressed very untidily. When his therapist finally understood and interpreted that he felt *she* felt he was ugly, he was tremendously relieved. He "began to talk about a snail whose little house had magnetic powers which enabled it to attract the therapist to him". With the new thought that someone might value him, the devaluation stopped. But note that he felt that he had to take on magnetic powers (omnipotent, illusory?) to attract someone.

Forgetting

In her chapter on child sexual abuse, Alvarez discusses healthy forgetting as a form of survival. For Alvarez, forgetting can be one way of overcoming the tyranny of the past. Analysts working with trauma survivors have made similar observations. They note not only the "magnetic" power of the past and its constant intrusion into the present, but also the way in which "*future* events are drawn *back* and absorbed into the single trauma long after it occurred" (Yorke, 1986: 234). In their paper on post-traumatic memory as "pathway" and "obstacle" to recovery, Auerhahn and Laub (1984) describe the way that concentration-camp survivors are "burdened" by memories. Recovery is intertwined with being able to forget. Here, Alvarez draws our attention to the wisdom of forgetting and again reverses the tendency among psychoanalysts to equate forgetting with repression, denial and neurotic outcome. Analysts such as Bowlby and Emmanuel Peterfreund, who are familiar with a cybernetic approach to learning and cognition, have viewed defence and memory in a non-linear, systemic way. In the years when John

Bowlby's teaching formed part of the child psychotherapy training at the Tavistock Clinic, he stressed the importance of looking at what the child or infant was turning *towards* when he turned away from his mother. Bowlby (1980) described defence as "*selective exclusion*" and substituted the term "*redirected*" for what has traditionally been referred to as "displacement". It was a great step when Robbie came to learn that he *could* forget – that is, "when he *wanted* to and when he decided something else was well worth putting there" (p. 210). Alvarez discusses the ways in which the attention of traumatised children needs to be "redirected" so that development can take place. "Concentration on a thought, a task, a subject requires the focusing of attention, but it also requires the capacity to ignore other thoughts, tasks and subjects, the capacity to put aside those others" (p. 160). Alvarez gives a poignant example of a latency boy who had been anally penetrated regularly at the age of two. One day in treatment, he tried to tell his therapist about a bun but to his distress the word "bum" kept slipping out. Alvarez looks at this moment not in terms of how the word "bun" masked the latent truer meaning of "bum" but in terms of the struggle between the boy's attempt to forget about the abuse and his exclusive focus upon it. Alvarez, like Sinason, suggests that the "unmasking" trend in psychoanalysis may have little to offer the abused child (Sinason, 1988). These children are flowers "that have to be opened too soon". In working with such children, "it is usually they who succeed in unmasking the workers. Their rescuers often have little to teach them about human evil, selfishness, greed and lust. Their task is somewhat different" (p. 153).

Identification

Alvarez's thoughts on the process of identification are a *tour de force* and bring psychoanalytic thinking on identification much closer to the views of contemporary philosophers as well as developmental psychologists. The philosopher Donald Davidson and the infant researcher Colwyn Trevarthen have both described the ways in which we arrive at self-knowledge. Human beings are interpreters who come to understand their own mental states through their ability to interpret the states of others. Wollheim, commenting on Freud's study of Leonardo in which Freud linked Leonardo's homosexuality with his identification with his mother, states: "In identifying himself with his mother, Leonardo imagines himself doing this or that, but what he imagines himself doing is determined not by his knowledge of himself, but by his knowledge of her" (Wollheim, 1974: 75). In other words, imagination is not a result of projective identification but rather the accompaniment or precursor of introjective identification. These few points are amply illustrated in Alvarez's book. For instance, before Robbie "becomes vertebrate" when he was 21, he looked at Alvarez, and on being questioned as to what he had seen, replied, "You-looking-straight and stiff".

He said this gently, admiringly and without fear. A few days later, he told her, "I've been to the Natural History Museum and I have bones and muscle and they are how I move" (p. 47). In Chapter 6, entitled "Making the thought thinkable", Alvarez discusses introjection and projection as this has been incorporated into the alimentary-digestive model of the development of the mind. Alvarez points to the other modalities in which experience is assimilated – visual, tactile, auditory as well as the important dimensions of "perspective, proximity, graspability and accessibility" (p. 79). She observes, "The fact, for example, that an experience can be assimilated only when it is located in someone else *may have more to do with questions of perspective, than with questions of projection.* Such locating may actually involve the *beginnings of an introjective process rather than a projective one*" (p. 79). Quoting Trevarthen's views on the "first identification of live company", Alvarez discusses the autistic child's preoccupation with inanimate objects, linking this to the lack of "vitality affects" in the mother. Mothers who are chronically depressed or absent-minded are unlikely to interact in what Trevarthen has called "motherese" – the musical, rhythmic, harmonic, surging, flowing conversation-like exchanges of early infancy. Harriet, a withdrawn adolescent in treatment with Alvarez, "began to say with surprise that it was odd that someone else often had to feel things for her first, before she could feel them for herself". Alvarez comments that she did not believe that Harriet was using other people as vehicles for ridding herself of unwanted parts of herself. Rather, "she was using them as places for the exploration of whether or not it was safe to have feelingful states of mind at all" (p. 88).

Live Company is a book which child and adult psychoanalysts will treasure. Its only shortcoming results from the author's tendency to tie her own explorations too closely to pre-existing theory. The thrust of Alvarez's book is not only to present new findings and ideas, but to disentangle us from the normative concepts – the good/bad, true/false dichotomies – which limit the thinking and observations of the psychoanalyst. Alvarez does much to *reclaim* the side of life we therapists tend to overlook.

References

Auerhahn, N. and Laub, D. (1984) "Annihilation and Restoration: Post-traumatic memory as pathway and obstacle to recovery". *International Review of Psycho-Analysis*, 11, 327.

Bowlby, J. (1980) *Loss, Sadness and Depression*, Volume 3 of *Attachment and Loss*, London: Hogarth.

Sandler, J. (1959) "The background of safety". In *From Safety to Superego*, London: Karnac.

Sinason, V. (1988) "Smiling, swallowing, sickening and stupefying: the effect of abuse on the child", *Psychoanalytic Psychotherapy,* 3, 2.

Tinbergen, N. (1952) "Ethology". In *The Animal and Its World: Explorations of an Ethologist*, London: Allen & Unwin.

Trevarthen, C. (1978) "Modes of perceiving and codes of acting". In J.H. Pick (ed.) *Psychological Modes of Perceiving and Processing Information*, Hillsdale, N.J.: Erlbaum.

Wollheim, R. (1969) "The mind and the mind's image of itself". *International Journal of Psycho-Analysis*, 50, 209.

Wollheim, R. (1974) "Imagination and identification". In *On Art and the Mind*, Cambridge, Mass.: Harvard University Press.

Yorke, C. (1986) "Reflections on the problem of psychic trauma'. *Psychoanalytic Study of the Child*, 41, 221.

Acknowledgements

The editor would like to thank all the contributors to this book for their enthusiasm and energy in offering their work, and particularly Victoria Hamilton for her early encouragement. Thanks too to Kate Hawes and her colleagues at Routledge/Taylor & Francis for their support and help throughout the project. Thanks to my husband Andrew Baldwin for his tolerance, and for his technological skills which were fortunately rather in advance of my own.

Introduction

It has been a pleasure and a privilege to collect together the chapters which make up this appreciation of the work of Anne Alvarez. I, like so many others in this volume, have been enriched by her clear thinking, her clinical work and her warm friendship, and it is my hope that this international Festschrift will not only be read by those to whom her work is already familiar, but will enable those interested in this field and perhaps taking their first steps along the road towards clinical training to find ideas which will enliven their progress, much in the way that she herself has enlivened the struggles in training of generations of students. Always forthright, often controversial, never dull, possessing a mind large enough to encompass paradox, Alvarez has an assured place in the history of developing ideas about the creation and evolution of minds.

At the beginning of Part I, the opening chapter by Neil Altman from New York, "Bridging the Atlantic for Psychoanalysis", locates Anne Alvarez firmly in the role in which she has commanded so much respect over the years. He describes her as "both a solid member of the Kleinian community, and among the most creative of border-crossers", and in this chapter he focuses on two specific areas out of many in Alvarez's thinking where she has offered a unique and original contribution to psychoanalytic thinking both about theory and about technique: the analyst's use of self and the developmentally progressive as opposed to the destructive view of narcissism. The author sees this split as being crystallised in differences in points of view between Kernberg and Kohut. What he describes as Alvarez's "characteristic complex-mindedness" offers an integrated view, through careful and precise attention to both simultaneous and differential functions of narcissism and idealisation as they unfold in the consulting room.

There follow two chapters by contemporary Freudians, which emphasise the increasing convergence between notions of psychic change and the internal world in Freudian and Kleinian perspectives. In "Changing Ideas of Change: The Dual Components of Therapeutic Action", Professor Peter Fonagy from London notes the key contribution made by Alvarez in the understanding of change as a matter of process rather than of remembering, and the expansion of both theory and technique which has ensued. His view is that "psychoanalysts should eschew the archaeological metaphor", and he draws on the most recent research into declarative and procedural memory in order to illuminate the contemporary debate where "unmasking" has been replaced by the notion of "unfolding", and deeper meanings may emerge from material that is in fact already conscious. As he notes, there has been a modification of deeply held theoretical views in the movement towards an interpersonal perspective.

In her chapter "A Contribution to a Technical Frame of Reference", Anne-Marie Sandler from London quotes her late husband's description of what he called "the happy co-existence" of contradictory psychoanalytic theories in the analyst's unconscious, which can only emerge when they can be framed in what he termed "a psychoanalytically socially acceptable way". She takes up the debate presented in the previous chapter by Fonagy, and offers a careful delineation of different theories of the unconscious, revisiting Freud's topographical model to retrieve what threatened to be lost in a rigid adherence to structural theory, and emphasising the radical shift from reconstruction of the past unconscious in the analytic setting to the construction of the present in the analytic relationship. This is, as she emphasises, only achieved by presenting the relationship in the consulting room to the patient in a way which is "consciousness syntonic". This issue of "hearability" at an unconscious and conscious level will be taken up later in Part II.

Professor Didier Houzel from Caen in France conceptualises Alvarez's notion of "live company" as originating in the psychic container of the mother's mind, where the capacity for reverie is seen to encompass both maternal and paternal features. In "Bisexual Qualities of the Psychic Envelope" he locates the reclaiming function of the therapist as being one of the vital paternal aspects of this capacity for reverie, and he describes the progress from what he calls "simple stability" towards "structural stability". He sees these two poles of stability as being vital for the promotion of psychic health, and gives a vignette of his little patient Cyril who came to experience these poles in the containing mind of his therapist "Zel".

Part I concludes with an important chapter which links the latest researches in developmental psychology and neuroscience with Alvarez's work in "developmental psychoanalysis", exploring and linking classical psychoanalytic formulations with those of the developmentalist in the exploration of primitive mental states. In "Neurobiology, Developmental Psychology and Psychoanalysis: Convergent Findings on the Subject of Projective Identification", Professor Allan Schore from the University of California explores what he calls "psycho-biological states", or primitive states of mind–body. He argues that the concept of projective identification links clinical psychoanalysis not only with developmental psychoanalysis and psychology but with developmental neuroscience, and indicates that affect regulation of "the emotional brain" is not simply an early-appearing mechanism, but plays an essential role, as does projective identification, throughout life, as we strive to communicate and to receive feelings and affective experiences.

Part II is opened by Peter Blake's chapter "Think Outside, Not Inside", where the author focuses on Alvarez's concept of "hearability" in work with deprived and borderline children. Alvarez's place in the long history of consideration about when, how much and in what way to interpret is clearly delineated, and Blake describes his own innovative work in Australia with two emotionally deprived boys. By "entering the play" in terms of verbalising the boys' displaced feelings located even in the dust on top of the cupboard, he gives space for playful projections to move around in a third area, so that genuinely lively interaction becomes a possibility, perhaps for the first time. Blake notes the careful discrimination needed in the here and now to differentiate genuine playfulness from psychic retreat, emphasising the crucial dual role of careful observation and "the play of the interpretation".

As anyone who has been exposed to extreme cold will know, coming inside and "thawing out" is a painful process. It is this process, on an emotional level, which Bianca Lechevalier-Haïm from France describes in her chapter "From Freezing to Thawing: Working Towards the Depressive Position in Long-term Therapy with Autistic Patients". Mental pain can be experienced as catastrophically overwhelming to those previously cut off from anguished internal states, and Dr Lechevalier shows through her work with a young girl progressing from childhood to adolescence how much can slowly and patiently be retrieved from "the autistic ice-age". Mental pain can gradually be borne, and the individual too can be born into her potential, both as an internally mothered infant and as a potential mother to an infant herself.

In her chapter "Deficits in the Object and Failures in Containment" Maria Teresa Gallo from Italy talks of the illumination shed on the material of her most disturbed patients by Alvarez, as she helped the author towards an understanding of original primary deficit in children who were possessed by primitive mental states that did not respond to the "classical" Kleinian technique of addressing and interpreting verbally the deepest anxieties. Gallo talks of the most primitive levels of ego development in her work with a three-year-old autistic boy and his mother, and an eight-year-old adopted boy, showing how earlier catastrophic failures in containment were able to some extent to be repaired in what the author calls "the intensive care" of detailed therapeutic work when the therapist gradually reclaims previously inaccessible areas so that hitherto paralysed mental functions can begin to have life.

Gabriella Pansini from Italy in her chapter "Thoughts About the Concepts of Cognitive Development, Reparation and the 'Manic Position'" also acknowledges her profound debt to Alvarez for what she calls her "evolutionary point of view" when working with deprived and borderline patients. Here classical notions of "mania" are superseded by the idea that it is not triumph over the object through destructive forces which is the issue, but the real need to overcome depression and despair in a previously barren internal world devoid of helpful objects. Her work with a four-year-old girl and a young adolescent demonstrates how she has used these ideas, both in recognising constitutional strengths and developmental needs in the journey towards psychic repair.

In "The Sense of Abundance in Relation to Technique" Maria Rhode from London takes as her starting point Alvarez's notion of the most important aspects of a mother's mental capacities which assist the baby's emotional and cognitive development: her prompt and appropriate response to him, her ability to keep him in mind while attending to something else, and her ability to wait while he too shows interest in something other than their relationship. Rhode discusses these vital functions in relation to children with autism, and extends Alvarez's view to include the development of symbolic speech where previously words have been experienced only concretely. Through her fine-grained work with a six-year-old boy she describes technical modifications which increase contact with dissociated patients, working towards the establishment of the Oedipal triangle and a concomitant theory of mind. She talks of the need for the normal developmental progress from primary to secondary intersubjectivity to be reversed in cases where direct attention might be felt to be persecutory, and in this case she opens the way for the child's defensive use of stories and songs to be used in the service of making rather than repudiating a relationship.

Elsa First from New York continues the theme in her chapter "Liking *Liking* Doing", in which she gives us a vivid and touching example in work with six-year-old Ian, isolated and odd, who after years of "deleting" his own liveliness and that of his internal and external objects began to have an idea of his own agency and relatedness to people in his world. The author notes her indebtedness to Alvarez as she makes the therapeutic journey with Ian from primary inter-subjectivity to intra-subjectivity, and from rigid time-lessness to a sense of duration and the durability of good experiences.

In "First Love Unfolding", Judith Edwards from London underlines the bridge-building aspect of Alvarez's thinking between psychoanalytic concepts and the continuing evidence offered by child development research, from the notion of primary inter-subjectivity to the most recent revelations from neuro-biologists that early experience does indeed become encoded in our right brains, and it is these often pre-verbal areas we need to draw on in work with profound disturbance. Revisiting work with a post-autistic adolescent, the author thinks further about the impact of traumatic birth on a sensitive constitution, with resultant change in the "primitive mind" of a premature infant.

It is with the encouragement of Alvarez's ideas that therapists can dare to work with the most profound disturbance, as Trudy Klauber from London shows us in her moving description of intensive work with "Billy" over seven years, where she has indeed, after much struggle, obtained "Glimpses of What Might Have Been". What she illustrates is that it requires great courage and endurance to work with patients who actually seem to repudiate the live company of an object relationship; courage coupled with gradually accumulating insight which enables the patient, perhaps only fleetingly at first, to face their terror. This involved in this case relating to an object which could help transfer "the washing machine" of somatised terror into thinkable thoughts.

This book closes with a chapter by Suzanne Maiello, "On Temporal Shapes", where she further emphasises the vital links made by Alvarez between psychoanalytic and developmental formulations. Alvarez's most recent thinking has concerned the inevitable connection between the classical concentration on absence as a stimulator to thought and to mental growth and the notion of dynamic *presence*, where the modifiability of the present object in space and time has an equally important impact. Maiello's work further develops Alvarez's thinking about the temporal and dynamic qualities of objects and relates it to her own explorations of possible prenatal precursors to the later maternal object, specifically in terms of sound and rhythm as an underlying structure or matrix for later development. Her discussions use material from the early development of two premature babies in neonatal care, where the rhythms of safety had been dramatically interrupted, and where the impact of the earliest experiences outside the womb had been slowly metabolised in different ways. Using in addition material from work with a five-year-old autistic girl, she shows how oscillating temporal shapes can evolve from being symptoms of pathology to become the rhythmical background of safety which sustains us throughout life. As she insists: "Creative thinking is not the result of *overcoming* the circular, oscillating and rhythmic aspects of internalised experiences, but of their *integration* with the mature awareness of the linear reality of time."

It seems fitting to end this book at a point where both Alvarez and the last author, in common with others in the book, are continuing their explorations into the earliest reaches of human experience. What I hope this wide-ranging collection illustrates is how powerfully and in their different ways the authors have been interested in and often shaped by Alvarez's work as the evolution of psychoanalytic deliberations progressively unfolds over time. By keeping company with Alvarez and her thinking, as she argues with herself and struggles for understanding in integrating different points of view, we participate in and enter the heart of what is entailed in being fully alive.

Judith Edwards

Part I

Mainly theoretical

Chapter 1

Bridging the Atlantic for psychoanalysis

An appreciation of the contributions of Anne Alvarez

Neil Altman

In the evolution of a field such as psychoanalysis there need to be both close-knit subcommunities with a common vision and commitment, and cross-fertilization between and among subcommunities. Subcommunities create the conditions under which people feel they are working on a common project, inspiring each other and feeling inspired and nurtured by one or more intellectual leaders. Synergy and enthusiasm develop as people, excited by a unique or novel point of view, spell out the view's clinical and theoretical implications. The very solidarity that creates a sense of community, however, can also give rise to onesidedness, an ingrown tendency. Cross-fertilization, promoted by people who cross borders between communities, creates the potential for something new, unexpected, creative.

Anne Alvarez is both a solid member of the Kleinian community, and among the most creative of border-crossers. As such, her work enriches us all. Her writing, firmly rooted in the Kleinian tradition, shows the influence of recent North American psychoanalytic thinking in the self-psychological and relational traditions. I like to think that this particular theoretical integration reflects a generative marriage, within Alvarez, between the cultures of her Canadian roots and her British life-of-choice. Alvarez has not only received and integrated these psychoanalytic and national traditions; she has also picked, chosen, and used that which is available in these traditions to express her own values and clinical commitments. England and the British Kleinian community must have felt like home to her, a place where she could be, or become, herself. But then Alvarez became her own kind of Kleinian. I would like to highlight two areas that stand out for me in her writing: (1) the analyst's use of self in the analytic process, and (2) the way Alvarez integrates, or transcends, a split in psychoanalytic thinking about the relative primacy of destructive vs. developmentally progressive factors in human psychic life, a split that had crystallized in differences between Kernberg's and Kohut's points of view about narcissism. I pick only two areas out of many I might have chosen in which Alvarez has been especially original, and in which she has made unique contributions reflecting who she is and what she has become. My reading of Alvarez's work, of course, will reflect who I am, the use that I, a North American analyst working in the relational tradition, have made of her work.

Use of self in the analytic process

The analyst as interpreter, container, and reclaimer

Alvarez's way of working with autistic and severely disturbed children is, to my mind, strikingly bold. Confronted with these most inaccessible of children, she refused to give up, refused to accept that behavioral modifications were the best that could be hoped for. She insisted on connecting with them, human being to human being. Using a Kleinian conceptual framework, Alvarez thought that the internal objects of these children must seem dead if they treat other people as inanimate objects. Interpretation, the standard Kleinian technique, seemed futile. So Alvarez developed the idea that the analyst must be "live company" (Alvarez, 1992) for these children, must "reclaim" them for the human world by making active efforts to engage them, especially when the attachment to their withdrawal and their rituals becomes addictive. It is only too easy to respond to an autistic child's inaccessibility with a reciprocal withdrawal, to respond to their "deadness" with a reciprocally dead ritual of interpretation that has no meaning to the child. In my view, a large and crucial part of Alvarez's achievement with autistic children is the analysis and transcendence of countertransference that would otherwise lead us to abandon them or to join them in their deadness rather than seeking ways to help them join us in life among human beings.

In claiming a place for this work in the psychoanalytic repertoire, Alvarez became a trail-blazer for the Kleinians in seeing the analyst as a "real" object for the child. She saw that the traditional, interpreting, analyst is not necessarily neutral and anonymous for the autistic child. To the contrary, the abstinent analyst positively confirms, or at least fails to provide a contrast with, the child's projected internal object. The analyst who reaches out, who actively seeks to engage the child, is more neutral than the more reserved analyst in the sense that such an analyst may have successfully transcended a defensive countertransference withdrawal, rationalized as proper technique. Not incidentally, the actively engaged analyst is more likely to help the child, as is clearly demonstrated by the many case presentations in *Autism and Personality* (Alvarez and Reid, 1999). So, for me, the more general question arises, how does Alvarez view the balance in the analytic process between the analyst's participation as a "real" external object, and as a more detached commentator on the person's internal world? Since Alvarez's clinical presentations are mostly of autistic and severely disturbed children, the following comments will apply specifically to these patients. I think Alvarez probably believes that a more traditional, interpretive, approach is more suitable for the relatively healthy patient, child or adult; however, her staking a claim within the analytic repertoire for her participatory stance as a "real" external object leaves open the possibility that such a stance may be useful at times, if not at all times, with any patient in analytic work.

Contemporary Kleinian thinking (e.g. Joseph, 1989) has recognized that interpretation is not always the best technical approach. Following Bion's (1961) idea that the analyst may need to function as "container," the idea has gained currency that the analyst may sometimes need to "hold" the patient's projections until such time as the patient is able to reintegrate them. It has been recognized that to interpret too quickly can serve a defensive function for the analyst, in terms of the analyst's intolerance for the patient's projection. (Alvarez, 1997, cites Grotstein, 1981, who refers to this phenomenon as a "deficit in the object.")

Two-person psychologies in the inner and outer worlds

Alvarez's work has thus been part of a general move in Kleinian thinking toward recognizing an expanded use of the analyst's self in the clinical situation. We now have the analyst as reclaimer and the analyst as container. As the analyst's participation becomes more of a factor, Alvarez invoked the concept of "two person psychology" (Alvarez, 1992) to describe her evolving view of the analytic situation. This concept, originating with the British middle group (Rickman, 1928; Winnicott, 1965; Balint, 1950), has been used extensively by North American relational analysts. In this literature, as relational analysts have struggled to integrate British object relations and American interpersonal concepts, a wide variety of ways of integrating one- and two-person factors have become available. Briefly, two-person perspectives have entered analytic thinking as follows: neo-Kleinian analysts have tended to apply two-person perspectives to the inner world by seeing the inner world as structured by object-*relationships*; a two-person perspective is applied to a lesser degree with respect to the outer world, e.g. the actual interaction between patient and analyst.[1] American interpersonal analysts tend to focus on a two-person perspective applied to the outer world of the patient with others, while relational analysts try to apply the two-person perspective to both inner and outer worlds in defining the field within which one attempts to understand and help the patient.[2] In a sense, traditional Kleinians apply a one-person perspective to the interpersonal field by seeing the analyst, through the patient's eyes, as the patient's internal object. Many relational analysts (e.g. Benjamin, 1995) invoke a two-person perspective in the analytic situation by emphasizing the analyst's separate subjectivity, as well as the interactions between subjectivities of patient and analyst, in the process of trying to understand the patient. What is at stake in the choice of these perspectives has to do with how we, as analysts, see the role of our subjective experience and our participation, interpretive or otherwise, in understanding and helping the patient. An interpretation, for example, can be conceived of as a detached commentary with minimal input from the analyst's personal subjectivity. Or interpretation can be conceived of as a process of intersubjective recognition, or as reflecting a process of containment and metabolization (Bion, 1988) of a projected psychic content or internal object. In both these latter cases the transformation of a patient's internal world depends on the analyst's active reception and transformation of an experience within her own subjectivity, followed by a communication to the patient which conveys the psychic work done by the analyst on that which the patient has projected.

The analyst as container holds and explores

Consider now how Alvarez views the role of the analyst's subjectivity. In much of her writing (e.g. Alvarez, 1999) she emphasizes two-person factors in the inner world rather than the outer world; for example, she refers, in speaking about projective identification, to projections into an *internal* object. She emphasizes the analyst's separate subjectivity in terms of the analyst's "holding and exploring" (1997, p. 755) within herself the patient's projections, rather than immediately attempting to return them to the patient via interpretation. Let us focus here on what exactly is entailed by such "holding" and "exploring" within oneself, and what sort of intersubjective analytic process is being described. If the patient sees the analyst as depriving or persecutory, the analyst may, on this account, have to allow that bad object to remain "out there" in the analyst, far enough away from the patient so that the patient can explore it. Alvarez (1997), using the "grammar of rightful need" (p. 766) advocates sometimes saying things like: "(You) must feel I should be sorry about not being strong enough to persuade (your) parents to let (you) stay (in analysis)" (1995, p. 178) to convey a recognition and to enact, in a sense, that from the patient's point of view, the analyst has been ineffectual in providing for the patient that to which he is entitled. Clearly, in making a statement such as this one, the analyst is containing the patient's projection of an ineffectual internal object.

But is the analyst also saying that she experiences herself as ineffectual from her own point of view in such a case? In the "as if" space of psychoanalysis this question is left open. One can only say "yes and no." The question of the analyst's subjectivity touches on what Alvarez means when she speaks of "exploring" the patient's projection within herself. On the one hand, the phrase "within oneself" might seem to imply that Alvarez expects to find the patient's internal object in her own subjective experience to some extent, and in some way. One can imagine that the analyst, from a relatively detached perspective, could recognize that, from the patient's point of view, the analyst is ineffectual, while retaining a sense of being effective enough from her own point of view. Or, one could imagine that a sense of being ineffectual, from her own point of view, is part of the mixture of subjective experiences that the analyst is juggling at the moment. A particularly illuminating clinical example here is in Alvarez (1995). Alvarez, as analyst, has been unable to prevent her 4-year-old patient Tom's parents from pulling him out of treatment. She says to him that "he must feel that I ought to be sorry about not being strong enough to have persuaded his parents to let him stay" (p. 178). It is easy to imagine that Alvarez did, in fact, feel sorry that she could not persuade them to let him stay, even as she knows that she has done all anyone could do under the circumstances. Here, I believe, good use is made of her *own* distress and sense of helplessness to convey to the patient a *powerful* sense of recognition of the patient's experience.[3] What follows is particularly illuminating. The patient orders the analyst to clean up the mess he has made in the play room. Alvarez decides to enact the part of the helpless victim, the slave, projected into her by Tom, because she feels that he "actually needed me to pick the things up, and to show him that I was willing to do it because I liked him, not forced to do it because I feared his tantrums. Also, he was finally engaging me in a joint activity, in however bullying a manner" (p. 178). Accordingly, Alvarez cleans up, all the while maintaining eye contact with the boy, in my reading so as to retain her sense of dignity, but more than that, to convey that she is, and is not, identifying with his sense of helplessness. Alvarez thus holds and explores within herself the sense of being helpless, while simultaneously functioning very effectively as a containing and metabolizing analyst by integrating the helpless feeling with her liking for the boy, and her understanding of what he needs at the moment. The balance seems to be right, since at this point the boy is freed up from his one-sided role as persecutor, as he is startled by a noise from upstairs and Alvarez is able to say that "he was afraid someone up there didn't like him bullying me like this" (p. 178). Alvarez thus seizes the opportunity to help the boy begin to integrate his own sense of empathy for himself as victim and misgivings about his defensive sadism (though still at a safe-enough distance).

How the analyst's subjectivity is inevitably implicated

Alvarez refers to this sequence of events as "what is really happening between the patient's self and his object" (1995, p. 179). The word "really" in this context generally refers to what is happening in external reality, but in referring to the patient's "self" and "objects" Alvarez appears to be referring to what is "really" happening in internal reality. But to me it seems clear that external (from the patient's perspective) reality, in the form of the analyst's separate subjectivity, is also operative and clinically significant in a variety of ways that remain implicit in Alvarez's discussion of the case. I would add to her statement that this sequence of events is also what is really happening between the patient and his analyst. For example, the analyst must draw on her own experiences seeing other people as ineffectual or persecutory or deadened, in imagining the patient's experience of the analyst. She must draw on her own experience of *herself* in these ways. In this case, Alvarez conveys something of her subjective world in the way she enacts her identification with Tom in the role of helpless victim.[4] In thus drawing on her own experience, the analyst's own life-experience would seem necessarily to color her sense of the patient's experience even though the analyst would, of course, be listening carefully and with objectivity, as well as subjectivity, as the patient describes or enacts her experience of the analyst directly or indirectly. It would also seem likely that the analyst's reaction to being experienced in any particular way by the patient will be open to being experienced by the patient to one degree or another. In particular, Alvarez's ability to feel victimized while also feeling in control provides the boy with a model for how to metabolize, to keep in perspective and to integrate, his own sense of helplessness. The fact that Alvarez is working out of her *own* experience, as well as Tom's experience, means that the boy has the opportunity to internalize, to identify with, some of Alvarez's *own* strength and ego functioning. Some not-me sustenance is available to him. In these senses, then, it seems to me that two-person factors in the interpersonal domain are always operative. At the very least, the analyst's internal world is always interacting with the patient's internal world in the sense that the analyst's experience of the patient's internal world reflects, in part, the analyst's internal world.

Unconscious countertransference

In the case discussed so far, we are concerned with the analyst's conscious experience of the projection of, say, helplessness. What of cases in which the projection is received without conscious awareness by the analyst? Alvarez does not believe that such induced countertransference takes place inevitably. In her discussion of papers by Seligman and by Silverman and Lieberman (Alvarez, 1999), in discussing projective identification from parent to child, Alvarez mentions that some projections are more powerful than others, and some potential "recipients" are more or less thin- or thick-skinned, solid or vulnerable, than others. Granted that analysts are, as a rule, less vulnerable than children with their parents, I assume that Alvarez would reason similarly about patients and analysts. That is, in any particular case, a patient's projective identification may or may not, or to a greater or lesser degree, affect the analyst's subjective experience, depending on the nature of the projection and its interaction with the personality of the analyst. Therefore, the analyst would always have to take account of a unique clinical situation in determining the degree to which her subjective experience needed to be a factor in exploring a particular projection. In this sense, Alvarez's point of view is very flexible, makes room for many possibilities, and so requires careful thought and discrimination in determining how to explore each instance of projective identification. This complexity creates complications in terms of distinguishing between cases in which there *is* no induced countertransference, and those in which the analyst is not conscious of this countertransference. This is where the authoritative stance of the Kleinian analyst runs foul of the inevitable uncertainty and ambiguity in the intersubjective realm, and where social constructivism (Hoffman, 1998) becomes helpful, in my view.

Summary with respect to two-person factors

One of the most fascinating aspects of psychoanalytic work, very much brought to the fore in Kleinian thinking, is the coincidence that tends to occur between the patient's internal object and the external person (i.e., the analyst). The lines blur, the analyst finds herself playing the part of the patient's internal object. Even as Alvarez has brought a new emphasis on the analyst as an external person to the Kleinian repertoire, I sense that she feels that American relationalists may have gone too far in emphasizing the analyst's separate subjectivity. Thus, she reminds us that projective identification does not inevitably affect the analyst's countertransference, and that projective identification can be into an internal as well as an external object (Alvarez, 1999). This is an interesting and valuable complementary perspective for those of us who have been strongly influenced by interpersonal psychoanalysis. On the other hand, I think Alvarez occasionally understates how large a role the analyst plays as a person in the external world in her own work. For example, in the work with Tom referred to above, she says "I think you feel I'm glad you're going" (i.e. leaving the analysis). She says that she did not say "You are afraid that I'm glad you're going" because "the verb containing doubt – 'afraid that' – can serve to deny what is really happening between the patient's self and his object. It is important to contain the reality of his emotional experience, and I find the word 'feel' to be less denying" (1995, p. 179). If I understand correctly what Alvarez is saying here, she wants to validate the patient's experience with his object, an object that truly cannot contain the patient. But, from my point of view, if this object is conceived of as solely internal to the patient, i.e. as being unrelated to what is "really happening" between patient and analyst, then it is hard to avoid a sense of invalidating the patient's experience. Of course, it would not do simply to say that the analyst is indeed glad that the patient is leaving; such a claim would leave out how much the patient's inner world does indeed structure his experience in the outer world; furthermore, it vastly oversimplifies the analyst's subjective state. To grant the plausibility of the patient's experience of this particular analyst as one partial "take" on reality, it seems to me, leaves room for both validation of the patient's experience and for the influence of the internal world of the patient. In my view, then, we need to focus on both the patient's internal object, and the external analyst, in order to avoid invalidating the patient's experience.

Integrating the split between Kleinian and self-psychological thinking in North America

One of the major forks in the road faced by North American analysts has to do with the contrasting views of narcissism in the work of Otto Kernberg (1975) and Heinz Kohut (1971) and the self psychologists who have followed him. Kernberg, following Freud in viewing narcissism as developmentally primitive compared to object-related libido, tends to focus on the defensive, pathological aspects of narcissistic phenomena. Kohut, by contrast, saw narcissism as a separate developmental line, with healthy as well as pathological manifestations. Crucially, Kohut recognized healthy narcissistic needs as part of the developmental, and analytic, processes. To take the specific example of idealization, Kernberg sees idealization of the analyst as defensive with respect to primitive destructiveness and envy. Self psychologists, by contrast, see idealization as a developmental need, necessary for healthy self-esteem. Faced with an idealizing patient, the clinical stances of these two analysts could not lead in more different directions.

Among analytic writers I cannot think of one who so fully takes account of human destructiveness and defenses against it, and human developmental needs, as does Anne Alvarez. In true depressive position fashion, Alvarez's writing encompasses both an unflinching focus on destructiveness and on the positive forces for growth and development in the human personality. In the case of Tom, cited above, recall how Alvarez manages to take account of the destructiveness inherent in his tyrannical attitude toward her, *and* to appreciate the developmental needs contained in his wish to order her about. Most significantly, her actions, the way she goes about following his orders, convey recognition of his destructiveness *and* of his needs.

In *Live Company* (1992) and elsewhere, one of Alvarez's central points is that traditional Kleinian interpretations tend to have a negative focus; they tend to frame as defensive behaviors that could otherwise be seen as growth seeking. For example, when Richard (Alvarez, 1997) first enters Alvarez's home-office, he hears painters upstairs. He begins to pretend to paint, and Alvarez says "perhaps he was showing me how he would like to be able to paint like the grown up workmen." Richard says "Yes I do, I do want to, but I do work, this is what I do, you see" (p. 759). Alvarez notes that at first she takes Richard's action to indicate an "omnipotent defensive identification, a desire." But then she wonders whether Richard was communicating a "desperate need to be seen by me as being capable of being, or at least of becoming like, a potent and reparative father" (p. 759). To interpret his "painting" as defensive omnipotence, she says, could serve as a "crushing reminder of lifelong impotence and maybe lifelong humiliation" (p. 759). She concludes by considering how it would have been if she had said "Well, I think I should notice that you can paint too, not so differently from those fellows upstairs" (p. 759). Here is where I think Alvarez's work has a kinship with the North American self-psychological tradition, in which a good deal of human behavior is recognized as developmentally progressive and self-esteem building, as opposed to being defensive and regressive. Alvarez seems to take account, here, of how the analyst's recognition of growth-promoting forces furthers growth, while the failure to recognize these positive forces can thwart growth, perhaps promoting, iatrogenically, the very defensiveness and anger that had been posited.

Taking Alvarez's work as a whole, however, the power of aggression, and the defenses against aggression, are not neglected. Far from it. Her 1995 paper, "Motiveless Malignity: problems in the psychotherapy of psychopathic patients," is perhaps the most unflinching consideration of primary destructiveness that I have seen in the psychoanalytic literature. In this paper, Alvarez differentiates a kind of destructiveness, which she calls "psychopathic," which is not a product of conflict, or of the segregation and protection of the good object that occurs in splitting, but is, rather, the destructiveness of a person who has known little else in life. Psychopathic destructiveness is not defensive, and it is not deployed in the service of an underlying developmental need; there is little or no underlying love being warded off. Alvarez urges us to recognize this kind of destructiveness, to recognize it unflinchingly, for it is only by doing so that we can begin to build any kind of relationship with a psychopathic patient. To look for the underlying love or developmental need in these cases would be precisely to fail to recognize who the patient is. With her characteristic complex-mindedness, Alvarez recognizes that there is more than one kind of destructiveness; in some cases we are confronted with neurotic destructiveness, a product of conflict, or borderline destructiveness, a product of splitting. In the case of neurotic destructiveness, loving feelings may, in fact, be warded off; in the case of borderline destructiveness, a need to protect the good object through splitting may, in fact, be present. As in her recognition of various subtypes of projective identification, her recognition of subtypes of destructiveness encompasses an unusually wide range of clinically encountered phenomena with great subtlety and respect for the uniqueness of each patient, avoids dogmatic overgeneralization about clinical approaches, and requires great thoughtfulness on the part of the clinician.

Alvarez's work, then, transcends many of the splits, the either/or thinking, in our field. She does so by a precise attention to the particular person with whom she is working, that person's developmental status and needs, and the system of meanings in that person's psychic world. Returning to the example of idealization as defensive and pathological, vs. idealization as developmental need, an approach such as Alvarez's makes room for recognizing that idealization in any particular case can serve either or both functions (even, perhaps usually, both simultaneously). Alvarez's work is an example for us all of respect for all patients, including the most impaired, of attention to subtle yet crucial distinctions in the psychic worlds of patients, and of complex mindedness and absence of dogmatism with respect to theory and technique.

Notes

1 In the context of the intrapsychic or internal world, the relationship between a patient and his internal object is a two-person factor, whereas when the context is the external or interpersonal world, the very same self-internal object relationship is a one-person factor, given that the second person's role is de-emphasized.
2 I am using the term "two-person" here to subsume, rather than exclude, "one-person" factors, in that reference is made to each person, as well as to their interaction.
3 This is a good example of what Gill (1982) has spoken of as a recognition of the "plausibility" of the patient's transference experience of the analyst. The word "plausible" conveys the analyst's recognition and validation of the patient's experience of the analyst, without being fully taken over by this experience, i.e. feeling that the patient's way of experiencing the analyst is the *only* way to experience her.
4 As Racker (1968) points out, the analyst identifies with the patient's projections, thus making the analyst's experience an amalgam of the patient's experience and her own.

References

Alvarez, A. (1992) *Live Company*. London and New York: Tavistock/Routledge.

Alvarez, A. (1995) Motiveless malignity: problems in the psychotherapy of psychopathic patients. *Journal of Child Psychotherapy*, 21(2): 167–182.

Alvarez, A. (1997) Projective identification as a communication: its grammar in borderline psychotic children. *Psychoanalytic Dialogues*, 7(6): 753–768.

Alvarez, A. (1999) Widening the bridge: commentary on papers by Stephen Seligman and by Robin C. Silverman and Alicia F. Lieberman. *Psychoanalytic Dialogues*, 9(2): 205–217.

Alvarez, A. and Reid, S. (1999) *Autism and Personality*. London and New York: Routledge.

Balint, M. (1950) Changing therapeutic aims and techniques in psychoanalysis. *International Journal of Psychoanalysis*, 31: 117–124.

Benjamin, J. (1995) *Like Subjects, Love Objects*. New Haven and London: Yale University Press.

Bion, W.R. (1988) Attacks on linking. In E. Bott-Spillius (ed.) *Melanie Klein Today*, vol.1. London: Routledge.

Gill, M. (1982) *Analysis of Transference*, vol.1. New York: International Universities Press.

Grotstein, J. (1981) Wilfred R. Bion: the man, the psychoanalyst, the mystic: a perspective on his life and work. In J. Grotstein (ed.) *Do I Dare Disturb the Universe*. Beverly Hills, Calif.: Caesura Press.

Hoffman, I.Z. (1998) *Ritual and Spontaneity in the Psychoanalytic Process*. Hillsdale, N.J.: The Analytic Press.

Joseph, B. (1989) *Psychic Equilibrium and Psychic Change*. London and New York: Tavistock/Routledge.

Kernberg, O. (1975) *Borderline Conditions and Pathological Narcissism*. New York: Jason Aronson.

Kohut, H. (1971) *The Analysis of the Self*. New York: International Universities Press.

Racker, H. (1968) *Transference and Countertransference*. New York: International Universities Press.

Rickman, J. (1928) The development of the psychoanalytic theory of the psychoses. *International Journal of Psychoanalysis* (Supplement). London: Bailliere.

Winnicott, D.W. (1965) The capacity to be alone. In *The Maturational Processes and the Facilitating Environment*. New York: International Universities Press.

Chapter 2

Changing ideas of change
The dual components of therapeutic action

Peter Fonagy

Introduction

Change in deeply held theoretical views amongst clinicians may be much harder to produce than psychic change in our patients. Yet our understanding of the change process has changed markedly over the last three decades. We have moved away from a simplistic mechanistic understanding of change (e.g. in terms of shifts in the balance of forces between ego, id, and superego), and begun to understand change more as a process involving modifications in intrapsychic representations of relationships, both with and between our internal objects. Anne Alvarez's contribution has been key. In her wonderful book, *Live Company* (Alvarez, 1992), she traces the development of psychoanalytic ideas of therapeutic action from a one-person depth psychology to an interpersonal perspective, modifying Kleinian thought as she goes in the direction of increasing concern with live relationships. She draws our attention to two changes in our understanding of therapeutic action: (a) the way in which the aim of lifting repressive barriers has been supplanted by a process that involves extending the boundaries of the self to include the regaining of lost, split-off parts by means of analytic containment, and (b) the development of a meta-theory which is more relational, less mechanistic and more able to accommodate novelty and the "mentalness of mind" (p. 11).

Concurrently, from a Freudian perspective, our views have also changed to a point where few regard the classical ego-psychological model of psychic change as viable. These changes are instances of a more general shift in interest that has brought opposing psychoanalytic perspectives closer together. The aim of this tribute to the brilliant contribution of Anne Alvarez is to highlight the distinction drawn by her from the perspective of a Freudian analyst and to show how there is a convergence of views concerning psychic change between Alvarez's updating of Kleinian ideas and our attempts at restating the Freudian tradition – how from the two extreme poles of psychoanalysis in Britain a common thread has emerged concerned with, as Alvarez describes it: "making the thought thinkable". Increasingly, regardless of perspective, we focus not simply on the content of mental function but on the form of psychic activity, and, even more specifically, on the ways we may facilitate the growth of these forms. In this domain, where Kleinians and Freudians have come together from different points of origin, Anne Alvarez's contribution has been most significant.

Therapeutic action and memory

Ever since the fourteenth IPA Congress in Marienbad (Panel, 1937), where Glover, Fenichel, Strachey, Nunberg and Bibring crossed swords, the nature of therapeutic change has been a perennial topic for psychoanalytic debate. Since that time, at about ten-year intervals, alternating between the International and the American, there have been regular symposiums on this topic. Uncharitable commentators on psychoanalysis might suggest that our endless consideration of the "WHY" issue ("why is psychoanalysis effective?") masks our uncertainty about the "WHAT" question ("what precisely are the expected effects of this intensive and expensive treatment?"). Yet there are those who, against opposition from within and without, are beginning the painful task of empirically demonstrating the unique therapeutic benefits of psychoanalytic treatment (e.g. Fonagy *et al.*, 1999; Sandell *et al.*, 2000).

Changing ideas about therapeutic action have developed out of the clinical realities of the outcome of psychoanalytic therapy. Alvarez (1992) observes that "These sobering reflections about the sheer amount of time it takes to change one's nature have also been accompanied by changes in the theory of how the therapeutic action of psychoanalysis takes place and the manner in which the so called insight is gained" (p. 2). The slow rate of psychic change was also the starting point for George Moran's and my explorations of the subject ten years ago (Fonagy and Moran, 1991). In one of the least-read papers in the psychoanalytic literature we advanced a tentative model of the therapeutic action of psychoanalysis (Fonagy *et al.*, 1993). We suggested that therapeutic action should be considered, first and foremost, in terms of the mechanisms underlying psychic change. We outlined two schematic models to highlight distinct aspects of the curative factors in the psychoanalytic treatment of mental disturbance. The first, which we called the *representational model*, focused on the recovery of threatening ideas and feelings and the consequent reorganization of mental structures commonly invoked in explanations of psychoanalytic process. The second, the *mental process model*, drew attention to the therapeutic benefits of engaging previously inhibited mental processes in the here and now of the psychoanalytic encounter. We sought a framework to replace the outmoded notion, implicitly present in the minds of many psychotherapists, that the release of inhibition of depressed and repressed patients was the path to psychic change and cure. In a similar way, Alvarez (1992) eschewed the "early theories [which] had to do with catharsis and with the liberating effect of uncovering and unmasking repressed material" (p. 3).

Our representational model of change, the first of the two models, is strikingly similar to Matte Blanco's (1975) notion of the "unfolding" or "translating" function where the patient is helped to see new or deeper meanings in ideas which may in fact be quite conscious. We consider three methods by means of which developmentally primitive mental representations may be assimilated into higher order organizations in the course of treatment: (1) by enhancing the integrity and coherence of mental organizations, (2) through the elaboration of their connections with other systems, and (3) by creating new representations of both internal and external states. The representational system is restructured so that previously isolated, unintegrated, incompatible representations cease to be pathogens. Within this framework, pathogenic parts of the dynamic unconscious are seen as distinct sets of mental representations that are incompatible with evolving mental structures in some important way. The representational model assumes that therapeutic action enables the harmonization of mental representations through analytic clarification and interpretation, as well as through the patient's inherent capacity to achieve increasingly sophisticated constructions concerning experience, given felicitous circumstances. The patient's perception of the analyst as having empathy (Emde, 1990) or healing intentions (Stone, 1961) may alter their object representations through the same mechanism of change as interpretations. Regardless of the agent of change, therapeutic action mediated through changes of mental representations will be relatively rapid and self-evident.

To give an example, a somewhat narcissistic young man who presented with sexual problems and anxieties about the superficial quality of his relationships with women spent the first year of his analysis describing in depth and with some sophistication his rivalrous and ambivalent feelings about his father, whom he greatly admired. During this time his problems with women remained unchanged. The analyst deliberately waited 18 months before pointing out that, although the patient was talking of his complex feelings toward his father, he had never once mentioned his mother in the analysis. This recognition shook the patient. Over subsequent sessions he began to recall his feelings of having been neglected and ignored by her, and linked this to his anxiety about being abandoned by any woman he intensely desired. Gradually, his terrifying perception of women as in total control of life and death was integrated in his conscious feelings and his behaviour toward them changed. His potency problems disappeared and he established a deep friendship with a junior colleague, whom he later married.

The representational perspective, while compatible with the work of Bion and Matte Blanco, also has a substantial history in Freudian writings. Joseph Sandler and Walter Joffee advanced the notion of the representational world in the 1960s (Joffe and Sandler, 1969; Sandler and Joffe, 1966). The most comprehensive Contemporary Freudian formulation based on these assumptions is the "schematic model" proposed by Sam Abrams (Abrams, 1987, 1990). These models and others like them attribute therapeutic action to changes in long-term memory, which underpins the representational system. Alvarez (1992), drawing on Kleinian sources (e.g. Joseph, 1989), points out that links with the past, while important, are no substitutes for the study of the living interaction and the "dangerous erosion of the personality that can take place in these interactions" (p. 3). Her argument was radical, claiming that it is just not sufficient to look for missing aspects of the patient in his repressed and buried unconscious as these missing parts may lie further afield, often in someone else's feeling.

More recently, in the light of new models of memory in cognitive science, we have reconsidered which aspects of the memory system underpinning mental representations are likely to generate therapeutic change (Fonagy and Target, 1997). Advances in the debate on the aims of psychoanalysis since Freud's original model of undoing repression and recovering memory into consciousness (Freud and Breuer, 1895), have not included updating the role of memory in the therapeutic process. We now know that memory is not a singular mechanism but is made up of a number of different systems. Cognitive science distinguishes two kinds of memory system, both of which have important functions in psychoanalytic treatment. *Declarative* or *explicit memory* is the conscious retrieval of information about the past. Information may be retrieved *without* the experience of remembering from the so-called *procedural* or *implicit* memory system. The distinction was originally made by Cohen (Cohen, 1984; Cohen and Squire, 1980) to distinguish knowledge characterized by content from the kind of content-independent information involved in acquiring skills such as playing the piano (regardless of the specific piece) or driving (independent of destination).

Declarative memory relates to remembering events and information. Procedural memory has to do with acquiring processes. Schachter (1987, 1992b) suggested that the declarative–procedural distinction overlaps the more general distinction between explicit and implicit memory systems. Schachter (1992a) defines explicit memory as "intentional or conscious recollections of prior experiences" (p. 244) and implicit memory as "changes in performance or behaviour that are produced by prior experiences (on tests) that do not require any intentional or conscious recollection of those experiences" (p. 244). Neuropsychological work has demonstrated the complete independence of these two systems. It is generally agreed that, whereas the hippocampus and the temporal lobes are directly involved in the recall of personally experienced autobiographical events which compose an individual's life history (Alvarez and Squire, 1994; Damasio and Damasio, 1994; Ungerleider, 1995), implicit memory is mediated by sub-cortical structures such as the putamen and caudate nucleus of the basal ganglia (Mishkin *et al.*, 1984; Saint-Cyr and Taylor, 1992) and the cerebellum

(Glickstein and Yeo, 1990). A further sub-cortical system that has been implicated in implicit learning of emotionally charged experiences is the amygdala (LeDoux, 1995). Implicit memory is evident earlier in development than declarative memory (DiGiulio *et al.*, 1994). It is a non-voluntary system. It is non-reflective and non-declarative. It appears relatively early but is constructed relatively slowly, and is capable of storing behavioural procedures whose origins may have been lost or have never been retained. Recently, a group of psychoanalysts in Boston, including Daniel Stern, Ed Tronick, Karlen Lyons-Ruth, Alexander Morgan and Alexie Harrison, have been working intensively to integrate the concept of implicit memory with ideas about the therapeutic process[1] (Lyons-Ruth, 1999; Stern *et al.*, 1998).

It seems then that experiences contributing to internal representations of object relationships are not, by and large, stored in declarative memory. The extent to which episodes of interaction with the caregiver may be remembered (encoded and stored in autobiographical memory) may be incidental in the development of internal representations of relationships.[2] What lies at the root of interpersonal problems, the transference relationship and quite possibly all aspects of the personality that we loosely denote by the term "unconscious", is not a series of episodes of caregiver interaction stored in the explicit memory but a set of procedures or implicit memories of interactional experience. These may be represented as self–other–affect triads, as Otto Kernberg (1988) has suggested, as a network of unconscious expectations, as Bowlby (1988) conceived, or they may simply be emergent properties of the nervous system, abstracting invariant information through the tendency of nerve-cells to survive together if activated together (Edelman, 1987; Stern, 1994). This emphasis on the living interaction does not deny the importance of the therapeutic exploration of the past, but it highlights the fact that it cannot substitute for the study of living interactions ("live company" to borrow Alvarez's catchphrase).

Kleinian psychoanalysis has worked with the implicit assumption of the primacy of procedural change over declarative change as the psychic motor of therapeutic action for many years (Joseph, 1989). The shift away from earlier techniques which involved interpretations of a more explanatory kind and which focused on the exchange of one content for another has characterized modern Kleinian technique, which Anne Alvarez's work brilliantly exemplifies. Alvarez (1992) describes the move away from an interpretation such as "you think you feel this but you really feel that" to a more cautious and respectful approach where the analyst "feels his way through to whatever is the patient's experience of the moment, and ... allows time for such experience to be explored fully" (p. 6). Similarly, in her paper on transference, Betty Joseph (1985), explicitly eschews the consideration of specific associations in favour of attempts to understand the patient's current internal state in terms of the total interpersonal situation created in the transference with the analyst. "If we work only with the part that is verbalised, we do not really take into account the object relationships being acted out in the transference; for example, the relationship between the uncomprehending mother and the infant who feels unable to be understood, and it is this that forms the bedrock of her personality." She goes on, "interpretations dealing only with the individual associations would touch only the more adult part of the personality, while the part that is really needing to be understood is communicated through the pressures brought on the analyst" (p. 448). Joseph points out that the inner world built up from infancy is conveyed only through the feelings aroused in us. As the commentators Feldman and Bott Spillius point out: "Gradually Joseph has become convinced that these experiences of psychic reality in the session, however uncomfortable for the analyst and patient, should come before intellectual links are made with the patient's remembered past or the 'facts' of his life outside analysis" (Feldman and Bott Spillius, 1989, pp. 6–7).

Arguably in consequence of the pervasive influence of the Kleinian approach on other traditions, the idea that change was a matter of process rather than remembering came to dominate some clinicians from the Freudian tradition. For example, from a Contemporary Freudian perspective, Joseph Sandler made broadly the same points as Joseph in his paper on role-responsiveness (Sandler, 1976). He expanded this argument in the distinction between past and present unconscious (Sandler and; Sandler, 1987), and more recently in a paper on the false memory controversy (Sandler and Sandler, 1997). Thus both Freudian and Kleinian clinicians independently recognized that patients cannot possibly *remember* why they behave as they do. Nor will they necessarily learn about the events or experiences that have caused them to be this way, even in the longest of analyses. The particular experiences which lead to deeply pathological ways of experiencing the other may antedate the development of the memory system which is needed to encode and retain the experience in a way which can be represented, consciously or unconsciously, as a story (Gathercole, 1998). The Sandlers described this as the past unconscious – a system to which neither patient nor analyst can have direct experiential access, even at an unconscious level. Frequently analysts and patients make the understandable error of ascribing causal significance to the memory recovered as agent of cure. Non-Kleinian analysts have frequently assumed that remembering in and of itself has caused change. The return of such memories is best considered as an epiphenomenon, an inevitable consequence of exploring mental models of relationships. The memory may or may not be one of the experiences to have brought about the pathogenic way-of-experiencing oneself or another in a particular relationship. Either way, the significance of its recovery is the same. It provides an explanation, but therapeutically it is inert. *Therapeutic action lies in the conscious elaboration of preconscious relationship representations, principally through the analyst's attention to the transference.* The events which patients report as "recovered memories" may or may not have happened. They are recalled because they most closely fit with one or other of the non-conscious structures organizing their current relationships. The enactment of procedures already laid down before the formation of narrative memory will lay down episodic memories that give this enactment meaning and texture. Naturally, the experience brought about by the enactment of implicit procedural memory may then be experienced as its cause.

The only way we can know what might have happened to our patients is through their interaction with us in the transference. They come to us with a kind of model – a network of unconscious expectations or mental models of self–other relationships. If we are serious about object relations theory, and consider these relations as psychic structures organizing behaviour, then the focus of psychoanalytic work ought to be these structures and not the events which might have contributed to them. Psychoanalysis modifies ways of thinking. By themselves new ideas cannot sustain change, although they may prompt new ways of experiencing the self with other, which can. To focus on the recovery of memory is therefore to pursue a false god: psychoanalysts should eschew the archaeological metaphor. A significant revision of our implicit and explicit models of therapeutic action is called for. The removal of repression should no longer be viewed as the key to therapeutic action. Psychic change is a function of a shift of emphasis between different mental models of object relationships. Change must occur in implicit memory for the procedures the person uses in living with himself and with others to change. Memory is of tremendous importance, but as a mediator, a valuable channel for communicating about the nature of internal representations of object relationships, not as an account of history, be it accurate or inaccurate. It fleshes out the skeleton of the internal structure, but should not be confused with the structure itself; that is, the procedures underpinning ways of experiencing the self with the object. The "recovery" of emotionally charged memories may indeed be central to a person's experience of a psychoanalysis, even if the change this analysis achieved was through an improved understanding of pathological modes of relating, and through this a more integrated set of representations of object relationships. Intensive work within the transference aims to modify implicit memories, rather than to effect relatively superficial changes in autobiographical memory. Experiences constructed in autobiographical memory are more likely to be inaccurate than accurate. Truth in psychotherapy makes sense only in the context of psychic reality. *Beyond the creation of a narrative, psychoanalysis is the active construction of a new way of experiencing self with other.*

The patient's implicit memory or procedural representation of an experience of self with other lies in what Sandler and Joffe (1969) have called the non-experiential realm. This realm is "intrinsically unknowable, except insofar as it can become known through the creation or occurrence of a phenomenal event in the realm of subjective experience" (p. 82). It becomes explicit and knowable when it is enacted or instantiated as an unconscious fantasy. Frequently we can infer the presence of such a fantasy from the patient's behaviour. For example, the fantasy that "I am filled with badness" may manifest in the transference as a constant vigilance for critical comments or a defence against this in arrogance and grandiosity. The distinction between enactment and unconscious experience is critical because an emotional reaction (conscious or unconscious) to the implicit memory will only arise once it has entered the experiential realm (Sandler and Joffe, 1967). The distinction proposed by Sandler has much in common with Ron Britton's (1995) more recent distinction between unconscious fantasy and belief, from a Kleinian perspective. Here fantasy may be thought to exist in the non-experiential realm of implicit memory and belief in the mental contents generated by this procedure, normally activated in the context of an object relationship (for us the transference). In making the experiential unconscious conscious, the analyst is struggling against resistance. This resistance, however, is not the residue of the original affective charge marshalled to keep the fantasy or experience from being represented in autobiographical memory. This battle has been fought and lost. Psycho-analysis is not therapeutic because it provides access once again to memories, however painful and conflict-ridden, whether accurate or inaccurate. The repression which is so much part of our everyday work is in the present unconscious (Sandler and Sandler, 1987), assisting the patient in the struggle with the painful current implications of an unconscious idea (the shame, humiliation and guilt of the second censorship against what is currently conflictual). Consciousness of the beliefs generated by such implicit memory models is crucial if the patient is to acquire the power to inhibit or modify them through the creation of a second order representation of their inner experience (Fonagy et al., 1995).

On the basis of this model, we would anticipate substantial and enduring change from a psychoanalytic process which has directly tackled ways of experiencing the other that were acquired defensively, through direct experience or through defensive distortions of such experience regardless of the extent or accuracy of autobiographical reconstructions. Any psycho-analysis will activate numerous models of self–other relationships. Given the activation of a particular relationship model, autobiographical memories consistent with it will be *secondarily* activated. But this is not the curative factor. The emergence of the memory is due not to the undoing of repression but to a process of active construction, the creation of an experience con-gruent with the pattern of self–other relationships close to awareness. The analysand works backwards, pulling together elements of early experience consistent with a freshly discovered perception of himself in relation to the other. It is not surprising then that memories from adolescence and latency will dominate a patient's material despite our conviction that earlier experiences were the formative ones. The mental model uncovered by the patient in analysis is likely to have been generated by early experiences which antedate the development of autobiographical memory and therefore will never be retrieved.

What is the status then of memories recovered in analysis? Freud's (1900) notion of screen memories was a remarkable insight into memory processes. He noted that the striking feature of screen memories was their apparent capacity to contain numerous important aspects of interpersonal experiences encoded into a single remembered event. We might now see screen memories as manifestations of the implicit memory system which can otherwise achieve no phenomenal representation. Screen memories provide a bridge between the two memory systems.

Therapeutic action and the "mentalness of mind"

There are of course individuals whose entire memory system has come under attack or, to put it slightly less dramatically, individuals whose experience has led to a disruption of the entire memory system. Such individuals are most common amongst those with persistent and pervasive experiences of trauma (Allen, 1995). In these people, the barrier between physical and psychic reality has been breached, disrupting the accurate encoding of events (Fonagy, 1995; Fonagy and Target, 1996; Target and Fonagy, 1996). This is not a regression to a childlike state, since the young child is, if anything, hypersensitive to the distinction between actual and imaginary (Gopnik, 1993). Paradoxically, perhaps one of the surest signs of actual trauma may be irremediable damage to memory processes. But the treatment of these individuals involves the second of Alvarez's descriptions of developments in the theory of change: the meta-theory of change concerning the mentalness of mind, or what we have termed "mentalization" (Fonagy and Target, 1998).

The limitations of the representational model of therapeutic action via changes in implicit or procedural memory become most clearly apparent when the analyst is confronted with a patient whose representational model is fixed. In such patients alternative ways of viewing things are either dismissed or entered into in superficial and meaningless ways, lack of coherence and consistency between representations apparently causes little distress, and the representational system seems immutable to change. I vividly remember my first analytic experience with a borderline patient. Early in his analysis, following a lengthy discussion of his anxieties concerning competitiveness, I ventured to point out that these might be related to unresolved conflicts about his sexual competition with his father as a little boy (I am still ashamed of the degree of my naivety). He seemed thoughtful about my interpretation and returned proudly the next day with an account of a dream where he and his father were fighting; he had a knife and after a struggle managed to cut his father's penis off which he held up victoriously, reminding himself of the Statue of Liberty. By then I had the presence of mind to make the more appropriate interpretation that his anxiety the day before concerned his feeling of being in competition with me, and now, having witnessed my inadequacy, he could, indeed, afford to feel triumphant. While clearly reducing his anxiety momentarily, these and other interpretations had little impact on his ways of seeing things.

The ongoing discussion on therapeutic action has generally acknowledged individual developmental deviations, impairments, deficits or underlying structural deficiencies that fit poorly with the representational model of therapeutic action. From the late 1970s a number of writers shifted the emphasis from "structural change" as the focus of therapeutic action to the transaction between patient and analyst as a curative experience and the early mother–child relationship as the most appropriate analogue for the therapeutic encounter. Developmental processes are invoked by those who link therapeutic action to the holding environment (Modell, 1976), separation–individuation (Stolorow and Lachmann, 1978; Blatt and Behrends, 1987), a sense of union with the primary object (Loewald, 1979), social referencing (Viederman, 1991), empathy (Emde, 1990), or other aspects of developmental processes (Goodman, 1977; Schlessinger and Robbins, 1983).

These developmental models are insufficient for a satisfactory account of therapeutic action with the difficult patient. Christopher Bollas (1987) noted that analysts were in no sense parents of the analysand, rather they possessed the "generative paradigmatic skills that reach the child element in the adult analysand" (p. 115). Linda Mayes and Donald Spence (1994) make the important counter-intuitive observation that the developmental metaphor applies more to relatively well-endowed adults who historically probably had the benefit of the kind of care-giving experiences that re-emerge in the transference, whilst the group of patients with whom these metaphors are most often used simply do not have the capacities which might make the developmental metaphor applicable. From a Kleinian perspective, development in therapy is not seen as a retracing of ontogenetic steps. Alvarez's chapter in *Live Company* on the "Growth of the Mind" (Alvarez, 1992) is subtitled: "The function of reclamation". Within a classical Kleinian frame of reference the primitive functioning of the adult mind was not a developmental residue of earlier forms of thought. Rather, primitive (paranoid–schizoid) forms of mentation were thought to exist side by side with more mature functioning as part of normal adult thought process (Bion, 1962; Rosenfeld, 1987). Yet Alvarez (1992, chapter 5) also recognized that working with severe disorders in psychoanalysis has normal counterparts in the caretaker–infant relationship and she accepted that "notions of growth, learning, inadequacy or even defect seem to offer a better description of the therapeutic problems" (p. 57).

In my view psychoanalysts of all schools have resorted to the developmental metaphor to point to a qualitatively different type of change we observe in our patients, one which clearly does not involve remembering and memory but rather the recovery (or reclamation) of a psychological function.

Strangely, whilst analysts have relatively readily accepted that all mind is representation, they have been curiously unconcerned about the mechanisms that generate and organize these: mental processes. Mental representations are the products of mental processes. A mental process is the violin from which the melody of mental representation originates. A fantasy is a mental representation and it is the product of the process of fantasizing. The distinction is well established, both in philosophy of mind and cognitive science (Bolton and Hill, 1996; Mandler, 1985). Though not explicitly discussed, the notion that mental processes are as vulnerable to the vicissitudes of conflict as mental representation is implicit in many Kleinian psychoanalytic writings. Hanna Segal (1978), for example, illustrated how thinking puts a limit on the omnipotence of fantasy and can therefore be despised and fervently resisted. The Ecole Psicosomatique of Paris described patients who commonly present with somatic disorders, whose experience of life appears concrete, devoid of sentiment or affect and who insist on seeing things "as they are" (De M'Uzan, 1974; Marty, 1990; McDougall, 1974, 1986). Their history, as it emerges in treatment, tends to be one of having been overwhelmed by affect at a time when their capacity to deliberately exclude affect-laden representation is not yet available. Prior to the development of representational capacities which can selectively exclude ideas associated with unmanageable feelings, these individuals may have coped by disengaging or inhibiting mental processes critical to the generation and recognition of affect. Others have described this clinical picture as alexithymia (Sifneos, 1977).

The notion of recovery of mental processes is central to the therapeutic action of psychoanalysis. Alvarez (1992) noted that the failure of some patients to understand the analyst's comments may have less to do with questions of projection and more to do with questions of perspective (p. 79). Importantly, she initiated a move away from the alimentary model of taking in and digesting understanding favoured by some Kleinian writers (Meltzer, 1975) and adopted a metaphor of infant caretaker interaction in the context of perspective taking. "The way in which a patient may or may not be able to follow a the therapist's train of thought, or pursue one of his own, may be as analogous to the problem of the visual tracking of the trajectory of moving objects as to his response to the flow of milk in his throat" (p. 79). She has propelled Kleinian theory away from the notion of therapy as helping the patient "re-introject" lost parts: she considered this an inappropriate metaphor for patients who needed to "grow [these capacities] for the first time" (p. 91).

A related, but less metaphorical way of formulating this idea draws on the developmental psychological concept of theory of mind (Astington and Jenkins, 1995) or mentalization (Fonagy, 1997). Mary Target and I have argued that patients with severe personality disorder have little reliable access to an accurate picture of their own mental experience, their representational world (Fonagy *et al.*, 2000). They are unable to take a "step back", and respond flexibly and adaptively to the symbolic, meaningful qualities of other people's behaviour. Instead, they find themselves caught in fixed patterns of attribution, rigid stereotypes of response, non-symbolic, instrumental use of affect – mental patterns that are not amenable to either reflection or modulation. They inhibit their capacity to mentalize, to think in terms of thoughts and feelings in themselves and in others, prototypically as an adaptation to severe and chronic maltreatment. The vulnerable child, confronted with a caregiver who harbours frankly malevolent affects and thoughts about him, may have no other option than to disavow thinking in terms of mental states altogether. Therapeutic action concerns the recovery (or what Alvarez might call the reclaiming) of this function through the dyadic interaction between patient and therapist.

The curtailment of mental process has more drastic consequences for psychic functioning than the defensive distortion of specific representational structures. Inhibitions of mental processes enable the individual to avoid a whole class of painful conflictual mental representations. Biological factors (constitutional vulnerability) or specific categories of developmental history (developmental vulnerability) may predispose an individual to respond in this way. For example, where mentalization is inhibited in particular interpersonal contexts (e.g. affect-laden interpersonal relationships) we have argued that genetic vulnerability as well as deficiencies in maternal sensitivity leading to poorly established meta-representations of affect can predispose a child to respond to later trauma by actively inhibiting this capacity.

The concept of selectively inhibited mental process enables us to think about therapeutic action in a somewhat more sophisticated manner. Psychoanalytic treatment works not only by reorganizing representational structures, but also by making a fuller range of mental functions available to the patient. Of course, we can only observe both these changes by observing changes in ideas (representations), as mental functions are inevitably part of the non-experiential realm. However, the manner in which the change is achieved, as well as the nature of change, is different in these models. We believe that inhibited mental functions are reactivated through the active involvement of the analyst in the mental functioning of the patient and the reciprocal involvement of the patient in the mind of the analyst. This removes the threat of the overwhelming mental anguish that originally led to the abandonment of the mental process concerned. This involvement, combined with interpretations of the anxieties that originally led the patient to curtail mental functioning, can reactivate inhibited mental processes. For example, Alvarez (1992) suggests that the observation of something "different and new or even renewed but unexpected" (p. 81) examined for a location or point of view that permits it to be explored, makes the thought thinkable again.

Optimally, the patient's mental work recapitulates that of the analyst. These kinds of patients have a desperate need for what Alvarez (1992) has termed an "intelligent animate object". The analyst's thinking, even if initially neither understood nor appreciated by the patient, continually challenges the patient's mind, stimulating a need for conceiving of ideas in new ways. Alvarez (1992) writes: "The thought may not be thinkable until it is recognized as being precisely that: a thought and only a thought, a noise and only a noise" (p. 90). What is crucial, then, is the active engagement of one mind with another, inconceivable without empathy, holding and containment. Yet none of these is directly responsible for the therapeutic action. The process model should not be claimed to be unique to psychoanalysis. There are probably a wide range of interpersonal situations which make the individual feel safe once again in using biologically canalized capacities (Waddington, 1966). However, it is likely that these contexts are restricted to attachment relationships, as these prototypically engage the widest range of cognitive and affective capacities and thus minimise the opportunity for finding alternative means to achieve adaptation without the inhibited psychological process.

Conclusion

This brief essay has sought to demonstrate the increasing convergence between notions of psychic change rooted in a Kleinian and a Freudian orientation. I have attempted to link Alvarez's illuminating contributions to this topic to the work of myself and my colleagues at the Anna Freud Centre. It seems that both the contemporary Kleinian and the Freudian notions of change through psychoanalytic therapy de-emphasize the role of memory, insight and the recovery of lost parts of the mental world in favour of a model where psychoanalysis, at least with the more severe patient, aids by recovering psychological capacities never developed or repudiated as adaptations to early conflict. The centrality of the study of early development is accepted in both these traditions. These new formulations also highlight the importance of the interpersonal aspect of the treatment process, the centrality of the respectful attuned relationship with the patient for which Anne Alvarez's work is justly renowned.

Notes

1 A "Work in Progress" review of their contribution is about to appear in a special issue of the *Infant Mental Health Journal*.
2 At this time controversy surrounds the chronology of the development of auto-biographical memory (see review by Gathercole, 1998). An influential research team headed by Nelson has proposed that autobiographical memories are not formed at all during the first four years, not until children have developed an extensive repertoire of generic knowledge about the event structure of their lives and they learn to talk about their memories, having formulated them as narratives

(Fivush *et al.*, 1996; Nelson, 1993a, 1993b). Others propose that autobiographical memory is present typically by two years of age, as soon as the "cognitive self" (the awareness of oneself as having particular cognitive capacities) emerges between 18 and 24 months (Howe and Courage, 1997).

References

Abrams, S. (1987). The psychoanalytic process: A schematic model. *International Journal of Psycho-Analysis*, 68, 441–452.

Abrams, S. (1990). The psychoanalytic process: The developmental and the integrative. *Psychoanalytic Quarterly*, 59, 650–677.

Allen, J. G. (1995). The spectrum of accuracy in memories of childhood trauma. *Harvard Review of Psychiatry*, 3, 84–95.

Alvarez, A. (1992). *Live Company: Psychoanalytic Psychotherapy with Autistic, Borderline, Deprived and Abused Children*. London: Routledge.

Alvarez, P. and Squire, L. R. (1994). Memory consolidation and the medial temporal lobe: A simple network model. *Proceedings of the National Academy of Sciences*, 91, 7041–7045.

Astington, J. and Jenkins, J. M. (1995). Theory of mind development and social understanding. *Cognition and Emotion*, 9, 151–165.

Bion, W. R. (1962). A theory of thinking. *International Journal of Psycho-Analysis*, 43, 306–310.

Blatt, S. J. and Behrends, R. S. (1987). Internalization, separation-individuation, and the nature of therapeutic action. *International Journal of Psycho-Analysis*, 68, 279–297.

Bollas, C. (1987). *The Shadow of the Object: Psychoanalysis of the Unthought Known*. New York: Columbia University Press.

Bolton, D. and Hill, J. (1996). *Mind, Meaning and Mental Disorder*. Oxford: Oxford University Press.

Bowlby, J. (1988). *A Secure Base: Clinical Applications of Attachment Theory*. London: Routledge.

Britton, R. (1995). Psychic reality and unconscious belief. *International Journal of Psycho-Analysis*, 76, 19–23.

Cohen, N. (1984). Preserved learning capacity in amnesia: Evidence for multiple memory systems. In L. R. Squires and N. Butters (eds), *Neuropsychology of Memory*. New York: Guilford, pp. 83–103.

Cohen, N. and Squire, L. R. (1980). Preserved learning and retention of pattern-analyzing skill in amnesia: Dissociation of knowing how and knowing that. *Science*, 210, 207–209.

Damasio, A. R. and Damasio, H. (1994). Cortical systems underlying knowledge retrieval: Evidence from human lesion studies. In T. A. Poggio and A. D. Glaser (eds), *Exploring Brain Functions: Models in Neuroscience*. New York: John Wiley.

De M'Uzan, M. (1974). Psychodynamic mechanisms in psychosomatic symptom formation. *Psychotherapy and Psychosomatics*, 23, 103–110.

DiGiulio, D. V., Seidenberg, M., O'Leary, D. S. and Raz, N. (1994). Procedural and declarative memory: A developmental study. *Brain and Cognition*, 25, 79–91.

Edelman, G. M. (1987). *Neural Darwinism: The Theory of Neuronal Group Selection.* New York: Basic Books.

Emde, R. N. (1990). Mobilizing fundamental modes of development: Empathic availability and therapeutic action. *Journal of the American Psychoanalytic Association*, 38, 881–913.

Feldman, M. and Bott Spillius, E. (1989). General introduction. In M. Feldman and E. Bott Spillius (eds), *Psychic Equilibrium and psychic change: Selected Papers of Betty Joseph.* London: Routledge, pp. 1–15).

Fivush, R., Haden, C. and Reese, E. (1996). Autobiographical knowledge and autobiographical memories. In D. C. Rubin (Ed.), *Remembering Our Past: Studies in Autobiographical Memory.* New York: Cambridge University Press, pp. 341–359.

Fonagy, P. (1995). Playing with reality: The development of psychic reality and its malfunction in borderline patients. *International Journal of Psycho-Analysis*, 76, 39–44.

Fonagy, P. (1997). Where cure was inconceivable. The aims of modern psychoanalysis with borderline patients. *Texte*, Heft 3, 17 Jahrgang, 11–25.

Fonagy, P., Kachele, H., Krause, R., Jones, E., Perron, R. and Lopez, L. (1999). *An Open Door Review of Outcome Studies in Psychoanalysis.* London: International Psychoanalytical Association.

Fonagy, P. and Moran, G. S. (1991). Understanding psychic change in child analysis. *International Journal of Psycho-Analysis*, 72, 15–22.

Fonagy, P., Moran, G. S., Edgcumbe, R., Kennedy, H. and Target, M. (1993). The roles of mental representations and mental processes in therapeutic action. *The Psychoanalytic Study of the Child*, 48, 9–48.

Fonagy, P., Steele, M., Steele, H., Leigh, T., Kennedy, R., Mattoon, G. and Target, M. (1995). Attachment, the reflective self, and borderline states: The predictive specificity of the Adult Attachment Interview and pathological emotional development. In S. Goldberg, R. Muir and J. Kerr (eds), *Attachment Theory: Social, Developmental and Clinical Perspectives* New York: Analytic Press, pp. 233–278.

Fonagy, P. and Target, M. (1996). Playing with reality: I. Theory of mind and the normal development of psychic reality. *International Journal of Psycho-Analysis*, 77, 217–233.

Fonagy, P. and Target, M. (1997). Perspectives on the recovered memories debate. In J. Sandler and P. Fonagy (eds), *Recovered Memories of Abuse: True or False?* London: Karnac Books, pp. 183–216.

Fonagy, P. and Target, M. (1998). Mentalization and the changing aims of child psychoanalysis. *Psychoanalytic Dialogues*, 8, 87–114.

Fonagy, P., Target, M. and Gergely, G. (2000). Attachment and borderline personality disorder: A theory and some evidence. *Psychiatric Clinics of North America*, 23, 103–122.

Freud, S. (1900). *The Interpretation of Dreams.* In J. Strachey (ed.), *The Standard Edition of the Complete Psychological Works of Sigmund Freud* (Vol. 4,5). London: Hogarth Press, pp. 1–715.

Freud, S. and Breuer, J. (1895). Studies on hysteria. In J. Strachey (ed.), *The Standard Edition of the Complete Psychological Works of Sigmund Freud* (Vol. 2). London: Hogarth Press, pp. 1–305.

Gathercole, S. E. (1998). The development of memory. *Journal of Child Psychology and Psychiatry*, 39, 3–27.

Glickstein, M. and Yeo, C. (1990). The cerebellum and motor learning. *Journal of Cognitive Neuroscience*, 2, 69–80.

Goodman, S. (1977). *Psychoanalytic Education and Research. The Current Situation and Future Possibilities*. New York: International University Press.

Gopnik, A. (1993). How we know our minds: The illusion of first-person knowledge of intentionality. *Behavioral and Brain Sciences*, 16, 1–14, 29–113.

Howe, M. L. and Courage, M. L. (1997). The emergence and early development of autobiographical memory. *Psychological Review*, 104, 499–523.

Joffe, W. G. and Sandler, J. (1969). Comments on the psychoanalytic psychology of adaptation, with special reference to the role of affects and the representational world. *International Journal of Psychoanalysis*, 49, 445–454.

Joseph, B. (1985). Transference: The total situation. *International Journal of Psycho-Analysis*, 66, 447–454.

Joseph, B. (1989). *Psychic Equilibrium and Psychic Change*. London: Routledge.

Kernberg, O. F. (1988). Psychic structure and structural change: An ego psychology–object relations theory viewpoint. *Journal of the American Psychoanalytic Association*, 36 (suppl.), 315–337.

LeDoux, J. E. (1995). Emotion: Clues from the brain. *Annual Review of Psychology*, 46, 209–235.

Loewald, H. W. (1979). Reflections on the psychoanalytic process and its therapeutic potential. *The Psychoanalytic Study of the Child*, 34, 155–167.

Lyons-Ruth, K. (1999). The two person unconscious: Intersubjective dialogue, enactive relational representation and the emergence of new forms of relational organisation. *Psychoanalytic Inquiry*, 19(4), 576–617.

McDougall, J. (1974). The psycho-soma and the psychoanalytic process. *International Review of Psycho-Analysis*, 1, 437–460.

McDougall, J. (1986). *Theater of the Mind*. New York: Basic Books.

Mandler, G. (1985). *Cognitive Psychology. An Essay in Cognitive Science*. Hillsdale, N.J.: Lawrence Erlbaum Associates.

Marty, P. (1990). *La Psychosomatique de l'Adulte*. Paris: Presses Universitaire de France.

Matte Blanco, I. (1975). *The Unconscious As Infinite Sets*. London: Duckworth.

Mayes, L. C. and Spence, D. P. (1994). Understanding therapeutic action in the analytic situation: A second look at the developmental metaphor. *Journal of the American Psychoanalytic Association*, 42, 789–816.

Meltzer, D. (1975). *Explorations in Autism: A Psycho-Analytical Study*. Strath Tay: Clunie Press.

Mishkin, M., Malamut, B. and Bachevalier, J. (1984). Memories and habits: Two neural systems. In G. Lynch and J. L. McGaugh (eds).

Modell, A. H. (1976). "The Holding Environment" and the Therapeutic Action of Psychoanalysis. *Journal of the American Psychoanalytic Association*, 24, 285–307.

Nelson, K. (1993a). Explaining the emergence of autobiographical memory in early childhood. In A. Collins, S. E. Gathercole, M. A. Conway and P. E. Morris (eds), *Theories of Memory*. Hove, U.K.: Erlbaum, pp. 355–385.

Nelson, K. (1993b). The psychological and social origins of autobiographical memory. *Psychological Science*, 4, 7–14.

Panel. (1937). Symposium on the theory of the therapeutic results of psychoanalysis. *International Journal of Psycho-Analysis*, 18, 125–184.

Rosenfeld, H. (1987). *Impasse and Interpretation*. London: Tavistock Publications.

Saint-Cyr, J. A. and Taylor, A. E. (1992). The mobilization of procedural learning: The "key signature" of the basal ganglia. In L. R. Squire and N. Butters (eds), *Neuropsychology of Memory* (2nd edn). New York: Guilford Press, pp. 188–202.

Sandell, R., Blomberg, J., Lazar, A., Carlsson, J., Broberg, J. and Rand, H. (2000). Varieties of long-term outcome among patients in psychoanalysis and long-term psychotherapy: a review of findings in the Stockholm outcome of psychoanalysis and psychotherapy project (STOPP). *International Journal of Psychoanalysis*, 81(5), 921–943.

Sandler, J. (1976). Countertransference and role-responsiveness. *International Review of Psycho-Analysis*, 3, 43–47.

Sandler, J. and Joffe, W. G. (1966). On skill and sublimation. *Journal of American Psychoanalytic Association*, 14, 335–355.

Sandler, J. and Joffe, W. G. (1967). The tendency to persistence in psychological function and development, with special reference to fixation and regression. *Bulletin of the Menninger Clinic*, 31, 257–271.

Sandler, J. and Joffe, W. G. (1969). Towards a basic psychoanalytic model. *International Journal of Psycho-Analysis*, 50, 79–90.

Sandler, J. and Sandler, A.-M. (1987). The past unconscious, the present unconscious and the vicissitudes of guilt. *International Journal of Psycho-Analysis*, 68, 331–341.

Sandler, J. and Sandler, A.-M. (1997). A psychoanalytic theory of repression and the unconscious. In J. Sandler and P. Fonagy (eds), *Recovered Memories of Abuse: True or False?* London: Karnac Books, pp. 163–181.

Schachter, D. L. (1987). Implicit expressions of memory in organic amnesia: Learning of new facts and associations. *Human Neurobiology*, 6, 107–118.

Schachter, D. L. (1992a). Priming and multiple memory systems: Perceptual mechanisms of implicit memory. *Journal of Cognitive Neuroscience*, 4, 244–256.

Schachter, D. L. (1992b). Understanding implicit memory: A cognitive neuroscience approach. *American Psychologist*, 47, 559–569.

Schlessinger, N. and Robbins, F. (1983). *A Developmental View of the Psychoanalytic Process*. New York: International Universities Press.

Segal, H. (1978). On Symbolism. *International Journal of Psycho-Analysis*, 59, 315–319.

Sifneos, P. E. (1977). The phenomenon of "alexithymia". *Psychotherapy and Psychosomatics*, 28, 47–57.

Stern, D., Sander, L., Nahum, J., Harrison, A., Lyons-Ruth, K., Morgan, A., Bruschweilerstern, N. and Tronick, E. (1998). Non-interpretive mechanisms in psychoanalytic therapy: The "something more" than interpretation. *International Journal of Psycho-Analysis*, 79(5), 903–921.

Stern, D. N. (1994). One way to build a clinically relevant baby. *Infant Mental Health Journal*, 15, 36–54.

Stolorow, R. and Lachmann, F. (1978). The developmental prestages of defenses: diagnostic and therapeutic implications. *Psychoanalytic Quarterly*, 47, 73–102.

Stone, L. (1961). *The Psychoanalytic Situation. An Examination of its Development and Essential Nature*. New York: International Universities Press.

Target, M. and Fonagy, P. (1996). Playing with reality II: The development of psychic reality from a theoretical perspective. *International Journal of Psycho-Analysis*, 77, 459–479.

Ungerleider, L. G. (1995). Functional rain imaging studies of cortical mechanisms for memory. *Science*, 270, 769–775.

Viederman, M. (1991). The impact of the real person of the analyst on the psychoanalytic cure. *Journal of the American Psychoanalytic Association*, 39, 451–489.

Waddington, C. H. (1966). *Principles of Development and Differentiation*. New York: Macmillan.

Chapter 3

A contribution to a technical frame of reference

Anne-Marie Sandler

When some time ago my husband and I were approached with a request to contribute to a Festschrift in honour of Anne Alvarez, we were both touched and delighted. We had always admired her enthusiasm, her clinical giftedness as well as her interest in theoretical issues. We felt that colleagues who could write so clearly and with such lucidity and, most of all, who could think truly independently were exceedingly rare. Anne felt to us to be such a person. When more recently contact was renewed in order to get the book together, I decided to re-work a joint paper that my late husband and I had in fact earmarked for this volume. In it we do attempt to present a theoretical frame of reference which we think would illustrate and contain the way we actually work with adults or children in analysis. Unfortunately, limitation of length does not permit me to include additional clinical material.

From the vantage point of today we can see that the conflicts within the British Society are significantly different from what they were a few decades ago, although they are, in a certain sense, derivatives of the conflicts of the past. Thus the Kleinians no longer place the same emphasis on the interpretation of deep anxieties and the Contemporary Freudians are much more sensitive to the subtleties of transference than they were years ago. And certainly both groups have influenced the Independents, who represent a very wide spectrum of views, and in turn members of both groups have been made increasingly aware of the interpersonal factors coming from the object relations theorists of the Independent group. There can be little doubt that much of the impetus for this cross-fertilization has come from the systematic discussion of clinical material, with the fine details of psychoanalytic theory taking second place.

In spite of the fact that changes in theory and technique have occurred in the British Society as a result of the different groups having stayed together under one roof, there are still substantial differences among the theories professed by members of these groups. Yet the members are close in their evaluation of what constitutes good clinical analytic work. This implies that there is an underlying theory or set of theories relating to clinical psycho-analytic practice, an essentially unconscious, i.e. private or latent body of theory that can be a basis for common understanding and communication, even though the so-called public theories may not show the same correspondences.

Let me say a few words about this issue of public and private theories. Some years ago, in a paper on the relation between psychoanalytic concepts and psychoanalytic practice, my husband put forward the view that

> With increasing clinical experience the analyst, as he grows more competent, will preconsciously (descriptively speaking, unconsciously) construct a whole variety of theoretical segments which relate directly to his clinical work. They are the products of unconscious thinking, are very much partial theories, models or schemata ... That they may contradict one another is no problem. They coexist happily as long as they are unconscious. They do not appear in consciousness unless they are consonant with what I have called official or public theory, and can be described in suitable words. Such partial theories may in fact represent better (i.e. more useful and appropriate) theories than the official ones, and it is likely that many valuable additions to psychoanalytic theory have come about because conditions have arisen that have allowed preconscious part-theories to come together and emerge in a psychoanalytically socially acceptable way.
>
> (Sandler, 1983)

In this chapter I hope to present a theoretical frame of reference which has emerged as a consequence of joint work with my husband on the basis of examining what we actually do when we work with our analytic patients and the technical stance we take in supervision and case seminars.

Very briefly, I shall be describing the need to reabsorb quite explicitly the topographical dimension (one that we in fact use all the time, i.e., the dimension of depth to surface) into our technical frame of reference, as well as adopt an essentially developmental point of view in our thinking about technique. In this context "developmental" refers both to development from infancy to early childhood, latency, adolescence, adulthood and old age and also to the inner developmental process in regard to movement from depths to surface, from the primitive to the more sophisticated, that is constantly going on in the present. After some comments about the concepts of the unconscious and the preconscious as they were formulated in Freud's topographical theory, I shall refer to a distinction that my husband and I have been suggesting between what can be called the past unconscious and the present unconscious. The present unconscious resembles Freud's Pcs. system in some ways, and has some features of the unconscious ego of his structural theory as well. What will be emphasized in regard to the present unconscious is the fact that its contents are not freely accessible to consciousness. Although these contents are the product of defensive and adaptive processes, they are still subject to a further censorship before being allowed into conscious awareness. The area of this censorship, which is related to what Freud called the second censorship, one between the pre-conscious and consciousness, can be regarded as the primary focus of our analytic work.

The *past unconscious* can be viewed as "the child within' and is very different from the system Ucs. of the topographical theory, and equally very different from the id. This child within (the past unconscious) can be conceived of as structuring, as giving form to all the intrapsychic content that arises in the depths – in particular unconscious wishes and wishful fantasies. This unconscious content then becomes modified in the present unconscious as it moves from the depths to the surface. I hope that what is meant by this will become clearer later, as it has important technical implications.

I would like to emphasize that what is being described in this chapter is not a theory intended to replace other theories, but rather a frame of reference to supplement other psychoanalytic models of mental functioning. It is a frame of reference aimed specifically at trying to narrow the gap between theory and practice. It is, of course, inevitable that in trying to do this I shall point to a few of the conceptual problems and contradictions that have hampered our psychoanalytic theories since the time of Freud onwards.

It is useful to begin by considering the concept usually referred to as "the unconscious". By now we must all be aware of the conceptual distinction between the system Ucs. of the topographical theory and the broader descriptive notion of the term, something we can call the "descriptive" unconscious, a term which, in Freud's topographical theory, referred to both the system Ucs. (the dynamic Ucs.) and the Pcs. The failure to distinguish between the dynamic Unconscious and the descriptive concept has been a source of endless confusion, and although many hoped that the structural theory would eliminate the problem the notion of "the unconscious" has not disappeared, and has remained as a noun referring to all that is, descriptively speaking, unconscious. An equal source of confusion has existed from the very beginning in regard to the system Pcs. and to preconscious mental processes. These mental processes were considered as if their content were easily accessible to consciousness while at the same time they were described as belonging to the unconscious. Because of this muddle some authors urged the abandonment of the term "preconscious" because of its ambiguity.

This suggestion did not appear to convince Anna Freud, who commented some years afterwards that

> I definitely belong to the people who feel free to fall back on the topo-graphical aspects whenever convenient and to leave them aside and to speak purely structurally when that is convenient ... this bad habit of mine of living between the two frames of reference – the topographical

and the structural – is much to be recommended because it simplifies thinking enormously, and simplifies description when necessary ... I tried to keep what has been lost [with the structural theory] by reverting whenever I feel it necessary to the former [i.e. the topographical theory], because we got along quite well with the former for a long time.

(Freud, 1985: 31)

Anna Freud's use of two psychoanalytic models of the mind does not make her an eclectic. Indeed, I believe that her position makes much more sense than the idea that one should use only one model of mental functioning. Those who criticize so-called two-track or multi-track theorists have, in my view, driven alternative or supplementary models, theories or frames of reference underground; that is, they are used by them unconsciously. One example of this is the way we as psychoanalysts for the most part move quite unconsciously between an intrapsychic view and an interpersonal one, without realizing that we are changing our frames of reference. A theory is good if it does the work it is intended to do, but there are many sorts of work we have to do as analysts. A one-track approach, if it is thought to be comprehensive and strictly adhered to, would of necessity be severely limiting, and the demands placed on it must inevitably lead to its breakdown, just as the topographical theory broke down and the structural model is showing signs of age. The approach I shall take in this chapter is that, for purposes of clinical psychoanalysis, the theoretical models we have and work with need to be supplemented – not replaced – by an additional technically oriented frame of reference.

Quite clearly a topographical point of view is inherent in our clinical thinking, a point of view which seems to have been lost in Freud's structural theory. We cannot work psychoanalytically without making use of notions of surface and depth, of movement from the depths to the surface. It seems as if the notions of the unconscious and the preconscious are here to stay, but they need some adjustment if we are not to revert to the topographical theory with all its attendant difficulties.

What are these adjustments? Consider the descriptive term "preconscious", referring to content in the system Pcs., located just below consciousness. It is, I believe, not generally appreciated that Freud used the term "preconscious" in a number of very different ways. The first is in reference to a psychic system which tends to function according to the secondary process, i.e. to make use of formal thought processes of greater or lesser complexity. Next, there is the descriptive sense of "preconscious", referring to mental content that is readily accessible to consciousness (this is perhaps one sense in which it might be useful to retain the term "preconscious"). But there is a third sense in which the term was used by Freud, one which does not fit with the more general use of the term but which is of the utmost importance. This is the concept of preconscious content which is not freely accessible to consciousness. As Freud put it in 1900, in *The Interpretation of Dreams*, "The second agency [the Pcs.] allows nothing to pass without exercising its rights and making such modifications as it thinks fit in the thought which is seeking admission to consciousness."

In his 1915 paper on "The Unconscious" Freud makes a number of further references to a *censorship* lying between the preconscious and consciousness. He speaks there, for example, of a "new frontier of censorship", and says that "One might suppose that in the course of individual development the censorship had taken a step forward ... in psycho-analytic treatment the existence of a second censorship, located between the systems *Pcs.* and *Cs.* is proved beyond question".

Freud here posits a second censorship in addition to the one he saw existing between the systems Ucs. and Pcs. in his topographical theory, and for the time being in our model we shall continue to refer to it as the second censorship, although we would now say that it is useful to consider it as lying between the present unconscious and consciousness.

By now the impression may have been gained that a return to Freud's topographical model of 1900 or 1915 is being advocated. Let me dispel that impression by saying that what is proposed is a visit rather than a permanent return, a visit aimed at retrieving, to use Anna Freud's words, what has been lost with the structural theory.

All practising analysts must be mindful of the resistance to conscious awareness that people have in regard to preconscious thoughts, impulses and feelings or, as I prefer to say, to contents of the present unconscious. It is clinically appropriate to describe this resistance as being due to a censorship that has as its fundamental motivation the avoidance of conscious feelings of shame, embarrassment and humiliation. Developmentally it can be linked first with the step of substituting conscious fantasying for play, and the need to keep such fantasies secret. What happens then has been described as follows:

> As the child develops the increasing capacity to anticipate the shaming and humiliating reactions of others (with all the additions he has made to his expectations arising from his own projections), so he will become *his own* disapproving audience and will continually internalize the social situation in the form of the second censorship. Only content that is acceptable will be permitted through to consciousness. It must be *plausible* and not ridiculous or "silly". In a way the second censorship is much more of a *narcissistic* censorship than the first, but the narcissism involved often tends to centre around fears of being laughed at, of being thought to be silly, crazy, ridiculous or childish – essentially fears of being humiliated
>
> (Sandler and Sandler, 1988).

That part of the unconscious which we can refer to as the present unconscious can be thought of as having a very different type of functional organization from that of the *system Ucs.*; that is, the dynamic unconscious of Freud's topographical theory. In many respects the present unconscious resembles the Preconscious of the topographical model or the unconscious ego of the structural theory, but it differs from the structural ego in having a dimension of depth. The contents of the present unconscious are accessible in analysis if we can verbalize the latent content closest to the surface, giving our interpretations in such a way as to make the latent content consciousness-syntonic, i.e. acceptable to consciousness.

The *present unconscious* can be distinguished from the *past unconscious*, a notion that may well prove to be the most controversial part of the argument. But first it is necessary to say something more about the functioning of the present unconscious. For the sake of convenience I shall refer to unconscious fantasy, using this term – for the time being at any rate – as a convenient representative of all thoughts, wishes, and impulses; that is, all mental representations and their accompanying feeling states as they exist in the present unconscious. As unconscious fantasies arise in the depths of the present unconscious – fantasies which can be considered to be, to varying degree, derivatives of the past unconscious – they have to be dealt with by *the person of the present*, with the aim of maintaining equilibrium in the present. These fantasies can be regarded as being different in structure from the fantasies of early childhood. The fantasies in the present unconscious are closely linked with representations of present-day persons, and are subject to a higher level of unconscious secondary process functioning than exists in the past unconscious. Thus, unconscious transference thoughts or fantasies exist in the *present* unconscious, not in the past unconscious. The fantasies or impulses arising in the present unconscious, *to the extent that they arouse conflict*, disturb the equilibrium of the present unconscious, have to be dealt with, *outside* consciousness, and have to be modified, disguised or repressed. It is here that the whole range of the mechanisms of defence, and indeed all varieties of other compensatory and adaptive mechanisms, all sorts of compromise formations, come in.

These mechanisms serve to disguise the unconscious fantasy by means of manipulations of the self and object representations as well as feelings involved in the fantasy. Parts of the self-representation will be split off and displaced to the object representation, and parts of the object representation absorbed into the representation of the self. All this is a reflection of what can be regarded as *the stabilizing function of the present unconscious*. This function involves a response in the present unconscious to all sorts of affective disturbances of inner equilibrium, whatever the sources of these disturbances may be, no matter whether they arise from the external world, from the past unconscious, or – as happens most frequently – from a combination of the two. The stabilizing function works essentially to maintain inner equilibrium, to maintain a feeling of safety and integrity of the self, by *reorganizing* the unconscious representations of the threatening content, through the use of a variety of defensive measures – essentially measures by which unconscious content is transformed. These defences may be all sorts of projections, identifications and projective identifications, displacements, externalizations, as well as reversals of one kind or another.

Although an unconscious wishful fantasy may have been substantially modified within the present unconscious in order to render it less disruptive, less conflictual, its path to the surface, to conscious awareness, may well still be impeded by resistance due to what we can regard as the operation of the censorship between the present unconscious and consciousness. In order to pass the second censorship, the products of the stabilizing function have to be modified further. They must have to undergo a sort of secondary revision in order to be made plausible, non-silly, non-stupid (except in perhaps specially licensed forms such as dreams and humour, in which forms of irrationality are permitted).

So, for example, a hostile wish towards the analyst arising within the present unconscious may be a source of conflict, and might then be modified by projection or other displacements within the content of the unconscious thought or fantasy. A revised thought or fantasy will be formed. What this means is that the hostile part of the self-representation might have been allocated to the representation of the analyst, and the result of this may be the thought that the analyst is hostile to the analysand. The conscious awareness of such a thought, however, may meet with resistance (here is our second censorship). The patient may talk, for example, of someone else who is disliked by an employer, but this is a consequence of the patient's unconscious internalized social anxieties, in the form of the censorship, not allowing the thought that *the analyst* is hostile, to enter consciousness. It is then the analyst's task, if he understands what is going on, to interpret the unconscious fantasy that exists just below the surface – that the analyst is hostile – in such a way as to make it acceptable to the patient, to make it consciousness-syntonic. Once this has been done, and the patient can accept and tolerate the previously unconscious transference thought, the opportunity should arise for further work to allow the original hostile transference thought itself to become acceptable to consciousness. It would have been, of course, a technical error on the part of the analyst to interpret the hostile thought directly without going through the intervening step of interpreting, what was being kept at bay, by the so-called second censorship.

In the very active work that occurs continuously in the present unconscious, a great deal of fantasy dialogue is involved. This dialogue can be said to be with one's introjects (Sandler and Sandler, 1978), but more precisely they are dialogues in fantasy with the *representatives* of one's introjects in one's unconscious fantasy life. It is worth commenting that there is always pressure to anchor the wishful thoughts or fantasies that exist in the present unconscious in reality. In some way we try to *actualize* our unconscious wishful fantasies (Sandler, 1976a, 1976b), but we do this in an unconscious way by making extensive use of what is perhaps the most overworked function of the mental apparatus – rationalization – in order to make our implausible actions plausible to ourselves and to others. We have a pressure to anchor, to externalize, to fit our unconscious fantasies into reality in one way or another.

It was relatively late in the development of psychoanalytic theory that defences began to be explicitly linked with representations of self and object (Sandler and Rosenblatt, 1962), and this understanding has been heightened as analysts came to understand those resistances in which defensive displacement between self and object representations occurred in the general context of transference. It is such representational displacements that will occur in the process of defensively modifying unconscious fantasies in order to restore the subject's feeling of cohesion and of integrity of the self.

I have given a rather sketchy outline of the way the present unconscious functions. Perhaps it might help to visualize it as a structural ego that has depth, that has, as a major aim, the protection of consciousness, that maintains an inner affective equilibrium through resolving conflicts and has established a special censorship in addition to the defences used in the resolution of conflict. This censorship, which functions just below the level of consciousness, serves to protect the individual from mental content that might generate conscious feelings of unpleasure, predominant among these being shame, embarrassment, humiliation and other forms of internalized social anxiety.

What I have referred to as the *past unconscious* – or the child within – is very different, not only from the present unconscious but also from the dynamic Unconscious of the topographical model and the id of the structural theory. Before going on to describe the past unconscious, however, I should like to make one or two preliminary observations. The first concerns the psychoanalytic theory of motivation, the second the presumed age of the hypothetical child within.

Most of us realize that the psychoanalytic theory of motivation is far more complex than it has tended to be seen in the past. We have taken the view that not all unconscious wishes can be regarded as being motivated by instinctual drives seeking discharge. Nor can we dodge the issue by referring to instinctual drives and their derivatives, as if all wish-fulfilling behaviour is, in the final analysis, powered by libido and aggression. From a clinical point of view it is of the greatest importance to recognize that anxiety, or indeed any unpleasant affect, can be an extremely powerful motivation for an unconscious wish, at times even more powerful than the instinctual drives themselves. Further, if a solution to some particular conflict has been found during the course of an individual's development, perhaps – but not necessarily – a compromise formation, *the pressure to impose that solution acquires a peremptory quality in the face of similar conflicts later on*. So, for example, if a child deals effectively with a conflict over separation by becoming clinging, then developmental adaptation in the urge to cling will have a powerful force behind it in the face of threatened separation. Of course, such a solution, such a wish, which was syntonic in childhood, may become dystonic later in development and create further conflict as it arises in the present unconscious – conflict that might have to be resolved in a new way, for example by being the one who rejects.

It is, I believe, a fundamental error to consider every unconscious wish as an instinctual wish or even as a drive derivative. (So, for example, the urge to cling to a maternal object, or simply to what is familiar as a response to anxiety, should not be regarded as always being motivated by a partial oral drive or as some form of drive derivative.) The motivating force is much more likely to be anxiety. This view in no way detracts from the importance of the drives in development and in the individual's current functioning, but the psychoanalytic theory of motivation should not be reduced to the functioning of the id.

As far as the age of our hypothetical "child within" is concerned, we would suggest that it be put more or less at the age of five, give or take a year. The reasons for what might look like an arbitrary choice are as follows. Five is more or less the age at which we date the infantile amnesia, owing perhaps to the massive repression responsible for Freud's first censorship. We are all aware of how little can be remembered from the first four or five years of life. What we do remember or recall in analysis tends to be in the form of isolated fragments which have been revised in the process of later remembering – if they have coherence this has usually been added later. In addition, much that is recalled from the first few years has been acquired second hand.

Five is the age at which we see serious attempts to deal with oedipal conflict, resulting in important identifications and other internalizations of significant figures in the child's life. It is the age at which we see a major crystallization of the superego. It is the age at which the child's level of cognition changes radically – in the Piagetian model, from pre-operational to operational thinking. It is the age when the child normally takes a major step forward in regard to separation–individuation. And last, but not least, it is the age at which there is a significant development in the child's theory of mind. By this I mean the attainment by the child of the capacity to attribute to others beliefs, thoughts or feelings *different* from his own (Mayes and Cohen, 1993), the capacity to put oneself in another person's shoes, so to speak, without losing the awareness of one's own feelings.

We cannot regard this hypothetical child as an id-child, as a purely instinctually driven child, whose psychic organization is dominated by primary process functioning. It is a child who has passed through important developmental phases, which may or may not have been mastered successfully, one who may or may not have had a deviant development, whose instinctual drives have undergone many vicissitudes, whose cognitive development has been marked by successive phases of secondary process functioning, who has narcissistic assets and vulnerabilities, who has specific fears and anxieties, who may have achieved useful sublimations, and who has devised a number of solutions to conflict and adaptations to his or her specific environment. It is a child who is, above all, an object-related child, who has made significant identifications, a child with a fantasy life profoundly affected by his structured internal objects, including those that constitute the superego. It is a child with specific strengths and vulnerabilities, who will have a greater or lesser tendency to regress in the face of conflict or any other source of unpleasant affect. It is a child who is expected to be ready for school and to put childish things behind. It is a specific individual child, with his or her own individual personality reflecting individual development.

What then is the relation of the child within to the present unconscious of the older child or adult? In previous formulations the view was taken that impulses and wishes enter the present unconscious from the past unconscious, and have to be dealt with *there* by the stabilizing function, because *they may be no longer appropriate*, and therefore disruptive. Somewhat later my husband and I put it somewhat differently. What happens, we believe, is that the initial unconscious reactions or impulses of the individual are formed *as if* the person were a particular five-year-old child; and these reactions then have to be dealt with in the present unconscious *by the person of the present*. The child within acts as a *template*, a structuring organization, a set of rules, for the immediate here-and-now unconscious strivings and responses of the older individual. We might even be tempted to call it a psychic agency, a macrostructure. The impulse or wish that arises in the depths of the present unconscious need not be regarded as one that has been passed through a censorship from the child within. The censoring, if one wants to call it that, takes place throughout the present unconscious, with a final censorship or defensive transformation – Freud's second censorship – occurring before admission to conscious awareness. The unconscious wish arising in the present unconscious is modelled on the inner child's wishes, *but the objects involved are objects of the present*. This can be put in another way by reference to the example I quoted previously. If an unconscious hostile wish towards the analyst arises in a patient's present unconscious, then it is not a death wish towards the father displaced on to the analyst in the transference. Rather, it is a hostile impulse arising in the here-and-now towards the analyst, quite possibly *modelled* on the inner child's hostile wishes towards the father.

However, we are not only dealing with impulses or wishes in this context. Reactions to promptings and demands of the external world can be regarded as being initially responded to *as if* by the child within, but to the extent that the responses in the present modelled on the past unconscious are trial actions found to be inappropriate to the present or threatening to the individual's equilibrium, they will be defended against and censored, either inhibited or allowed to proceed to action and conscious experience in a modified form. All of this occurs, of course, extremely quickly.

One may well ask what all these ideas have to do with analytic work, and I shall attempt to provide a partial answer. The first point is that the primary field of action in the analytic engagement is located around the censorship between the present unconscious and consciousness. It is vital that the analyst give *first priority* to understanding, and if possible interpreting, what is going on in the here-and-now of the analysis. Much of the material defended against by the second censorship – if we can still call it that – will relate to the analytic transference, and interpretation of the transference has, of course, first priority. By this I do not mean that the analyst should engage in compulsive transference interpretation, but I *do* mean interpretation that will allow the most intensely affect-laden material that is near the surface, but being warded off, to become acceptable to the analysand. If, in certain cases, it may be necessary to refer to the past *before* speaking of the present, then this should be done *with the aim of showing the patient what is going on in the present*. If interpretation of the here-and-now conflict of the patient is successful, and the patient can accept the censored, warded-off wishful aspect of himself, then we have, of course, the opportunity to *anchor* the understanding of the patient both in *constructions* (that is showing the patient his current habitual patterns of functioning) and in *reconstructions of the past*. But here we should remember that our knowledge of the child within is based almost entirely on informed reconstruction. We reconstruct the past, we do not excavate it. And, let me add, of the greatest importance in regard to all of this is the need to avoid reducing all conflict to conflict between drives and defence, to avoid the simplistic reductionism that has been responsible for so much bad analysis in the past.

The frame of reference outlined here is, I hope, a useful approach to the development of a theory of psychoanalytic technique. It is essentially a developmental approach to technique, but also allows for the absorption of our increased awareness of the importance of the interaction between analyst and patient. And certainly there are many directions in which it needs to be elaborated and extended. Psychoanalytic theory as well as psychoanalytic practice is in a state of continual development, and I am grateful for the chance that this publication gives me to try and contribute to the dialectic of this development.

References

Freud, Anna (1985) in A. Freud, with J. Sandler. *The Analysis of Defense: The Ego and the Mechanisms of Defense Revisited*. New York: International Universities Press.

Freud, S. (1900). The Interpretation of Dreams. In J. Strachey (ed.) *The Standard Edition of the Complete Psychological Works of Sigmund Freud*, Vols 4–5, London: Hogarth Press.

Freud, S. (1915). The Unconscious. In J. Strachey (ed.) *The Standard Edition of the Complete Psychological Works of Sigmund Freud*, Vol. 14, London: Hogarth Press.

Mayes, L. and Cohen, D. (1993). "The child's emerging understanding of other minds", Paper delivered to Third International Psychoanalytical Association Conference on Psychoanalytic Research on "The Observed Child and the Reconstructed Child". University College, London, 12–13 March 1993.

Sandler, J. (1976a). "Countertransference and role-responsiveness", *International Review of Psycho-Analysis*, 3: 43–47.

Sandler, J. (1976b) "Dreams, unconscious phantasies and 'identity of perception'", *International Review of Psycho-Analysis*, 3: 33–42.

Sandler, J. (1983). "Reflections on some relations between psychoanalytic concepts and psychoanalytic practice", *International Journal of Psycho-Analysis*, 64: 35–46.

Sandler, J. (1984). "The id – or the child within", in J. Sandler (ed.) *Dimensions of Psychoanalysis*, London: Karnac, and Madison: International Universities Press.

Sandler, J. (1986). "Reality and the stabilising function of unconscious phantasy", *Bull. Anna Freud Centre*, 10: 33–509.

Sandler, J. and Rosenblatt, B. (1962). "The concept of the representational world", *Psychoanal. Study Child*, 17: 128–145.

Sandler, J. and Sandler, A.-M. (1978). "On the development of object relationships and affects", *International Journal of Psycho-Analysis*, 59: 285–296.

Sandler, J. and Sandler, A.-M. (1983). "The 'second censorship', the 'three-box model' and some technical implications", *International Journal of Psycho-Analysis*, 64: 413–425.

Sandler, J. and Sandler, A.-M. (1987). "The past unconscious, the present unconscious and the vicissitudes of guilt", *International Journal of Psycho-Analysis*, 68: 331–341.

Chapter 4

Bisexual qualities of the psychic envelope[1]

Didier Houzel

When Bion introduced the concept of the containing relationship, for the purposes of description he used the symbols that designate male and female: ♂ ♀. "I shall use the sign ♀ for the abstraction representing the container and ♂ for the contained" (1962: 90).

It is quite clear that this was a reference to the idea of psychic bisexuality that had already appeared in 1896 in one of Freud's letters to Fliess (Freud 1950a). Indeed, Bion went on to specify that "♂ is projected into ♀" (1962). He was therefore indicating that the relationship between these two elements is one of penetration, hence the analogy with sexual penetration. It is interesting to note that he used this model to describe the link he called K (Knowledge): the conjunction between container and contained enables transformation not only in what is projected but also in what receives these projections. Hence the containing relationship is a "commensal" one: container and contained both benefit from it, and they are involved in a process of growth.

According to Tustin (1972) it is precisely the commensal relationship that is lacking in infantile autism and in the autistic enclaves found in many patients. As an example of this, Bion cites the containing relationship between mother and baby, as well as the part–object relationship between mouth and breast. For Tustin (1972, 1981), this part–object relationship is profoundly disrupted in autistic pathology as a result of an anomalous integration of psychic bisexuality:

> Work with Encapsulated Secondary Autism children gives us clues as to what may be going on during this desultory period. One child told me that he had been "making shapes" in his mouth with his spit, just as he made shapes in his bottom with his "poohs". He said these shapes were "monsters". He drew one of these monsters which in the second picture bifurcated into male and female monsters. This differentiation of body stuff in terms of his bisexuality seemed to be experienced in terms of thrustingness and receptivity ... Clinical material implies that all this happened in relation to the mouth (the primary receptor) and his tongue

(the primary thruster); later notions of male and female, mother and father, seem to develop from this primal basis.

(Tustin 1972: 118–119)

The reader will recall that Tustin described in children with autism a kind of splitting that divides up contrasting sensory qualities into hard/soft, rough/smooth, bright/dark, etc. She related these contrasting sensory aspects to the male and female poles of psychic bisexuality:

> Gradually, "soft" sensations become associated with "taking-in", with receptivity. "Hard" sensations become associated with "entering" and "thrusting". At some point, these become associated with the infant's bisexuality. "Hard" thrusting becomes "male", and "soft" receptivity becomes "female". When, on the basis of co-operative suckling experience, the "hard" entering nipple and tongue are experienced as working together with the "soft" receptive mouth and breast, then a "marriage" between "male" and "female" elements takes place.

(Tustin 1992: 100–101)

My own experience of the psychoanalytical treatment of children with autism has led me to suggest that deficiencies in psychic bisexuality integration should be related to two levels rather than to a single one: psychic envelope (or container – for me, the two concepts are equivalent) *and* part–object relations. If we add to this the level corresponding to whole objects – the Oedipal organization as Freud described it – then we can distinguish three levels of psychic bisexuality integration. I would suggest that, in autism, if the male and female elements of bisexuality are not integrated but rather felt as being in a potentially destructive relationship, this is because of the lack of a container with the correct balance between closely interwoven maternal and paternal elements. Integration of these elements of bisexuality at this level seems to be a prerequisite for the containing function; without it, the object destined to be the container will either be engulfing or hard and impenetrable. The container must have some degree of elasticity: it should not be too inflexible, otherwise it will prevent the child projecting anything that can leave a trace or an imprint, but at the same time it must not be too soft because then the child's projections would be forever swallowed up with no hope of ever re-emerging.

At this level of integration of psychic bisexuality, my hypothesis is that the paternal elements do not penetrate the maternal ones as in Bion's (1962) and in Tustin's (1972) model; there is more of an interwoven pattern, in which the paternal elements buttress, as it were, the maternal container. If this interweaving fails, the encounter with the paternal object will inevitably be experienced as strange and threatening. This is what Tustin meant when she described "a rudimentary 'Oedipus complex' out of phase and shot through with polymorphously perverse elements" (1972: 120). Tustin went on to give the example of a child with autism who, having managed, thanks to the treatment, to acquire a capacity for dreaming, described to his therapist "this oral-cum-sexual appearance of a phallic father [through] a dream about a bowl of creamy milk in which there suddenly appeared a tuft of male pubic hair, at the sight of which he felt sick and terrified" (ibid.).

To admit the existence of this primary level of psychic bisexuality integration, in which the relationship is not one of penetration but of support between the maternal/feminine and the paternal/masculine aspects, we should remember that the mother's mind, which provides a container for the baby, is itself made up of bisexual identifications – in other words, it includes maternal and paternal imagos that have to be in a commensal relationship for the containing function to be able to operate. The child must be able to experience, in the same object, not only maternal receptivity and flexibility but also paternal consistency and resilience. Generally speaking, the search for the container's bisexual qualities is expressed in the initial stages of therapy with autistic children, once they have begun to feel confident about the analyst's receptive capacity, via attempts at testing the limits of the setting: they stamp on the floor much as a mountaineer tests the solidity of a foothold before venturing on to it, they hit the walls of the room as if to test how solid they are, sometimes they climb on to the furniture or the therapist's lap in order to make a thorough check of the consistency of the setting. Later, their behaviour often takes on a provocative quality as they go to the limits of what is possible, allowed or forbidden, as though to test the resilience of the analyst's mind. Conversely, they may unconsciously test the analyst's receptivity by endlessly repeating the same behaviour patterns, the hypnotic effect of which is particularly difficult to tolerate. As therapists, we find ourselves wavering between two contrasting frames of mind: either tolerating and accepting everything, with no limits being imposed – the risk here is to find ourselves trapped in endless repetition so that we fall asleep both mentally and physically – or being very restrictive and forcing the child to behave in a way that leaves no room for his or her own communications. In my opinion, these swings are a counter-transference manifestation of the splitting between the bisexual aspects of the container: sometimes there is too much of a shift towards the maternal pole, at others the swing takes us too far to the paternal side.

Alvarez (1992) has drawn our attention to the fact that the child's carer plays a *double* role: that of receptacle *and* that of transformer. She reiterates Bion's hypotheses on the transformations to which the container subjects whatever is projected into it, thereby making these elements thinkable for the baby. But then she goes on to show how the carer plays a role in arousing the child, inviting entry into the world of human communication and actively urging the baby to make contact; this is what she calls "reclaiming". On the practical side, Alvarez argues that the therapist should take on this role and not let the patient with autism wander endlessly in a meaningless world of infinite repetition and absence of thought. Each time it is necessary to do so, the therapist must reclaim the child's presence and attention. She even suggests that, if required, the therapist should actively put a stop to repetition, whether it takes the form of stereotyped motor behaviour or recurrent themes in the child's discourse ("chuntering"). Above all, awareness of and working through the counter-transference enable the therapist to elude the traps of autistic behaviour patterns that are not only meaningless but also in fact destructive of meaning. She compares the role of mental alerting the therapist should play with young patients to what Klaus and Kennell (1982) have observed in mothers of new-born babies, who invite their child to open his or her eyes and show signs of physical and mental awakening. We could surmise that such mothers do not experience their babies as mere extensions of themselves from whom nothing new or unexpected can be hoped for; they urge their babies to show that they do have some autonomy and are not simply a mirror-image of maternal projections. In this way, babies manifest the creative expression of a new life, transmitted of course by the mother but over which she has no real control. In order to accomplish this, the mother's own internal world must be a place for mental creativity in which the internalized parental objects can come together in a productive manner. The capacity for reverie is not a purely maternal function; it must possess maternal *and* paternal features. The reclaiming function as described by Alvarez (1992) would, from this point of view, be one of the more primitive paternal aspects of the capacity for reverie. I would argue that it is based essentially on the introjection into the mother's mind of a good paternal object united in a productive way with an internalized maternal object.

The bisexual features of the psychic envelope make it possible for the infant to accede to otherness. In order to develop into an individuated and autonomous human being, separable from the primary object, the infant must have the experience of a bisexual container that lets itself be penetrated and modified by the projections into it, yet has its own consistency and ability to deal with the violence of these projections. Internalization of a container that possesses these bisexual features gives the infant the feeling of having an intrapsychic *locus* in which to place and process his or her own emotional experiences; there will also be the feeling that this locus has a boundary to ensure proper delimiting between internal and external worlds, between the infant's mind and that of others, between mental space as seat of the emotions and representations and bodily space as the seat of sensory experience. In children with autism, these distinctions are not established.

Psychic envelope and structural stability

The terms "container", "envelope" and "psychic skin" are metaphors for the mind's functions. In my view, we need such metaphors, and the ones we have are particularly apposite because they are taken from what patients themselves propose as mental images for describing their experience of these functions. It is, however, important to specify their meaning from the point of view of the mind – in other words, to identify the processes involved in mental development. In my opinion, these processes have mainly to do with stabilizing subjective experience in a very specific way – that which modern theoreticians refer to as *structural stability*.

Freud referred to the concept of stability when he introduced his second theory of the instinctual drives in "Beyond the Pleasure Principle" (Freud 1920), where he quoted the following passage from Fechner (1873):

> Insofar as conscious impulses always have some relation to pleasure or unpleasure, pleasure and unpleasure too can be regarded as having a psycho-physical relation to conditions of stability and instability. This provides a basis for a hypothesis into which I propose to enter in greater detail elsewhere. According to this hypothesis, every psycho-physical motion rising above the threshold of consciousness is attended by pleasure in proportion as, beyond a certain limit, it approximates to complete stability, and is attended by unpleasure in proportion as, beyond a certain limit, it deviates from complete stability; while between the two limits, which may be described as qualitative thresholds of pleasure and unpleasure, there is a certain margin of aesthetic indifference . . .
>
> (Fechner 1873)

The French psychoanalyst Michèle Porte has pointed out (1994) that in this extract Fechner was describing structural stability before the term was defined with all its necessary mathematical accuracy. He spoke in terms of threshold and range of stability, not in terms of precise point or location. As Porte herself makes clear, Freud was to convert these ideas into the concept of simple stability, one of the dimensions of the axis that defines the opposition between the life instinct at one end and the death instinct at the other. Freud defined the latter as a return to the minimum energy level of the dynamic system constituted by a mind subjected to the influence of the pleasure principle:

> The dominating tendency of mental life, and perhaps of nervous life in general, is the effort to reduce, to keep constant or to remove internal tension due to stimuli (the *Nirvana principle*, to borrow a term from Barbara Low [. . .]) – a tendency which finds expression in the pleasure principle; and our recognition of that fact is one of our strongest reasons for believing in the existence of death instincts.
>
> (Freud 1920: 55–56)

The reduction of tension and preservation at a constant energy level referred to by Freud are characteristic of *simple stability*, which we could define, in terms of space, as a return to a point or points of declivity in the system. It is customary to represent a dynamic system by graphs that map out the different energy levels in it. These contours take the form of valleys, wells, summits and mountain passes that resemble those on a map representing levels of altitude. There may be several points of declivity or downward slopes on such a map. The characteristic features of a system that reaches such a point are, firstly, that its energy level is lower than that of any neighbouring system, and, secondly, that any variation in energy levels will tend to be cancelled out by the system's return to its point of declivity. Imagine a marble at the bottom of a well: if an applied force causes it to move upwards, it will inevitably tend to fall back under the influence of gravity – unless the impetus is strong enough to cause the marble to pass over the rim of the well, whereupon it will fall into another area of the gravitational field to which it is subjected. As long as the input of external energy is insufficient to cause the marble to cross over that limit, it will fall back down into the well – the point of declivity that is, for the marble, a *locus* of stability in the sense of simple stability. This was the kind of stability Freud referred to in his description of the death instinct: the return to an inorganic state, de-fusion, and reduction of mental tension to a minimal level of energy.

Structural stability is quite another matter. This is the property whereby certain dynamic systems can maintain a stable shape even when their sub-strata are in constant movement. In such a case, it is no longer a question of stabilizing one element of the system at a fixed point, but of preserving its general shape whatever the vicissitudes of the constantly evolving system. We could note in passing that it was this kind of phenomenon that the Theory of Form (*Gestalttheorie*) studied: for example, even though the loudness, the pitch and even the harmonics of the various notes of a melody change, it can still be recognized and accurately identified if its overall structure stays the same. When the pitch and key of a melody are transposed, it remains structurally stable. However, all structurally stable phenomena remain so only within certain limits. If the changes they are subjected to go beyond a given threshold, the entire structure itself changes and the overall shape of the phenomena is modified. This is what the French mathematician René Thom called "catastrophe" (Thom 1972). Bion (1966) spoke of "catastrophic change" in describing the effect a new idea can have on the mind or the arrival of a genius can have on a social group – a subversive effect that modifies the whole structure. Bion's concept of catastrophic change is thus very close to the idea of catastrophe in Thom's theory, even though it would appear that neither was aware of the other's work.

Pascal said that Nature abhors a vacuum. I think that the mind abhors chaos, turbulence and instability. I do not feel that the main purpose of the mind, as Freud held, is to reduce tension to a minimum; rather, I feel that its main purpose is to diminish the instability of its experiences. This is the function that Fechner attributes to pleasure and unpleasure in the extract Freud quotes in "Beyond the Pleasure Principle".

> every psycho-physical motion rising above the threshold of conscious-ness is attended by pleasure in proportion as, beyond a certain limit, it approximates to complete stability, and is attended by unpleasure in proportion as, beyond a certain limit, it deviates from complete stability . . .

Nightmares give us a good picture of what is involved in psychic instability: a happy and serene representation is suddenly and without warning transformed into a vision of horror. The psychotic, no doubt, has to struggle against such a nightmarish world – as has the ordinary young infant who has not yet managed to create sufficient stability in his or her mind. Two roads lead to the establishment of the necessary degree of stability – that of simple stability and that of structural stability.

On the side of simple stability lies repetition, the neurotic aspects of which Freud described in his exploration of the *compulsion to repeat*. In infantile autism, this takes the form of ritual behaviour and motor or verbal stereo-types; through mechanisms such as these, the mind tries to keep itself in a stable state, functioning at as low an energy level as possible, with no evo-lution over time – and hence with no history. As Tustin pointed out, the child with autism has no experience of stable forms that could be subjected to the transpositions that are the hallmark of structural stability, as I mentioned earlier. The forms are vague, unstable and idiosyncratic. On the other hand, there are fixed sensations that appear to be located – in a spatial repre-sentation of the mental system – down in a well of energy, from which it is difficult to help the mind emerge. There is, of course, in the normal devel-opment of children, a time when they take pleasure in repetition and do demand to hear the same story, play the same game, etc. The carer's response to this demand for repetition will determine whether the child can move from one level of stability to another.

In fact, as far as I am concerned, the sole aim of Bion's containing function is to help the child climb ever higher up the steps towards structural stability. To illustrate the point I am trying to make, I will take the example of the child, already a few years old, who delights in repetition and ends up boring the adult carer by the sheer number of demands for the same song or the same game. It is important for the adult to show some tolerance towards the child's pleasure in repetition, otherwise the carer is likely to force the infant into a state of frustration and distress that he or she will be completely unable to process successfully. But it is just as important for the adult at some point to stop the repetition and propose – or even impose – change. Let us consider for a moment the point at which the adult feels change to be desirable. This

probably occurs when there is the feeling that repetition has become meaningless, that there is no longer any true pleasure in it, and that its only aim is
to protect the child against any change taking place. The carer, having lost all
quality as a human being, feels like a kind of robot in the all-powerful hands
of the child. The time is therefore ripe for change. If the moment is well-
chosen, the adult can help the infant move forward to a new stage in structural stability. In my view, structural stability is made up of many degrees.
The more mental growth develops, the more the internal world becomes able
to maintain its structural stability independently of context. I agree here with
Bion's model of the development of thinking, in which pride of place is given
to the infant's capacity for tolerating frustration in order to leave the door
open for thinking. I would nonetheless argue that there are degrees of tolerance which the infant has to work through step by step; reaching each
milestone depends on past experiences that will help or hinder the child's
attempts to go further along the road to structural stability.

The construction of a psychic envelope takes us only to the first of these
steps, where there is as yet no structural stability in the internal world; the
psychic envelope merely maps out the frontiers of the mental landscape in
which structural stability will be able to take root. In terms of the theory of
dynamic systems I find persuasive, this is called "a basin of attraction". An
attractor is a stable part of a system that drains surrounding phenomena into
certain given patterns, much as a magnet organizes a heap of iron filings into
a pattern according to the magnetic field it sets up. The basin of attraction is
the zone in which the attractor makes its influence felt.

To return to the containing function: the mother must be able to sort out
her baby's needs in order to make an appropriate response; she must also be
able to differentiate between her own desires and those of her infant so as not
to confuse them – this helps her to avoid projecting her own desires into her
baby; in addition, she will have to hold onto her own consistency whatever
the violence of her infant's projections in order to help her baby ride out the
storm and to avoid adding her own disorganization to that of the infant. I
would argue that the ability to accomplish all this requires integration of
psychic bisexuality at a very primary level – the level where its effects can be
observed for the first time: that of the psychic envelope. As I have said, this
envelope must be not only flexible and elastic but also consistent and resilient
– the paternal buttressing, as it were, reinforces the maternal containing
without causing it to lose its necessary flexibility.

Nipple-link and penis-link

Once the basins of attraction have been mapped out for the child's mind,
structural stability of the internal world can begin to be organized. This in
turn will help the infant to tolerate frustration, waiting and absence. In my
view, this stability becomes organized initially on a part–object basis, with

two kinds of link contributing to it: the first, proximal, which I call the nipple-link, puts the self in contact with the nourishing maternal object – the "feeding breast" as Klein put it; the second, distal, which I call the penis-link, sets up a relationship between self and object whatever the gap, the distance or the difference between them. Differentiation between nipple-link and penis-link enables a complex internal and external world to be set up. In the internal world, organization and construction of a body image involves differentiating between mental spaces as described by Meltzer (1973), acquisition of an axis, psychic verticality, left/right symmetry and top/bottom asymmetry. In the external world, it involves making contact with objects whatever the gaps created by frustration, absence and differences of all sorts: between self and other (otherness), between the sexes, and between generations. There is a kind of continuity between the *nipple-link* deriving from the masculine/paternal aspect of the combined nipple/breast object and the *penis-link*. It is as though the former prepares the advent of the latter. In my opinion, the shift from one to the other operates via the mother's paternal/masculine identifications.

The next task is to fill the internal world with structurally stable objects, in particular parental ones, on which will be based sexual differentiation and the construction of sexual identity. This takes place in the context of classic Oedipal dynamics as described by Freud and the first generation of psychoanalysts – in other words, at the whole-object level, which is the third level of integration of psychic bisexuality.

Clinical illustration

I would like now to give an example of the integration of bisexuality within the container or psychic envelope in the course of the analysis of a child with autism. The material is taken from the analysis of an autistic boy, which began when he was two and a half years old. I see him four times per week.

Extracts from Cyril's analysis

In his early sessions, Cyril scatters everything he can find in the room: pens, paper, toys, etc. But shortly after this, he is more concerned about bringing things together and controlling containers. He is particularly interested in the modelling-clay boxes that are part of his material and in the lids for keeping them shut. He soon says the word "lid". Two months later, he becomes interested in water. He mainly plays with the hot water, saying "hot", then "it's hot" when he puts his hand under the tap. I interpret that it's nice and warm when we are together. In the following sessions, he splashes water all around the room; he tries to suck on the tap, but he cannot reach it with his mouth. He says "mummy" several times as he plays with or looks at the water. One day, after playing with the water and trying to catch hold of it as it poured out of the tap, he puts his head right up against my stomach; I interpret this as his wish to get inside my stomach and be like a baby inside mummy. After this interpretation, he leans so far backwards that I have to hold him to stop him falling over (I had at that point the fantasy of a precipitate(d) birth). Then he turns round and leans his back against my body, as though looking for support. Then he empties the modelling-clay boxes and wants to leave. I interpret that perhaps he has the impression he is emptying me when he takes everything from me (when I wrote up my notes, I realized that this could correspond to a post-natal maternal depression, as though Cyril's birth had "emptied" his mother) – maybe he wants to leave because he feels I may then be dangerous.

In these initial sessions, we see Cyril building up in the transference a maternal container. Of course, what actually constitutes the container is the analyst's attentiveness, regularity and availability, but Cyril needs to represent it very concretely by coming physically close to me, thereby evoking a fantasy of going back inside the womb. I emphasize that this became possible for him only after repeated interpretations of the "warmth" and sometimes "too-hotness" of our meeting; this would suggest that what Cyril had come up against in his early years was not so much a deficit in the maternal container but too much violence, so that he could not get close enough to the container because of the danger the whole situation then carried with it.

Next, Cyril busies himself with the pens that are laid out on a little table, waiting for the moment when he feels able to draw. He plays at slipping them under the door, thereby pushing them outside. I comment that the pens seem to be dangerous, so he wants to push them out as if they were too-hard "daddy" things. (When he was pushing them out, he heard a noise coming from outside the room and said "daddy" in an anxious tone of voice – as though projecting on to a paternal object the danger connected with attacks against the maternal object.) On several occasions, Cyril finds it difficult to separate from his mother and come into the therapy room when there has been a wider gap than usual between two sessions. I say to him that we haven't seen each other for such a long time, so perhaps he feels I have become a bad Houzel, all empty and dangerous. He calms down and goes on with the session without crying at all – indeed, he seems really quite happy. He plays a lot with the water, and in particular tries to catch it as it flows out of the tap, saying "it's hot". I say he wants to take all the good hot-Houzel things home with him. He comes up to me and throws his arms around me, as if to catch me and hold me tightly. It is after this moving session that, for the first time, Cyril distinctly calls me "'Zel..." But then a new fear emerges: this good maternal aspect of the transference may turn out to be overwhelming and drown everything if it goes on flowing without any limits: he plays at filling up a cup then pouring the water onto the floor. At first he does this quite excitedly, then he seems terrified as the water flows into the cup; he comes close to me as though wanting to feel safe and reassured. He tells me he wants the window opened, as we did once in order to let the floor dry out; he takes a towel and begins to soak up the water on the floor. I interpret his fear that he will all run away like the water. I speak of his need for reassurance, by coming close to me, that it won't happen again, that we have not flowed away like a liquid, like the water, and that we won't be drowned and engulfed in the water that's flowing everywhere.

This material illustrates an aspect that I consider to be fundamental in the setting up of object relations. The maternal object is attractive and full of charm, but it also threatens the self with engulfment and annihilation. The first encounters with the transference, linked to the work of interpretation, enable the patient to break free of such fantasies and open up to a new relationship with the world. At that point, however, it is the child's own destructive impulses that are aimed at the object; in my view, these have the same origin as the libidinal impulses that make the self go in search of an object. In other words, it is the very violence of the drives that is the source of destructiveness.

Cyril continues to play with the water, though I gradually manage to limit the flooding: I ask him to pour the water into the wash-hand basin, not on the floor, and I put my hand in front of the cup so that he cannot pour the water onto the floor. Each time I do this, Cyril hits my hand hard; I say he is attacking the hands that say no. In a recent session, he again seems to be phobic: he moves back from the running tap, apparently afraid of it, as though the overflow of water was becoming threatening, and he has to come close to me, no doubt in a paternal transference role. I even hear him say " 'fraid". I speak of the water that runs everywhere, frightening him, and of his need for me to protect him like a daddy. In the following session, he sits for the first time on a big chair, saying "sit", before he goes to the child-sized seat to sit on that. He climbs on to the little table, sits on it, then climbs down again; he does this several times. Then he clambers on to my lap. I feel him to be very close and very much integrated with what is going on. Once or twice he gives me the impression of testing the solidity of the supports he is using, in particular of the little table. I comment on his need for solid things in Houzel so as to be supported by them as he grows up. He goes to the different items of furniture, including the cupboard, and strikes them with his hand; the cupboard makes a lot of noise. He asks me to open all the doors and windows of the room, including the cupboard doors. I comment that he wants to know what's inside my cupboard. On several occasions, I have the impression he is saying "Thierry", the first name of his little brother.

I have come to feel that the interest infants manifest for the interior of the mother's body, as described by Klein (1932), derives from their search for a container with the requisite qualities, in particular the bisexual qualities, that I imagine to take the form of a maternal container delimited and supported by a paternal buttress. There is an initial need to "sound out" these qualities, as it were, before going further along the path of mental growth, because if these qualities are not present there is a real danger of annihilation.

Cyril spends most of the following session putting the pens on the floor, picking them up again and placing them in my hands – which he is obviously using as a container. He takes the pens back, puts them on the floor, picks them up again and once more puts them into my hands. On several occasions, pointing to the pens lying on the floor, he says "Look!", and talks of eyes. I say that Houzel's eyes are there to pick up all Cyril's thoughts and keep them safe.

Cyril's trust in the container and in its bisexual qualities was increasing. He could entrust his precious contents to it, and the container became more and more part of his relationships, communication and sharing. It was in this sense that I made the interpretation concerning his reference to the analyst's looking: a look that can encompass and bring together without becoming engulfing.

Conclusion

For clarity of presentation, I have described the integration of psychic bisexuality as a series of stages. In fact, of course, this is not quite as linear as it seems. The interplay between the levels of integration I have described – psychic envelope, part–object relations, whole–object relations – are more dialectic and dynamic than my portrayal would have us believe. It is none-theless true that in healthy infants the main phases as I have described them are easily identifiable. Parents use the fact that they can observe these stages to adapt their emotional and educational attitudes towards the child: closely containing the baby who has no independent envelope at the very beginning of life, while differentiating between and acting differently towards his or her wishes and those of other people (in the family circle, for example); later, offering help with tolerating frustration, waiting and absence when they feel that their infant is beginning to be able to do so; and, later still, encouraging the complex interplay of Oedipal identifications to enable the child to sta-bilize the internal world and construct an appropriate sexual identification.

In very ill children, especially those with autism, this is not the case. In the first place, there is apparently no easily identifiable sequencing of stages. It is a long and patient task, entailing careful listening and observing, to unravel little by little the strands of an entangled ball and to locate the major dead-ends into which the child's mental development has wandered. Alvarez's work makes an essential contribution to this very precise task, in particular to the need for therapists to observe closely their own counter-transference. This observation will help therapists to realize when they are being pulled towards omnipotent maternal indulgence and when they are on the side of unacceptable paternal demands – both of these extreme positions being detrimental to the young patient's future mental growth. The adjustment of our counter-transference position in order to balance out the paternal and maternal poles is necessary if we are to offer the child that "live company" of which Alvarez writes (1992) – in other words, a proper container that is both flexible *and* resilient, able to take in the infant's projections while remaining solid enough to resist their destructive violence.

Note

1 Les Qualités Bisexuelles de l'Enveloppe Psychique, (translated by David Alcorn).

References

Alvarez, A. (1992) *Live Company*, London and New York: Routledge.
Bion, W.R. (1962) *Learning from Experience*, New York: Basic Books.
—— (1966) "Catastrophic change", *Scientific Bulletin of the British Psychoanalytical Society*, 5.
Freud, S. (1920) "Beyond the Pleasure Principle", London, 1961; (Standard Edn, 18, 7).
—— (1950 [1887–1902]) *The Origins of Psycho-Analysis*, London and New York: 1964. Also in *Extracts from the Fliess Papers*, (Standard Edn, 1, 175).
Klaus, M.H. and Kennell, J.H. (1982) *Parent–Infant Bonding*, London: C.H. Mosby.
Klein, M. (1932) "The psycho-analysis of children" in *The Writings of Melanie Klein*, Vol. 2, London: Hogarth (1975).
Meltzer, D. (1973) *Sexual States of Mind*, Strath Tay (Scotland): Clunie.
Porte, M. (1994) *La Dynamique Qualitative en Psychanalyse*, Paris: P.U.F.
Thom, R. (1972) *Stabilité structurelle et morphogenèse. Essai d'une théorie générale des modèles*, Reading, Mass.: W.A. Benjamin, Inc.
Tustin, F. (1972) *Autism and Childhood Psychosis*, London: Hogarth.
—— (1981) *Autistic States in Children*, London: Routledge & Kegan Paul.

Chapter 5

Neurobiology, developmental psychology, and psychoanalysis

Convergent findings on the subject of projective identification

Allan N. Schore

It is an honor and a pleasure to contribute to this volume dedicated to Anne Alvarez, master clinician and, to my mind, one of the true pioneers of developmental psychoanalytic explorations of the primitive mind. In venturing into largely unexplored unconscious realms of the minds of the early forming developmental psychopathologies, Alvarez has used the classical mappings of those who have preceded her – Freud, Klein, Bion, Winnicott and others. In addition, she has actively searched the literatures of disciplines contiguous to psychoanalysis, the science of the unconscious mind, for information that might be valuable to a greater understanding of the individuals in whom the deepest strata of the unconscious mind are so poorly developed. And so, a perusal of both *Live Company* (1992) and *Autism and Personality* (1999a) reveals relevant data from developmental psychology and neuroscience.

But perhaps what has allowed her to glean so much new information about the primitive realms of the human mind is that she is not only an objective observer but a subjective co-explorer who travels alongside her patients. In addition to her powerful curiosity, Alvarez's openness to be taught, indeed corrected, by her patients has been perhaps her greatest and most remarkable asset, and it has provided essential information about how to co-construct a therapeutic context that allows us to attend to even the faintest communications of an "undrawn," yet still nascent personality. It is no coincidence that along her journeys she has become intrigued with the primordial form of communication available to the developing psyche-soma – the theoretically enigmatic yet clinically useful process of projective identification (Alvarez, 1997, 1999b). Echoing her interdisciplinary approach to the understanding of clinical phenomena, in the following I would like to offer some thoughts about projective identification, which writers now describe as operating "in some mysterious way that we cannot begin to comprehend scientifically" (Sands, 1997: 653).

The concept, of course, derives from the work of Melanie Klein (1946), who defined projective identification as a process wherein largely unconscious information is projected from the sender to the recipient. Although this primitive process of communication between the unconscious of one person and the unconscious of another begins in early development, it continues throughout life. This phenomenon also refers to a primitive unconscious defense mechanism that is a central focus of the treatment of child and adult developmental psychopathologies.

In recent clinical work, Alvarez (1997), like Joseph (1997), stresses that projective identification is a form of communication. Morrison (1986) writes that it is "a communication to the recipient of what the unconscious fantasy feels like" (p. 59). Other current authors are asserting that projective identification involves the projection of affects associated with self and object representations (Adler and Rhine, 1992). Ogden (1990a) concludes "In projective identification, the projector by means of actual interpersonal interactions with the 'recipient' unconsciously induces feeling states in the recipient that are congruent with the 'ejected' feelings" (p. 79).

These clinical observations bear upon a long-debated issue concerning the specific nature of what is projected in this primitive communicative process. A commonly held belief is that Klein's sole emphasis was on the development of fantasy, on unconscious cognitions generated within the infant's mind. This seems inconsistent with current developmental research which reveals that the infant's states are less cognitively complex and more bodily based and sensoriaffective. Yet Brody (1982): asserts, "Melanie Klein contributed to psychoanalytic thought when she described the intensities that affects can reach during infancy." And Stein proposes, "The common thread running through all mental development, according to Klein, may be said to be that of "regulation of feelings" (1990: 508).

A major conclusion of my ongoing work on the "regulation of feelings," or "affect regulation" (Schore, 1994; 1996; 1997a, b, c; 1998; 1999; 2000a, b, c; 2001a, b; in press a, b) is that "primitive mental states" are much more than early appearing "mental" or "cognitive" states of mind. Rather, they are more precisely characterized as "psychobiological" states. Current interdisciplinary developmental research reveals that affective states are transacted within the mother–infant dyad, and that this highly efficient system of somatically driven fast-acting emotional communication is essentially nonverbal (Schore, 1994; Feldman et al., 1999). With such a perspective, those of us with a developmental framework are exploring not primitive states of mind, but primitive states of "mind–body."

Thus, both clinical and developmental models of projective identification are now stressing the critical role of the communication of internal affective states and process, rather than cognitions and content. This conception fits with a general trend within psychoanalysis, articulated by Kantrowitz (1999: 72), who discusses the centrality of "intense affective engagements" and concludes, "It is in the realm of preconscious communication that the interwovenness of intrapsychic and interpersonal phenomena become most apparent." With respect to the communications embedded in projective identification, Ryle (1994: 107) points out that this mechanism is essentially concerned with "the relationship between intrapsychic and interpersonal phenomena and with indirect forms of communication and influence."

Indeed, projective identification, a process that mediates what Loewald (1970) calls the transmission of "intrapsychic externalizations," is now being seen as a "bridge concept" between classical and interpersonal psychoanalysis (Migone, 1995). But more than this, the concept is linking developmental psychoanalysis with developmental psychology. An entire recent issue of the journal *Psychoanalytic Dialogues* (which includes a contribution by Alvarez) is devoted to a "Symposium on projective identification revisited: Integrating clinical infant research, attachment theory, and Kleinian concepts of phantasy."

Taking this integrative approach even further, I will argue here that projective identification links clinical psychoanalysis with not only developmental psychoanalysis and psychology, but also with developmental neuroscience. Watt has recently asserted that the nature of neurodevelopment is "the great frontier in neuroscience where all of our theories will be subject to the most acid of acid tests" (2000: 191). There is now a surge of research on emotional behavior, and an increasing number of studies on the psychobiology of affective states and the neurobiology of the emotion-processing right brain. A body of neurobiological research shows that the right hemisphere, or as the neuroscientist Ornstein (1997) calls it, "the right mind," is dominant for the perception and expression of nonverbal emotional expressions embedded in facial and prosodic stimuli at unconscious levels; that is, for nonverbal communication (Blonder, *et al.*, 1991; Dimberg and Petterson, 2000; George *et al.*, 1996; Schore, 1994, 1998, 1999). The continuous activation of early appearing right-lateralized mechanisms of the "emotional brain" over the course of the lifespan underlies Modell's (1994) assertion that although projective identification arises in the emotional communications within the mother–infant dyad, this "primitive" process plays an essential role in "the communication of affective experiences" in all later periods of development.

An integration of current developmental studies of infant–mother emotional communications and neurobiological research on the essential role of the right brain in emotional communications can offer us a deeper understanding of the mechanism of affective communications within projective identification. This rapidly expanding body of interdisciplinary studies can serve as a source pool for heuristic models of not only normal emotional development but also of how disorganizing forces in the early social environment can interfere with maturational processes. The early maturing right hemisphere is dominant for the first three years of life (Chiron *et al.*, 1997). The early social environment can positively and negatively influence the emergence of the early developing "primitive" right brain (Schore, 1997b, 2001b).

Indeed, this hemisphere is dominant for generating a sense of emotional and corporeal self (Devinsky, 2000) and the coping mechanisms that support survival and enable the individual to cope with stresses and challenges (Schore, 2001a). An interdisciplinary approach can thus model how developing systems organize primitive defense mechanisms such as projective identification and dissociation to cope with interactive forces that induce intensely stressful states that traumatically disorganize the infant's homeostatic equilibrium. Since these early events are imprinted into the maturing brain they become traits that endure as primitive defense mechanisms.

In two seminal papers, Klein conjectured that defensive projective identification is associated with the massive invasion of someone else's personality (1955) and represents an evacuation of unwanted parts of the self (1946). The use of a unique and restricted set of defenses in severely disturbed personalities has been long noted in the clinical literature. Indeed, a primary goal of treatment of such patients is to help them replace excessive use of projective identification with more mature defensive operations. Boyer (1990) describes a group of patients who have experienced an early defective relationship with the mother that results in a grossly deficient ego structure. Their excessive use of projective identification

> very heavily influences their relationships with others as well as their psychic equilibrium. Their principal conscious goal in therapy is to relieve themselves immediately of tension. Often they greatly fear that the experience of discomfort is intolerable and believe that failure to rid themselves of it will lead to physical or mental fragmentation or dissolution.
>
> (Boyer, 1990: 304)

With this introduction, I will use an interdisciplinary perspective to model projective identification as an early forming unconscious strategy for regulating right-brain to right-brain communications, especially of intense affective states. (Parts of this chapter and more detailed references appear in an upcoming paper, Schore, in press b.)

Current updatings of developmental and clinical conceptions of projective identification

Klein originally described projective identification as the projection of an unwanted part of the self onto an important other, together with identification of that part with the other. This is usually interpreted to mean the projecting out, in a controlling way, of "bad," *negative* parts that could be dangerous to the self into another person. However, a number of authors have recently emphasized that Klein also spoke about the role of projective identification in the child's positive relationship with the mother, stating that this process also involves the projection of a "valued" part of the self into another. Indeed, she also wrote that these processes are "of vital importance for the normal development as well as for abnormal object relations" (1946: 9).

Bion expanded this idea and emphasized the central role of this mechanism in all early developmental phenomena. In a far-sighted work (1962a) he described that when mother and infant are adjusted to each other the infant behaves in such a way that projective identification is a "realistic" rather than defensive phenomenon, and that this is its normal condition and function. This idea continues in the current literature, where the emphasis is on the adaptive aspects of projective identification – on more than just the valence or the content of the projected material, but rather on the underlying process of the communication of states.

The infant communicates both positive and negative states, and so the mother must also regulate infant distress. According to Carpy,

> [T]he normal infant needs to be able to sense that her mother is strug-gling to tolerate her projected distress without major disruption of her maternal function. [The mother] will be unable to avoid giving the infant slight indications of the way she is affected by [her infant], and it is these indications which allow the infant to see that the projected aspects of herself can indeed be tolerated.
>
> (Carpy, 1989: 293)

This mechanism is identical to Winnicott's "holding functions."

A conception of mother and infant adjusting to each other's commu-nications describes a model of mutual reciprocal influence. This clearly suggests that projective identification is not a unidirectional but a bidirec-tional interactive process. The interpersonal component of projective iden-tification has been advanced by clinical theoreticians such as Grotstein (1981) and Ogden (1979), the latter stating that "Projective identification does not exist where there is no interaction between projector and recipient" (p. 14). The concept moves from a monadic, one-way ejection of intrapsychic contents to a dyadic intersubjective communicative process. Current devel-opmental models thus emphasize the fact that projective identification, both in the developmental and the therapeutic context, is not a unidirectional but a bi-directional process in which both members of an emotionally commu-nicating dyad act in a context of mutual reciprocal influence.

These ideas are very similar to my own work, which indicates that when mother and infant synchronize the expression and reception of their affective communications, the ensuing resonance allows for an amplification of positive states in both members of the dyad (Schore, 2001a, c). The psy-chobiologically attuned dyad interactively generates positively valenced vitality affects (Stern, 1985), a context that represents what Alvarez (1992) calls "live company." But she also modulates negative states by participating in interactive repair (Schore, 1994). The regulating mother and her infant thus maximize positive and minimize negative affect and thereby co-create a secure attachment bond (Schore, 2000b). This allows for a developmental advance in the infant's capacity for self-regulation, the ability to regulate emotional states flexibly through interactions with other humans – interactive regulation in interconnected contexts, and without other humans – autoregulation in autonomous contexts. The adaptive capacity to shift between these dual regulatory modes, depending upon the social context, emerges out of a history of regulated interactions of a maturing biological organism and an early attuned social environment.

This mutually attuned process mediates all later intersubjective exchanges and empathic communications Developmental researchers are now defining the central role of the attachment relationship as "the dyadic regulation of emotion" (Sroufe, 1996), a concept that mirrors Klein's lifelong interest in "the regulation of feelings" (Stein, 1990). Thus the mechanism of Klein's adaptive projective identification is identical to the mechanism of Bowlby's (1969) secure attachment bond.

Developmental studies and the origin of dissociation and defensive projective identification

The ontogeny of both adaptive and defensive projective identification is deeply influenced by the events of the first year of life. Developmentally, adaptive projective identification is expressed in the "split-second world" of the mother–infant dyad in the securely attached infant's expression of a "spontaneous gesture," a somato-psychic expression of the burgeoning "true self," and the attuned mother's "giving back to the baby the baby's own self" (Winnicott, 1971a). This developmental mechanism continues to be used throughout the lifespan as a process of rapid, fast-acting, nonverbal, spontaneous emotional communications within a dyad.

As opposed to the interactive scenario of a secure attachment in which the caregiver contingently responds to the child's projective identifications, the insecurely attached child is often unable to induce affect-regulating responses and engage in empathic mutual regulatory processes because the primary object is not sufficiently attuned to the child's state and therefore unable to receive the infant's emotional communications (Schore, 1994, 1997b). This prevents the establishment of a dyadic system in which the infant can safely project "valued" parts of the self into the mother, i.e., aspects of adaptive projective identification. The insecurely attached organizations of developmental disorders thus have a greater tendency to use defensive rather than adaptive projective identification. Doucet (1992: 657) writes, "I consider that projective identification works in two ways: a normal way, in which the analyst-mother takes into herself a part of the patient-child's emotional identity in order to return it to him in a detoxified and hence assimilable form, and a pathological way in which the negative aspects are so plentiful that projective identification operates to excess."

More specifically, "primitive" personalities encode early traumatic experiences of being used as what Robbins (1996) calls "a projection screen for repudiated elements of parental identity, rather than having the parent act as a mirror for integration, and differentiation of nascent aspects of itself" (p. 764). These "negative maternal attributions" contain an intensely negative affective charge that is interactively amplified, and therefore rapidly dysregulate the infant. In fact, current developmental research is elucidating the effects of traumatic affect on the infant, and these studies are directly relevant to an understanding of the origins of defensive projective identification (Schore, in press b).

In important studies, Perry *et al.* (1995) demonstrate that the infant's psychobiological response to trauma is comprised of two separate response patterns: hyperarousal and dissociation. These two patterns are extreme forms of, respectively, Bowlby's protest and despair responses to attachment ruptures. The dual responses also represent activation of the two components of the autonomic nervous system (ANS) – first, the energy-expending sympathetic branch, and then, the energy-conserving parasympathetic branch (see Schore, 1994, 2001b).

During the initial stage of threat, a startle or alarm reaction is initiated, in which the sympathetic component of the ANS is suddenly and significantly activated, resulting in hyperarousal, somatically expressed in increased heart rate, blood pressure, respiration, and muscle tone, as well as hypervigilance. Distress is expressed in crying and then screaming. In very recent work, this dyadic transaction is described by Beebe as "mutually escalating over-arousal" of a disorganized attachment pair:

> Each one escalates the ante, as the infant builds to a frantic distress, may scream, and, in this example, finally throws up. In an escalating over-arousal pattern, even after extreme distress signals from the infant, such as ninety-degree head aversion, arching away ... or screaming, the mother keeps going.
>
> (Beebe, 2000: 436)

The infant's state of "frantic distress," or what Perry *et al.* (1995) term fear-terror, is mediated by sympathetic hyperarousal.

But a second, later-forming, longer-lasting reaction is seen in dissociation, a parasympathetic response of the ANS, in which the child disengages from stimuli in the external world and attends to an "internal" world. Traumatized infants are observed to be "staring into space with a glazed look." This behavioral strategy is described by Tronick and Weinberg:

[W]hen infants' attempts fail to repair the interaction infants often lose postural control, withdraw, and self-comfort. The disengagement is profound even with this short disruption of the mutual regulatory process and break in intersubjectivity. The infant's reaction is reminiscent of the withdrawal of Harlow's isolated monkey or of the infants in institutions observed by Bowlby and Spitz.

(Tronick and Weinberg, 1997: 66)

Meares concludes that "dissociation, at its first occurrence, is a consequence of a 'psychological shock' or high arousal" (1999: 1853). The traumatized child's hypoaroused dissociation in the midst of fear or terror involves numbing, avoidance, compliance and restricted affect, mediated by high levels of behavior-inhibiting cortisol, pain-numbing endogenous opioids, and especially high levels of parasympathetic vagal activity in the baby's developing brain (Schore, in press b, d). If early trauma is experienced as "psychic catastrophe" (Bion, 1962b), dissociation represents "a submission and resignation to the inevitability of overwhelming, even psychically deadening danger" (Davies and Frawley, 1994), "detachment from an unbearable situation" (Mollon, 1996), "the escape when there is no escape" (Putnam, 1997).

This primary parasympathetic regulatory process of conservation-withdrawal occurs in helpless and hopeless stressful situations in which the individual is hyperinhibited and therefore immobile in order to avoid attention by becoming "unseen," and it allows the infant to maintain homeostasis in the face of an internal state of accelerating hyperarousal (see Schore, 1994, 2001b). The dissociation from both contact with the external social environment and from the child's subjective physical experience is experienced as a discontinuity in what Winnicott calls the need for "going-on-being," and Kestenberg (1985) refers to as a "dead spot" in the infant's subjective experience. If adaptive projective identification mediates the onset of an intersubjective exchange, defensive projective identification signals a massive breach of subjectivity, the hallmark of a deficit in the processing of subjective information, both interpersonally and intrapsychically.

Type "D" disorganized/disoriented attachments are observed to use the primitive avoidant strategy of dissociation specifically in order to cope with relational trauma (Liotti, 1992). I suggest that an infant with an early history of "ambient trauma," especially one with a genetically encoded vulnerable psychobiological predisposition, must excessively utilize defensive projective identification in order to cope with all-too-frequent episodes of interactive stress and dense negative affect that disorganize the developing self.

In the first stage of trauma hyperaroused terror and screaming are triggered by "negative maternal attributions," which is equated with Spitz's (1965) "psychotoxic" maternal care, manifest in an overdose of affective stimulation, and Klein's "massive invasion of someone else's personality."

The second stage, the dissociative strategy to counter-regulate the hyperarousal, is expressed by "staring into space," and represents the mechanism that drives what Klein describes as an "evacuation" of the self. These dual mechanisms are described in a child therapy case by Joseph: "when projective identification was operating so powerfully," the patient "started to scream," and then "stared through the window with a vacant, lost expression" (1997: 104).

In other words, a stress-induced sudden counter-regulatory switch from an active state of sympathetic energy-expending, emotion-amplifying autonomic hyperarousal into an enduring passive state of parasympathetic energy-conserving, emotion-dampening hyperinhibition underlies the rapid onset of dissociation and represents the mechanism of projective identification as it operates in real time. The massively stressed child, with only primitive abilities to cope with overwhelming arousal induced by relational trauma and at the limit of her fragile regulatory capacities, experiences intense affect dysregulation, projects a distressing communication, and then instantly dissociates. States of autonomic hyperarousal are subjectively experienced as pain, and so this strategy represents a psychobiological mechanism by which psychic–physical pain is instantly inhibited.

In these traumatic moments of marked discontinuities in the caregiver–infant relationship, the child's attempts to use other-directed regulatory behaviors (such as crying, expressions of fear) are often met with continuing dysregulation by the misattuning caregiver; that is, further abuse. They therefore must be inhibited, and so, for adaptive goals, the infant must resort to an autoregulatory strategy to modulate overwhelming levels of distress. Furthermore, this rapid shift from a mode of interactive regulation into a long-lasting mode of autoregulation which the infant must access in order to maintain homeostatic equilibrium during traumatic assaults is imprinted into the maturing limbic system (Schore, 1996), the central nervous system (CNS) brain areas specialized for the organization of new learning and the capacity to adapt to a rapidly changing environment. It therefore endures as a (transferential) basic strategy of affect regulation, a characterological disposition to use defensive projective identification under future conditions of interpersonal stress. When activated, this mechanism takes the form of pathological "dissociative switches" between states, which occur rapidly, and are manifest in "inexplicable shifts in affect," changes in facial appearance, mannerisms and speech, and discontinuities in train of thought (Putnam, 1997). What is pathological is not only its excessive use, but also an inability to shift back out of the dissociative state that is heralded by defensive projective identification.

In the clinical literature, Stolorow and Atwood (1996) speak of "affect-dissociating defensive operations," rooted in early derailments, in which central affect states are walled off because they evoked "massive malattunement" from the caregiving surround. They assert that psychopathological phenomena unfold within an "intersubjectve field that includes the analyst as a codetermining influence" (p. 189). I suggest that the mechanism of defensive projective identification is overtly expressed in a context that resembles an early interactive derailment. This occurs in an affective transaction when the therapist exhibits a massive malattunement of the patient's disorganizing state. In this context high levels of dysregulated affect, codetermined by both members of the dyad, are rapidly amplified within the intersubjective field. This interactive stress will trigger, in real time, the patient's primitive defensive operations – projective identification and dissociation.

Projective identification as right-brain to right-brain communications of psychobiological states

It is important to note that the affective communications occurring within the dyadic processes that facilitate adaptive projective identification also impact the experience-dependent maturation of the infant's brain. Trevarthen notes that "the intrinsic regulators of human brain growth in a child are specifically adapted to be coupled, by emotional communication, to the regulators of adult brains" (Trevarthen, 1990: 357). I would amend this general statement to suggest that the regulators of both the infant's and mother's brains are located in specifically their right limbic brains (Schore, 1994, 2000b, c, 2001a).

Trevarthen's description of "emotional communication" as a traffic of visual, prosodic auditory, and gestural signals that induce instant emotional effects is paralleled by Buck's (1994) characterization of "spontaneous emotional communication":

> Spontaneous communication employs species-specific expressive displays in the sender that, given attention, activate emotional preattunements and are directly perceived by the receiver ... The "meaning" of the display is known directly by the receiver ... This spontaneous emotional communication constitutes a *conversation between limbic systems* ... It is a biologically-based communication system that involves individual organisms directly with one another: the individuals in spontaneous communication constitute literally a *biological unit*.
>
> (Buck, 1994: 266, my italics)

Buck (1994) emphasizes the importance of specifically the right limbic system, and localizes this biologically based spontaneous emotional communication system to the right hemisphere, in accord with other research that indicates a right lateralization of spontaneous gestures and emotional communication (Schore, 2000c).

Indeed, the activity of this "non-dominant" hemisphere, and not the later maturing "dominant" verbal-linguistic left, is instrumental to the perception of the emotional states of other selves; that is, for empathy (Schore, 1994, 2000b). Right cortical systems decode emotional stimuli by actual felt somatic emotional reactions to the stimuli; that is, by a form of empathic responding. According to Adolphs *et al.*, "recognizing emotions from visually presented facial expressions requires right somatosensory cortices," and in this manner "we recognize another individual's emotional state by internally generating somatosensory representations that stimulate how the individual would feel when displaying a certain facial expression" (2000: 2683). Current research suggests that the right hemisphere is more important than the left for broader aspects of communication (see Schore, in press c).

In addition, the right hemisphere plays a special role in the perception of the affective qualities of somatic signals coming from the body. The representation of visceral and somatic states and body sense is under primary control of this hemisphere. Recent neuropsychological studies indicate that self-related material is processed in the right hemisphere (Keenan *et al.*, 2000), and that the right hemisphere contains the most comprehensive and integrated map of the body state available to the brain (Damasio, 1994). Indeed, specifically right hemisphere functions maintain a coherent, continuous, and unified sense of self (Schore, 1994; Devinsky, 2000). This is due to the fact that right (and not left) hemisphere control exists over both the sympathetic and parasympathetic components of the ANS, and therefore the somatic expressions of all emotional states (see Schore, 2000c). The ANS has been called the "physiological bottom of the mind" (Jackson, 1931).

It is now established that instances of projective identification occur in "intimate or close relationships, such as the mother–child relationship or the patient–analyst relationship" (Migone, 1995: 626). A cardinal tenet of projective identification is that the infant projects parts or the whole of itself "into the mother's body," and like the empathic mother who matches her infant's internal state, the clinician's body is a primary instrument for psychobiological attunement. Since affects are psychobiological phenomena and the self is bodily based, projective identification represents not linguistic but mind–body communications. According to Basch (1976) "the language of mother and infant consists of signals produced by the autonomic, involuntary nervous system in both parties" (p. 766). Basch (1992) also points out the direct parallel of this to projective identification, which is manifest in "a situation in which the patient subtly causes the therapist to resonate autonomically with the patient's unconscious affect-laden fantasies" (p. 179).

In recent writings I have proposed that attachment is fundamentally the interactive regulation of biological synchronicity between organisms (Schore, 2000b). I suggest that adaptive projective identification involves a strategy of interactive regulation that is used in spontaneous right-brain to right-brain communications, a preverbal bodily based dialogue between right lateralized limbic systems, especially in intimate and intensely emotional contexts. This model supports Bion's (1967) assertion that projective identification is the most important form of interaction between patient and therapist.

More specifically, the chaotic somatic components of biologically "primitive emotions" represent the intrapsychic externalizations of projective identification. These biologically primitive emotions – excitement, elation, rage, terror, disgust, shame, and hopeless despair – appear early in development, are correlated with differentiable autonomic activity, arise quickly and automatically, and are processed in the right brain (Schore, 1994). This particular class of "primary" emotions are the "nonverbal" emotions in which Klein was interested, and they are specifically expressed in the rapid events of projective identification.

The right hemisphere is specifically impacted by early attachment experiences – in fact these object-relational, affect-communicating experiences act as a growth-facilitating environment for its experience-dependent maturation (Schore, 1994). In face-to-face interactions, the child uses the output of the mother's emotion-regulating right cortex as a template for the imprinting, the hard wiring of circuits in his own right cortex that will come to mediate his expanding capacities. In other words the regulated emotional transactions of adaptive projective identification that promote a secure attachment facilitate the organization of an internal structure involved in the relatively efficient processing, expression, and regulation of emotionally charged information.

On the other hand, a history of cumulative relational trauma represents a growth-inhibiting environment for the maturation of the right brain (Schore, 1997b, 2001b). Furthermore, the insecurely attached infant's all-too-common stressful experiences with a caregiver who chronically initiates but poorly repairs intense and long-lasting dysregulated states are incorporated in right-brain, long-term autobiographical memory as a pathological internal object relation, an interactive representation of a dysregulated-self-in-interaction-with-a-misattuning-object (Schore, 1997a). This unconscious internal working model encodes strategies of affect regulation, including major access to projective identification and dissociation. The result is, at later points of stress, a quicker entrance into and a longer duration within dissociated states. This represents a coping deficit, since adaptive coping is reflected by a termination of a stress response at an appropriate time in order to prevent an excessive reaction.

The structural defect of the organization of the right brain, the hemisphere dominant for dissociation (Weinberg, 2000; Schore, 2001b) and the stress response (Wittling, 1997), thus underlies the coping deficit associated with excessive use of defensive projective identification. Neuroimaging studies show that the right hemisphere is activated as traumatic emotional memories are activated and recalled (Schiffer et al., 1995). Furthermore, there is now evidence that early emotional learning occurring in the right hemisphere can be unknown to the left; learning and associated emotional responding may later be completely inaccessible to the language centers of the brain. This early learning includes "nonverbal presymbolic forms of relating" that "protect the infant from trauma and continue to be used by patients to avoid retraumatization" (Kiersky and Beebe, 1994: 389); that is, the right brain defensive regulatory strategies of dissociation and projective identification.

From this realm that stores split-off parts of the self also come projections that are directed outwards into the therapist. McDougall (1978) asserts that the patient who has suffered preverbal traumas transmits "primitive communications" that induce countertransferential emotional states in the analyst. Similarly, Modell states that in projective identification, "affects that are associated with the patient's past traumatic relationships are ... projected onto the therapist, so that these affects are also experienced by the therapist" (1993: 148).

It is well known that the infant's attachment system is activated when he or she is under stress, and this occurs even when the caregiver is the source of traumatic stress. Krystal (1978) notes that psychic trauma is the outcome of being confronted with overwhelming affect which produces "an unbearable psychic state which threatens to disorganize, perhaps even destroy all psychic functions" (p. 82). This means that during the interpersonal transmission of a stressful state the child is also bidding the mother interactively to regulate this stress. So at the "heightened affective moment" of the "defensive" projective identification the child in the developmental context (as well as the patient in the therapeutic context), due to a failure of interactive regulation, is in a dysregulated, and therefore a intolerable state. Ogden (1990b) describes how the projector induces a feeling state in the other that corresponds to a state that the projector is unable to tolerate.

Defensive projective identification is thus an early forming right-brain autoregulatory survival mechanism for coping with interactively generated overwhelming traumatic stress, and it is activated in response to subjectively perceived social stimuli (facial and prosodic) that potentially trigger imminent internal autonomic and therefore bodily dysregulation. At the moment of the projection, the patient's disorganizing right brain (fragmenting self) instantly switches state from a rapidly accelerating, intensely dysregulated, hyperactive distress state into a hypoactive dissociated state (collapsing self).

The essential defensive nature of this coping mechanism is echoed in the term "defensive" projective identification. The patient's sympathetically driven hyperarousal reaches a point of such intensity that a massive parasympathetic counterregulatory strategy must be activated. The fact that this stress-regulating mechanism represents a sudden transition from a hyperaroused into a hyperinhibited state indicates that the accelerating negative affect is not "emptied" or "discharged." The hyperarousal still remains and so the pain endures, but is now instantly dissociated, and thereby "anesthetized," or "numbed."

This bears upon some controversial aspects of the concept of projective identification. This primitive coping mechanism does represent an affective communication, and it does allow the precarious personality organization to disown parts of the self; that is, to "rid" the individual of contact with his or her own mind (and body!), but it does not represent a literal evacuation or expelling out into an other, so that the negative state no longer exists within. The tension is not relieved, because the state of hyperarousal remains. And the pain still exists within, but is dissociated by increased endogenous opioid release and experienced as an enduring "dead spot" in the patient's subjectivity. As a result of the sudden shift from a state of active coping into an inhibited state of passive coping, the projector will "implode" under stress, and further dissociate from the state, so that it appears as if only the recipient holds it. In other words, in the moments after the projective identification, the dissociating patient, now in a state of dense emotional inhibition, is no longer overtly expressing a dysregulating emotion, but the empathic non-dissociating therapist is still psychobiologically resonating with and therefore subjectively experiencing the amplified negative state.

An inefficient system to autoregulate or interactively regulate affective states will alter and impede the developmental trajectory of the self. Developmentalists have pointed out that "extreme" projective identification is associated with insecure attachments (Murray, 1991). Thus, for the rest of the lifespan, early forming self-pathologies, who manifest right hemispheric impairments (Schore, 1997b), overutilize primitive defenses such as dissociation and projective identification. Alvarez (1997) has proposed that "extreme" projective identification is associated with a "developmental delay." I suggest that this maturational delay is specifically of the right hemisphere, "the right mind."

It is important to note that the right hemisphere cycles back into growth phases throughout the lifespan, thereby allowing for the continuing experience-dependent maturation of the right brain within the growth-facilitating environment of an affect-regulating therapeutic relationship (Schore, 1997, 2001a, c). There is now consensus that the psychotherapy of "developmental arrests" is directed toward the mobilization of fundamental modes of development and the completion of interrupted developmental processes. I suggest that a "developmentally informed psychotherapy" (Alvarez, 1999a) can induce increased complexity of the patient's right-brain coping mechanisms – specifically, a developmental advance in the form of a mature personality organization that accesses adaptive over defensive projective identification. (For further discussion of the clinical implications of a psychoneurobiological model of projective identification, see Schore, in press b.)

Thirty years ago, in describing the dyadic nature of both the mother–infant and therapist–patient relationship, Winnicott wrote: "In order to use the mutual experience one must have in one's bones a theory of emotional development of the child and the relationship of the child to the environmental factors" (1971b: p. 3). This perspective is at the core of the writings of the major contributors to modern developmental psychoanalysis, including Anna Freud, Melanie Klein, and Anne Alvarez. In pushing out the frontiers of psychoanalysis into the most severe developmental disorders, her works serve as guidebooks for those who will follow into the deeper explorations of the primitive mind.

References

Adler, G. and Rhine, M.W. (1992). The selfobject function of projective identification. In *From Inner Sources: New Directions in Object Relations Psychotherapy*, ed. N.G. Hamilton. Northvale, N.J.: Jason Aronson, pp. 139–162.

Adolphs, R., Damasio, H., Tranel, D., Cooper, G., and Damasio, A.R. (2000). A role for somatosensory cortices in the visual recognition of emotion as revealed by three-dimensional lesion mapping. *Journal of Neuroscience*, 20: 2683–2690.

Alvarez, A. (1992). *Live Company: Psychoanalytic Psychotherapy with Autistic, Borderline, Deprived and Abused Children*. London: Routledge.

—— (1997). Projective identification as a communication: its grammar in borderline psychotic children. *Psychoanalytic Dialogues*, 7: 753–768.

—— (1999a). Addressing the deficit. Developmentally informed psychotherapy with passive, undrawn children. In *Autism and Personality: Findings From the Tavistock Autism Workshop*, eds A. Alvarez and S. Reid. London: Routledge, pp. 49–61.

—— (1999b). Widening the bridge. Commentary on papers by Stephen Seligman, Robin C. Silverman, and Alicia F. Lieberman. *Psychoanalytic Dialogues*, 9: 205–217.

Basch, M.F. (1976). The concept of affect: A re-examination. *Journal of the American Psychoanalytic Association*, 24: 759–777.

—— (1992). *Practicing Psychotherapy: A Casebook*. New York: Basic Books.

Bion, W.R. (1962a). The psychoanalytic study of thinking: II. A theory of thinking. *International Journal of Psycho-Analysis*, 43: 306–310.

—— (1962b). *Learning from Experience*. London: Heinemann.

—— (1967). *Second Thoughts*. New York: Basic Books.

Blonder, L.X., Bowers, D., and Heilman, K.M. (1991). The role of the right hemisphere in emotional communication. *Brain*, *114*: 1115–1127.

Bowlby, J. (1969). *Attachment and Loss*. Volume 1: *Attachment*. New York: Basic Books.

Boyer, L.B. (1990). Countertransference and technique. In *Master Clinicians on Treating the Regressed Patient*, eds L.B. Boyer and P.L. Giovacchini. Northvale, N.J.: Jason Aronson, pp. 303–324.

Brody, S. (1982). Psychoanalytic theories of infant development and disturbances: a critical evaluation. *Psychoanalytic Quarterly*, 51: 526–597.

Buck, R. (1994). The neuropsychology of communication: spontaneous and symbolic aspects. *Journal of Pragmatics*, 22: 265–278.

Carpy, D.V. (1989). Tolerating the countertransference: A mutative process. *International Journal of Psycho-Analysis*, 70: 287–294.

Chiron, C., Jambaque, I., Nabbout, R., Lounes, R., Syrota, A., and Dulac, O. (1997). The right brain hemisphere is dominant in human infants. *Brain*, 120: 1057–1065.

Davies, J.M. and Frawley, M.G. (1994). *Treating the Adult Survivor of Childhood Sexual Abuse. A Psychoanalytic Perspective*. New York: Basic Books.

Devinsky, O. (2000). Right cerebral hemispheric dominance for a sense of corporeal and emotional self. *Epilepsy & Behaviour*, *1*: 60–73.

Dimberg, U., and Patterson, M. (2000). Facial reactions to happy and angry facial expressions: Evidence for right hemisphere dominance. *Psychophysiology, 37*: 693–696.

Doucet, P. (1992). The analyst's transference imagery. *International Journal of Psycho-Analysis*, 73: 647–659.

Feldman, R., Greenbaum, C.W., and Yirmiya, N.´ (1999). Mother–infant affect synchrony as an antecedent of the emergence of self-control. *Developmental Psychology*, 35: 223–231.

George, M.S., Parekh, P.I., Rosinsky, N., Ketter, T.A., Kimbrell, T.A., Heilman, K.M., Herscovitch, P., and Post, R.M. (1996). Understanding emotional prosody activates right hemispheric regions. *Archives of Neurology, 53*: 665–670.

Grotstein, J.S. (1981). *Splitting and Projective Identification*. New York: Jason Aronson.

Jackson, J. Hughlings (1931). *Selected Writings of John Hughlings Jackson*, Volumes I and II. London: Hodder and Stoughton.

Joseph, B. (1997). Projective Identification. In *The Contemporary Kleinians of London*, ed. R. Schafer. Madison, Conn.: International Universities Press, pp. 100–116.

Kantrowitz, J.L. (1999). The role of the preconscious in psychoanalysis. *Journal of the American Psychoanalytic Association*, 47: 65–89.

Keenan, J.P., Wheeler, M.A., Gallup, G.G. Jr., and Pascual-Leone, A. (2000). Self-recognition and the right prefrontal cortex. *Trends in Cognitive Sciences, 4*: 338–344.

Kestenberg, J. (1985). The flow of empathy and trust between mother and child. In *Parental Influences in Health and Disease*, eds E.J. Anthony and G.H. Pollack. Boston, Mass.: Little Brown, pp. 137–163.

Kiersky, S. and Beebe, B. (1994). The reconstruction of early nonverbal relatedness in the treatment of difficult patients. A special form of empathy. *Psychoanalytic Dialogues*, 4: 389–408.

Klein, M. (1946). Notes on some schizoid mechanisms. *International Journal of Psycho-Analysis*, 27: 99–110.

—— (1955). On identification. In *Melanie Klein: Envy and Gratitude and Other Works 1946–1963*. London: Hogarth Press (1975), pp. 141–175.

Krystal, H. (1978). Trauma and affects. *Psychoanalytic Study of the Child*, 33: 81–116.

Liotti, G. (1992). Disorganized/disoriented attachment in the etiology of the dissociative disorders. *Dissociation*, 5: 196–204.

Loewald, H. (1970). Psychoanalytic theory and the psychoanalytic process. In *Papers on Psychoanalysis*. New Haven: Yale Universities Press, 1980, pp. 277–301.

McDougall, J. (1978). Countertransference and primitive communication. In *Plea for a Measure of Abnormality*. New York: International Universities Press, pp. 247–298.

Meares, R. (1999). The contribution of Hughlings Jackson to an understanding of dissociation. *American Journal of Psychiatry*, 156, 1850–1855.

Migone, P. (1995). Expressed emotion and projective identification: A bridge between psychiatric and psychoanalytic concepts? *Contemporary Psychoanalysis*, 31: 617–640.

Modell, A.H. (1993). *The Private Self*. Cambridge, Mass.: Harvard University Press.

—— (1994). Fairbairn's structural theory and the communication of affects. In *Fairbairn and the Origins of Object Relations*, eds J.S. Grotstein and D.B. Rinsley. New York: Guilford Press, pp. 195–207.

Mollon, P. (1996). *Multiple selves, multiple voices: working with trauma, violation and dissociation*. Chichester: John Wiley & Sons.

Morrison, A.P. (1986). On projective identification in couples' group. *International Journal of Group Psychotherapy*, 36: 55–73.

Murray, L. (1991). Intersubjectivity, object relations theory and empirical evidence from mother–infant interactions. *Infant Mental Health Journal*, 12: 219–232.

Ogden, T.H. (1979). On projective identification. *International Journal of Psycho-Analysis*, 60: 357–373.

—— (1990a). On the structure of experience. In *Master Clinicians on Treating the Regressed Patient*, eds L.B. Boyer and P.L. Giovacchini. Northvale, N.J.: Jason Aronson, pp. 69–95.

—— (1990b). *The Matrix of the Mind*. Northvale, N.J.: Jason Aronson.

Ornstein, R. (1997). *The Right Mind: Making Sense of the Hemispheres*. New York: Harcourt Brace.

Perry, B.D., Pollard, R.A., Blakley, T.L., Baker, W.L., and Vigilante, D. (1995). Childhood trauma, the neurobiology of adaptation, and "use-dependent" development of the brain: How states become traits. *Infant Mental Health Journal*, 16: 271–291.

Putnam, F.W. (1997). *Dissociation in Children and Adolescents*. New York: Guilford Press.

Robbins, M. (1996). The mental organization of primitive personalities and its treatment implications. *Journal of the American Psychoanalytic Association*, 44: 755–784.

Ryle, A. (1994). Projective identification: A particular form of reciprocal role procedure. *British Journal of Medical Psychology*, 67: 107–114.

Sands, S. (1997). Self psychology and projective identification – whither shall they meet? A reply to the editors (1995). *Psychoanalytic Dialogue*, 7: 651–668.

Schiffer, F., Teicher, M.H., and Papanicolaou, A.C. (1995). Evoked potential evidence for right brain activity during recall of traumatic memories. *Journal of Neuropsychiatry*, 7: 169–175.

Schore, A.N. (1994). *Affect Regulation and the Origin of the Self: The Neurobiology of Emotional Development*. Mahwah, N.J.: Erlbaum.

—— (1996). The experience-dependent maturation of a regulatory system in the orbital prefrontal cortex and the origin of developmental psychopathology. *Development and Psychopathology*, 8: 59–87.

—— (1997a). Interdisciplinary developmental research as a source of clinical models. In *The Neurobiological and Developmental Basis for Psychotherapeutic Intervention*, eds M. Moskowitz, C. Monk, C. Kaye, and S. Ellman. New York: Jason Aronson, pp. 1–71.

—— (1997b). Early organization of the nonlinear right brain and development of a predisposition to psychiatric disorders. *Development and Psychopathology*, 9: 595–631.

—— (1997c). A century after Freud's Project – Is a rapprochement between psychoanalysis and neurobiology at hand? *Journal of the American Psychoanalytic Association*, 45: 1–34.

—— (1998). The experience-dependent maturation of an evaluative system in the cortex. In *Fifth Appalachian Conference on Behavioral Neurodynamics, "Brain and Values,"* ed. Karl H. Pribram. Mahweh, NJ: Erlbaum, pp. 337–358.

—— (1999a). Invited commentary on "Freud's affect theory in light of contemporary neuroscience." *Neuro-Psychoanalysis*, 1: 115–128.

—— (2000a). Foreword to the reissue of *Attachment and Loss*, Vol. 1: *Attachment* by John Bowlby. New York: Basic Books.

—— (2000b). Attachment and the regulation of the right brain. *Attachment & Human Development*, 2: 23–47.

—— (2000c). The self-organization of the right brain and the neurobiology of emotional development. In *Emotion, Development, and Self-organization*, eds M.D. Lewis and I. Granic. New York: Cambridge University Press, pp. 155–185.

—— (2001a). The effects of a secure attachment relationship on right brain development, affect regulation, and infant mental health. *Infant Mental Health Journal*, 22: 7–66.

—— (2001b). The effects of early relational trauma on right brain development, affect regulation, and infant mental health. *Infant Mental Health Journal*, 22: 201–269.

—— (2001c). The Seventh Annual John Bowlby Memorial Lecture. Minds in the making: Attachment, the self-organizing brain, and developmentally-oriented psychoanalytic psychotherapy. *British Journal of Psychotherapy*, 17: 299–328.

—— (in press a). The right brain as the neurobiological substratum of Freud's dynamic unconscious. In *Freud at the Millennium: The Evolution and Application of Psychoanalysis*, eds D. Scharff and J. Scharff. New York: Other Press.

—— (in press b). Clinical implications of a psychoneurobiological model of projective identification. In *Primitive Mental States*, Vol. III. *Pre- and Peri-natal Influences on Personality Development*, ed. S. Alhanati. New York: Karnac.

Spitz, R.A. (1965). *The First Year of Life: A Psychoanalytic Study of Normal and Deviant Development of Object Relations*. New York: International Universities Press.

Sroufe, L.A. (1996). *Emotional Development: The Organization of Emotional Life in the Early Years*. New York: Cambridge Universty Press.

Stein, R. (1990). A new look at the theory of Melanie Klein. *International Journal of Psycho-Analysis*, 71: 499–511.

Stern, D.N. (1985). *The Interpersonal World of the Infant*. New York: Basic Books.

Stolorow, R.D. and Atwood, G.E. (1996). *Contexts of Being: The Intersubjective Foundations of Psychological Life*. Mahwah N.J.: Analytic Press.

Trevarthen, C. (1990). Growth and education of the hemispheres. In *Brain circuits and functions of the mind*, ed. C. Trevarthen. Cambridge, England: Cambridge University Press, pp. 334–363.

Tronick, E.Z. and Weinberg, M.K. (1997). Depressed mothers and infants: failure to form dyadic states of consciousness. In *Postpartum Depression in Child Development*, eds L. Murray and P.J. Cooper. New York: Guilford Press, pp. 54–81.

Watt, D. (200). The dialogue between psychoanalysis and neuroscience: Alienation and reparation. *Neuro-Psychoanalysis*, 2: 183–192.

Weinberg, I. (2000). The prisoners of despair: Right hemisphere deficiency and suicide. *Neuroscience & Biobehavioral Reviews*, 24: 799–815.

Winnicott, D. (1958). The capacity to be alone. *International Journal of Psycho-Analysis*, 39: 416–420.

—— (1971a). *Playing and Reality*. New York: Basic Books.

—— (1971b). *Therapeutic Consultations in Child Psychiatry*. New York: Basic Books.

Wittling, W. (1997). The right hemisphere and the human stress response. *Acta Physiologica Scandinavica* (Supplement), 640: 55–59.

Part II

Mainly clinical

Chapter 6

"Think outside, not inside"
Making an interpretation hearable

Peter Blake

Anne Alvarez's extension of the concept of containment by emphasising its energising features highlights the liveliness which is an essential characteristic of her work. The title of her publication *Live Company* reinforces the importance of this invigorating quality. It is needed to both awaken and sustain those patients for whom deadness has become a way of being. However, this aliveness is not only an upregulating presence, for it also needs to be accompanied by a sensitive awareness of how much liveliness the patient can tolerate. Continuous consideration to what the patient can manage is a crucial ingredient in Alvarez's "live" company.

This chapter will concentrate on this feature of her work by focusing on her concept of "hearability". It will examine how much a therapist needs to play with an interpretation, especially a transference interpretation, to make it more hearable and therefore more thinkable. A major thesis will be that interpretations are given too readily and forcefully and greater thought needs to be given to what is the appropriate distance and temperature, to use Meltzer's terms, of an interpretation (Meltzer, 1976). If it is too close or too hot it will overwhelm and be experienced as traumatic, while if it is too distant and cold it will fail to impact upon the patient. The "hearability" (Alvarez, 1992) of an interpretation will be examined in the context of working with children and the use of the play technique.

Alvarez has consistently addressed this issue in her questioning of the traditional Kleinian technique of interpreting early, deeply and to the area of most acute anxiety (see Alvarez, 1985, 1988, 1992, 1996; Alvarez et al., 1999; Alvarez and Reid, 1999). She has raised many questions about the appropriateness of the speed and type of interpretation we offer our patients. She argues some children do not have the ego strength to be able to listen and think about their anxieties if given in a standard way. Her experience, as has been mine, is that for some children the very mention of anxiety makes them more anxious – it does not open the door to unconscious constellations, either now or in the future. Moreover she feels that analytic workers run the risk of dwelling too much on the past and present and do not give enough attention to the future. Obviously with children this "anticipatory" identification, as she calls it (Alvarez, 1992), is especially important. This also influences the way she interprets. A statement like "You are worried about being alone on the weekend" is quite different from "It's hard to believe we will meet again on Monday." Here the focus on the future helps to distance the frightening present, as well as reinforcing the hope. Alvarez also plays with or modulates the anxiety by concentrating more on the need behind it. Again a statement, "You are showing me how important it is to be big" allows for greater space for thought than the anxiety-based interpretation of, "You are worried about being small." This way of interpreting puts more space between the child and his anxieties, while at the same time recognising that they exist. It affords more room for play without denying the work.

In a recent "Symposium on Frustration" Alvarez reinforces this view when she states, "Frustration promotes thinking only when it is not over the limits of the tolerable and thinkable; otherwise trauma and despair may produce dissociation and cognitive disorder" (Alvarez et al., 1999: 184).

Alvarez's ideas arise out of a long history of consideration as to when, how much, and in what way we should interpret. It can be found in Freud's earliest formulations in 1895 in "The Project for a Scientific Psychology" (Freud, 1895) and later in "Beyond the Pleasure Principle" (Freud, 1920). In these papers he talks, albeit in biological terms, about the need for a protective apparatus or shield so the system will not be overloaded or traumatised. In Freud's language the protective shield guarantees the system will not be over excited by having "periodic cathexis and decathexis of the perception–consciousness system" (Freud, 1920). That is, the system simply takes samples of the external world. This sampling of the world can be thought about in terms of giving patients some samples of an interpretation – not to give the full amount but to gauge the correct dosage. With children this can be achieved by keeping the anxieties in the play.

The idea of not overwhelming the patient is one which has been focused upon by Winnicott in his use of the concept of the third area, the in between, and his emphasis on play. In "The Use of an Object" (Winnicott, 1971) he highlights the infant being able to use the mother as an object so as to feel he has created her and not the other way round. From this initial omnipotence, and later gradual disillusionment, the infant's true sense of self can develop. He notes that the Transitional Object is the infant's first not-me "possession" rather than its first not-me "object". The infant must feel this ownership just as the patient must feel he owns and has helped to create the interpretation. Winnicott emphasises the importance of creating a space for both therapist and patient to play. From this position they can find the interpretation rather than the patient feeling it has been given to him. To quote Winnicott:

> it is only in recent years that I have become able to wait and wait for the natural evolution of the transference arising out of the patient's growing trust in the psychoanalytic technique and setting, and to avoid breaking

up this natural process by making interpretations. It will be noticed that I am talking about the making of interpretations and not about interpretations as such. It appals me to think how much deep change I have prevented or delayed in patients in a certain classification category by my personal need to interpret. If only we can wait, the patient arrives at understanding creatively and with immense joy, and I now enjoy this joy more than I used to enjoy the sense of having been clever. I think I interpret mainly to let the patient know the limits of my understanding. The principle is that it is the patient and only the patient who has the answers.

(Winnicott, 1971: 101–102)

Bion's model of containment is also helpful in considering whether an interpretation should be given, as well as its timing. It emphasises the interplay between the container and the contained and raises the question of how far a projection must travel before it can be felt to be safely expelled (Bion, 1962). The other side of this model, namely the function of the container, stresses the need not only of holding but of when to feed back the detoxified projection. Insufficient holding of the anxieties by interpreting too quickly can lead to clinical disasters, as a safe space has not been created for patient and therapist to play.

A clinical example of this process occurred with a thirteen-year-old boy who was highly anxious about his homosexual feelings. Such feelings threatened to overwhelm his fragile sense of a sexual identity and as such had to be evacuated. In the therapy I felt these feeling were projectively identified in me as he would accuse me of being a fucking poofter. I was despised and experienced as a horrible threat. He would often yell, "You fucking poofter Blake, I will kill you." Under this assault I would interpret back that I understood how frightened he was of his homosexual feelings. Interpretations of this kind led to me being physically attacked. Such interpretations did not allow him to feel such impulses were safely housed in me. With hindsight, an interpretation naming the anxiety as he was experiencing it – that is, that the homosexuality was in me and as such posed an awful threat to him – would have been more helpful, or perhaps to not have interpreted at all but rather to have thought about his terror of feeling so attacked.

Another influence on this issue of the hearability of an interpretation has been the practice of infant observation (Miller et al., 1989). Perhaps more than any other experience it has led to a much greater appreciation of the therapeutic value of thoughtful observation and raises the question of whether it is always necessary to interpret. Can there be therapeutic change without interpretation – of course we all know that there can. Are we interpreting too much? May a judicious use of being a "thoughtful audience" be more appropriate at times? Does this give more space to our patients as well as enabling them to feel they create the drama – that this is their creation and not ours?

We can learn about this question of how long an interpretation needs to be held in the therapist's mind and not given, or fed back, to the patient by looking at what we know from the infantile experience of being held and fed. Dilys Daws' paper, "The Perils of Intimacy" (Daws, 1997), highlights the dangers of being too close in a feeding situation. For some infants intimacy can feel like a traumatic intrusion. In discussing how an infant needs to be held she notes, "The regulating of distance may be a crucial way of managing emotional issues" (Daws, 1997: 180). We know from infant observation how the increased distance between mother and baby at the period of weaning can paradoxically allow some nursing couples to be more intimate (Blake, 1988; Daws, 1997; Lubbe, 1996). Moreover, the increased distance at this time promotes the infant's capacity for symbolisation and play.

Allowing a playful space in the clinical setting for the patient's communication, rather than giving a direct interpretation, is shown in Paul and Thomson-Salo's work with mothers and their infants (Paul and Thomson-Salo, 1997). They note that they were initially puzzled as to why they did not give many transference interpretations, but go on to conclude that their holding, in a thinking way, of the mothers' and babies' projections allowed the mothers to "find the answers within themselves".

A century ago psychoanalysis felt it had to find the answers. Freud's early therapeutic ambition (Freud, 1895) led to forceful interpretations. More understanding of the complexity of the mind and the fragility of the therapeutic relationship has led to a greater sensitivity in the use of interpretations. Alvarez's work with autistic, borderline and deprived children and its focus on what is hearable and thinkable continues the refinement of analytic technique. Her work, along with that of other clinicians such as Winnicott (1971), Casement (1985), Klauber (1986), Rosenfeld (1987), Lomas (1987), Joseph (1989), Steiner (1993) and Britton (1998), has made therapists more mindful of whether they should give an interpretation, and if so, should it include the transference? How much should it focus on process or content? Should it be client- or patient-centred? Does it concentrate on the need or the anxiety? How much of an interpretation should be given? Can it be diluted so anxieties can be addressed in a manner that does not overwhelm?

This issue was brought to my clinical attention several years ago when I was seeing an eight-year-old boy called Steven. He had been referred for being aggressive at home and at school. He was the only child of a wealthy older couple. His mother had suffered from depression after his birth, and both parents said they felt that they were too old to play with him. After several months of therapy I felt the process was quite blocked. His sessions were full of contempt for any interpretation I made. He presented as a hard, almost psychopathic child and I struggled with feelings of disliking him. Things changed quite dramatically, however, in one session. In this session he began playing with a ball of plasticine. He attached some string to the ball and began waving it about. This developed into flinging the ball on to a high ledge, as if he was fishing. He would pull the ball down and inspect the dust that had collected on it. He did this several times. After a while I found myself entering the play and speaking as a piece of dust. In a rather high-pitched voice I spoke about being dislodged from my home, that I wanted to stay with the rest of my dust family. Unlike all other attempts at communication Steven actually listened to this. Indeed, he seemed to enjoy it in a genuine rather than sarcastic or mocking way. At this time I was not sure why I was speaking in this manner nor why I was saying these particular things. It felt much more spontaneous and alive than an articulation of a processed counter-transference reaction. Steven continued to play with the plasticine and after a short time would ask me, "What is it saying now?" What was most remarkable was the change in Steven. He asked these questions like a small child, both enjoying and being curious about the play. The mocking, arrogant pseudo adult in him had gone. I further discovered a change had come over me. Being in the role of the dust I began to speak about being only a speck of dust, so small, so worthless and so unwanted. In speaking like this I began to realise how much vulnerability and pain hid behind his hard, superior self. Until I began to speak in this way I had not appreciated this. I found through the play, and I am not sure whether it was his play or my play, a side of Steven which had remained hidden to both of us.

After several sessions of entering the play, rather than interpreting it, or perhaps more accurately interpreting in the play, it became clear how Steven enjoyed my playing with his play, and I enjoyed it as well. There was now an excitement and energy in both of us as his play continued and I wondered what I might say in this high-pitched voice. We were now a lively couple. Usually I would address some form of anxiety or guilt in the play; for example, "Oh, what's happening now, I don't know when I will see my family again." (After this session I discovered there was some threat to him being sent away to boarding school.) I normally found myself acting out the role of the passive character in the play, the one to whom something was being done, although there were some moments when I spoke on behalf of the one per- forming the action (for example I became the car hitting the animal rather than the animal being hit). At other times I would speak for both sides of the action. I was never sure what determined which character I would identify with, although I suspect, or perhaps hope, I was picking up some message from Steven about this. What was clear was that I was always in the action. The verbs in his play were emphasised. Entering the play gave me the free- dom to name the action rather than being too concerned as to who was doing what to whom. The ease of projection in play lessens this distinction between subject and object. The projections can playfully move around.

I believe this change in technique worked with Steven for several reasons. With his history of being with a depressed mother, not being played with and surrounded by adults, my "formal" interpretations given from an observer's position were experienced as being too far away. He hated this distance. There were other times when my interpretations were experienced as critical and belittling. At these times he would belittle me back with his contempt. My entering the play allowed us to be together in this third in between area. In so doing there was undoubtedly an element of fun for both of us. It did not feel so serious. Playing detoxified the intensity of the experience. It was not too intimate and so could be held rather than denied or attacked. It also enabled Steven to feel that his material and he himself could be a source of fun and enjoyment. I experienced and treated his material as precious. I was always mindful of not taking over his play. I consciously tried to keep to the material he had given me, although by entering the play the therapist opens himself or herself up to many more levels of communication from the child. When I did elaborate his themes it still felt I was extending something that was primarily his creation. For children especially, who are so used to being taught by adults, an interpretation can so easily be felt to be the therapist's creation. While there is always the risk of taking over the play, I think child therapists have become too cautious in this area and run the opposite risk of losing touch with the child in themselves, or being too adult.

This technique of entering the play is one way to regulate the distance and temperature between therapist and patient. On one level it draws both therapist and child away from direct contact with each other, but at another level it can allow them to be very close in the safety of the play. Even when I do not enter the play, but rather simply think about doing this, I find myself wondering what it would be like to be this piece of paper that is being ripped or this piece of string that is being pulled. I find this helps me to tune into the child.

Entering the play also turns down the heat of the transference. I make no transference references while in the play. This does not mean I take no account of the transference, but work with it rather than in it.

In my experience entering the play is especially helpful for children under five. It can also be beneficial for certain obsessional children who are not so terrified of emotion. They can enjoy their play being given an emotionality by the therapist, while still being able to distance themselves from it.

Rather than entering the play a therapist can further distance the anxiety by commenting about the feelings which may be in it. To give an everyday example of a child cutting up some plasticine: a possible comment could be, "If I were the plasticine I'd be feeling in bits and pieces", or the slightly more playful, "I think the plasticine is feeling in bits and pieces." It is interesting to note that even Melanie Klein herself, who was such an advocate for interpretation, gets close to this in her account of the case of Ruth. This four-year-old girl was terrified of being alone in the room with Klein and for some time would only enter with her older sister. With such a level of distress Klein decided to interpret via the play. I quote:

All the while I began by applying my interpretations to the doll – showing her as I played with it that it was afraid and screaming, and telling her the reason – and then I proceeded to repeat the interpretation which I had given for the doll by applying them to her own person. In this way I established the analytical situation in its entirety.

(Klein, 1932: 28)

I would now have some doubts about the need or speed at which such interpretations had to be "applied to her person".

For some children even commenting on the feelings in the play can be too much. Here a more "technical" or real discussion may be as close as the child will allow. Continuing with the plasticine example, a discussion about how the plasticine is made or the ease with which it can be cut and separated may be as hot as the comments can be. I have spent many sessions talking about such things as the technical details of brakes and gears on bikes, how a volcano works, the life of a hermit crab, and so on. This seems to be especially so with latency aged children and young adolescents. In this situation the therapist has to be able to tolerate this distance – to contain his or her own therapeutic ambition. To be able to hold on to the belief in thinking about the anxieties in a symbolic form, without any overt therapeutic comment or intervention can be enormously difficult, especially when seeing a child on a once a week basis, and even more difficult in private practice when payment is involved.

In my experience there is a smaller group of children who cannot even tolerate safe and non-threatening comments: to ask about the plasticine or the gears on the bike would be too much. Any comment can feel an invasion, yet such children seem to be quite happy to draw or tell you about school, music, sport, and so on. This seems to be most common in the early adolescent group, between 12–14 years old. Here anxieties seem so raw and powerful that even touching them on a symbolic level is too much (Waddell, 1993).

David was a twelve-year old boy whom I saw three times a week for four years. For the first two years of therapy he would fill the sessions by dramatically telling me about movies, TV shows, pop stars, and so on. If I tried to ask any questions or make comments he would either ignore them or tell me politely to shut up. Normally, after some comment by me his material would quicken even more. He hated being disturbed and every song or story had to be completed without interruption. In one session after I commented on something he said, "Think inside, not outside." I did feel he wanted me to think, I was to be more than just a toilet breast (Meltzer, 1967), but I certainly was not to be a feeding one. For the first two years I felt I needed to be his audience, but I think that alone would not have been enough. He required a thinking audience, and when I realised this his analysis proceeded within me. Interpretations or even interpretative activity (questions, comments) were not appropriate. I literally had to shut up and think. For most sessions I did not say anything. (I must say it helped to be hearing his behaviour outside the sessions was improving.) Steiner's important distinction between understanding and being understood (Steiner, 1993) is helpful in maintaining this "thinking audience".

David came from a disturbing background. Like Steven, his mother was depressed and there was early abandonment, and I felt he had never been played with in his early years. However, my attempts to play with him felt like an intrusion and a negation of himself. His sense of self was very fragile and this was heightened in this early adolescent period. I felt he was showing me he needed to be allowed to play by himself. That I had to witness and appreciate this play so it could be authenticated, to be truly his. My comment, no matter how helpful, did not allow his thoughts to be fully his own. I remember thinking to myself it doesn't matter how crazy or confused these thoughts are, they are his. My trying to modify them prematurely took away their very essence.

During these two years I had periods of struggling to hold this role as a thinking audience. Was I being too gentle, too passive, colluding by not confronting his anxieties? In the third year of therapy things began to change. His stories became clearer, both in their presentation and symbolic content. They also began more clearly to relate to himself, although they were still symbolic. Often he would sing songs such as the Red Hot Chilli Peppers', "I don't ever want to feel like I did that day, I went to the place alone", and Jeff Buckley's, "This is our last goodbye". At this time he would say, "These are not about me." We both knew they were. I would just look and smile. The therapy developed further when after a song or a story he would offer what he called a "reflection" period, telling me what he thought it was about. Soon after this he would ask for my reflection. Subsequent to this came a period when he became very interested in Psychology, especially Freud. One day he asked me, "Did it all come from him?" Now when he would do something he would interpret it himself by saying this is what a psychiatrist would say about this. I felt now the thinking could be outside, and it was after this stage in the therapy that thoughts and feelings about our relationship could be acknowledged and discussed. He did not allow me to gather the transference (Meltzer, 1967), I had to wait for it.

Reviewing my experiences of being a thinking audience for David and on entering the play with Steven, it is clear that in both cases formal interpretations were experienced as intrusive and traumatic. I had to struggle to find some way to make interpretations hearable so that thought between us could eventually be tolerated. Thinking about this clinical difficulty, Britton's idea of a triangular space has been extremely helpful. In *Belief and Imagination* (Britton, 1998), he relates this idea to subjectivity and objectivity. He proposes that in the earliest developmental periods mother and infant are at one with each other and only subjectivity is known between them. With the emergence of the awareness of "the other" (which he relates to the earliest Oedipal situation) there is the capacity for the development of a triangular space. To quote Britton:

> If the link between the parents perceived in love and hate can be tolerated in the child's mind it provides the child with the prototype for an object relationship of a third kind in which he or she is a witness and not a participant. A third position then comes into existence from which object relationships can be observed. Given this, we can also envisage being observed. This provides us with a capacity for seeing ourselves in interaction with others and for entertaining another point of view while retaining our own – for observing ourselves while being ourselves. I call the mental freedom provided by this process triangular space.
>
> (Britton, 1998: 41–42).

While this movement from two to three is crucial, it can be very difficult if the security of the two has not been established. For both David and Steven the early relationship with their depressed mother (and uninvolved fathers) did not enable them to feel secure in this being at one with each other world. As such the other, or objective fact, poses an awful threat. In the therapy this was represented by any interpretation which was experienced as evidence of otherness. At times interpretations were also experienced as some sort of public display of a mental intercourse of ideas, like a mating of my observations with my thinking. Giving them my thoughts about how they may be feeling was like putting a distance between us. I had gone off and "observed" our interaction rather than stayed in it. From this position they felt they were excluded and forced to witness. Britton develops Rosenfeld's work on thin- and thick-skinned patients in discussing this clinical dilemma of how to interpret to someone who experiences an interpretation as an attack on their very existence. Britton states:

> The only way I discovered of finding a place to think that was helpful and not disruptive was to allow the evolution within myself of my own experience and to articulate this to myself while communicating to the patients my understanding of their point of view. This, I found, did enlarge the possibilities of co-existent thinking.
>
> (Britton 1998: 42)

This co-existent thinking is very close to what I am calling a thinking audience. In being a thinking audience there is certainly evidence of an "other" thinking, but it is only vaguely in the vicinity of the patient's thoughts and as such may not be perceived as an intrusive threat. I think the technique of entering the play is getting closer to the subjective experience of the child, but it is often not experienced as totally coming from the other and therefore can be more tolerated. It is not moving to a three, but there is a slight shift from the two; perhaps it is a position of two and a quarter! My clinical experiences suggest that this slight movement towards the recognition of the other can ultimately lead to a position of acceptance of triangular space. I certainly found this to be the case with David.

I would like to conclude by thinking about this issue of the hearability of an interpretation in relation to the transference, for no interpretation is closer or hotter than that which deals with the immediacy of the therapist–child relationship.

Therapists are taught at the beginning of their training about the primacy of the transference (Rosenbluth, 1970). While the dual questions of what is the child worried about and how are those worries manifested in our relationship are enormously helpful ones in the consulting room, there is a danger of over emphasising the use of the transference. As far back as 1934 Strachey reminds us that the transference interpretation is the one which brings about change. That is, it leads to real structural personality change; it is mutative. But he also notes, when comparing the transference interpretation to fruit in a fruit cake, that a fruit cake needs more than just fruit. I would like to go further and say there can be some cakes that can be highly nutritious and contain no fruit.

This urgency to interpret in the transference (especially promoted by early Kleinians) may dull one's sensitivity to what is the most appropriate level of intimacy for a particular patient. Just like other interpretations, transference interpretations need to be played with – by both therapist and patient. Clearly a transference interpretation can be powerfully helpful if it is hearable to the patient. But what if it is not?

This question raises the important distinction between working "with" and "in" the transference (Rustin, 1982). Working "in" the transference is when feelings experienced by the patient are taken up and related to, or placed inside the relationship of the therapist and the patient. The therapist directly refers to the transference. Working "with" the transference does not lead to this direct reference and as such can be used when the therapist feels the transference is too hot or close. In this situation the therapist is aware of the transference but does not speak to the patient about it. Rather this awareness is used to guide the therapist, to help him or her emphasise or highlight this feeling as it may arise in other relationships. For example, the therapist may feel the child is upset at seeing the therapist with another child, but feels the child is not able to hear about this feeling in relation to the therapist. This, however, alerts the therapist to the issue of jealousy so that this issue can be looked for in the play or in other relationships (for example, the child's jealousy of a younger sibling) as well as emphasising it in any discussion ("you really feel very jealous about your brother"). Working "with" the transference is most commonly applied in short-term work but it can also be used to dilute or distance the transference when it is felt to be necessary. This is not only in situations when the transference feels too hot but also when it may be too cold. That is when the child is a long way away from consciously feeling these feelings towards the therapist. This can easily occur with children who are seen on a once a week basis. The transference may also be played with in other ways. One way of diluting it is to mention it in the context of other relationships. This tends to soften the impact. For example, "You feel let down by your school and your mum and by me today." Another technique is to leave the transference in the air – to note the dynamic but not to relate it to anyone or anything. Using the above example of being let down one could say, "Being let down is horrible." I would normally speak to the air in this situation. I would not look at the child while saying this and my tone of voice would be vague. This allows such a communication to be picked up or left alone.

In this chapter I have concentrated on Alvarez's idea of the hearability of an interpretation. I have emphasised the importance of regulating the temperature or distance of an interpretation, of when and how to feed it back to the child. The third area of play can be an important go-between or no man's land in which anxieties can be safely explored. It should be briefly noted, however, that such a safe haven can be used as a retreat, or what I have described elsewhere as the "dangerous safety of play" (Blake, 1997b). This type of play has a very different type of quality to the playfulness I have been describing in this chapter. It does not feel like an exploration which is alive; rather, there is a sense that the child is losing him/herself in the play.

In concluding I would like to note that the child psychotherapist of today is one of the most highly trained of all child mental health workers. Years of reading, infant observation, supervision and personal analysis help to develop a depth of understanding of the child's mind which is not paralleled in any other paediatric area. While this level of refinement and sensitivity in observing is essential, it must be accompanied by a similar depth of understanding of what to do with such observations. The work of the observation must be combined with the play of the interpretation.

References

Alvarez, A. (1985) "The problem of neutrality: some reflections on the psychoanalytic attitude in the treatment of borderline and psychotic children". *Journal of Child Psychotherapy*, 11: 87–104.

Alvarez, A. (1988) "Beyond the unpleasure principle: some preconditions for thinking through play". *Journal of Child Psychotherapy*, 14: 1–14.

Alvarez, A. (1992) *Live Company: Psychoanalytic Psychotherapy with Autistic, Borderline, Deprived and Abused Children*. London and New York: Routledge.

Alvarez, A. (1996) "Interview with Mrs. Anne Alvarez". *Child Psychoanalytic Gazette*, 8: 5–12.

Alvarez, A., Harrison, A. and O'Shaughnessy, E. (1999) "Symposium on frustration". *Journal of Child Psychotherapy*, 25: 167–198.

Alvarez, A. and Reid, S. (1999) *Autism and Personality*. London: Routledge.

Bion, W. (1962) *Learning from Experience*. London: Heinemann.

Blake, P. (1997a) "Weaning revisited". *Australian Journal of Psychotherapy*, 7: 97–110.

Blake, P. (1997b) "The dangerous safety of play". *Child Psychoanalytic Gazette*, 9: 4–18.

Britton, R. (1998) *Belief and Imagination*. London: Routledge.

Casement, P. (1985) *On Learning From The Patient*. London: Tavistock.

Daws, D. (1997) "The perils of intimacy: closeness and distance in feeding and weaning". *Journal of Child Psychotherapy*, 23: 179–199.

Freud, S. (1895) "Project for a scientific psychology", Standard Edition 1.

Freud, S. (1920) "Beyond the pleasure principle", Standard Edition 18.

Freud, S. and Breuer, J. (1895) *Studies in Hysteria*. Standard Edition 2.

Joseph, B. (1978) "Different types of anxiety and their handling in the clinical situation". In M. Feldman and E. Spillius (eds) *Psychic Equilibrium and Psychic Change*. London: Tavistock.

Klauber, J. (1986) *Difficulties in the Analytic Situation*. London: Free Association.

Klein, M. (1932) *The Psychoanalysis of Children*. In *The Writings of Melanie Klein*, Vol. 2. London: Hogarth.

Lomas, P. (1987) *The Limits Of Interpretation*. London: Penguin.

Lubbe, T. (1996) "Who lets go first? Some observations on the struggles around weaning". *Journal of Child Psychotherapy*, 22: 195–213.

Meltzer, D. (1967) *The Psychoanalytical Process*. London: Heinemann.

Meltzer, D. (1976) "Temperature and distance as technical dimensions of interpretation". Paper read at the European Psychoanalytic Federation, Aix en Provence.

Miller, L., Rustin, M., Rustin, M., and Shuttleworth, J. (1989) *Closely Observed Infants*. London: Duckworth.

Paul, C. and Thomson-Salo, F. (1997) "Infant-led innovations in a mother–baby therapy group". *Journal of Child Psychotherapy*, 23: 219–244.

Rosenbluth, D. (1970) "Transference and Child Psychotherapy". *Journal of Child Psychotherapy*, 2: No. 4.

Rosenfeld, H. (1987) *Impasse and Interpretation*. London: Tavistock.

Rustin, M. (1982) "Finding a way to the child". *Journal of Child Psychotherapy*, 8: 145–150.

Steiner, J. (1993) *Psychic Retreats*. London: Routledge.

Strachey, J. (1934) "The nature of the therapeutic action of psychoanalysis". *International Journal of Psycho-Analysis*, 15: 127–159.

Waddell, M. (1993) *Understanding Your 12–14 Year Old*. London: Rosendale.

Winnicott, D.W. (1971) *Playing and Reality*. London: Pelican.

Chapter 7

From freezing to thawing

Working towards the depressive position in long-term therapy with autistic patients[1]

Bianca Lechevalier-Haïm

> I will be responsible
>   for watching over
>   the snow dogs
> I will follow my footsteps
>   and listen to
>   the howling in the evening
> And if I get lost
>   in the night
>   the wolves will help me
>   if I call on them softly
> And the wolves will once again become
>   my good friends
>   *"The snow dogs". Julia, age 14*

In the long-term treatment of autistic children, emotions only begin to thaw out after a great deal of time is spent on processing them; this is done in stages, once splitting mechanisms have diminished in intensity. Resnik (1999) says that there is a crucial moment in this process when mental pain begins to emerge once again. Thawing-out may at times appear to lead to a catastrophic emotional tidal wave. In every case, access to pain – the pain of despair at the very beginnings of life – in a context of emotional thaw requires the analyst, in the counter-transference, to be sufficiently receptive towards these very early life experiences (Bion 1970), without simply sending the projections back (Segal 1957; Grinberg 1963).

Receptivity implies being passive enough when faced with the unknown and the unfamiliar, with bodily perceptions that carry in their wake anxiety concerning death (Lechevalier 1987); but it implies also that there be libidinal forces full of hope that can cathect thinking in order to give body and meaning to emotions, enabling links to be made in the child's painful internal world without the kind of intrusion that would only tend to confirm the existence of persecutory images. It then becomes possible to hope that links may be established between two living beings able to communicate with and understand each other, able to continue their road through life with respect for each other's identity.

Thawing-out also poses problems concerning the way in which defences have to be modified. If therapy can be prolonged until adolescence, we see that defensive activity has to struggle against the overwhelming impact of eroticism and pain of separation as reactivated in the transference. This struggle is made even more complex by the anxiety and depression involved in Oedipal issues. Moreover, identification with the internal objects of depressed parents, who have been themselves unable to work through a mourning process, tells us something about the identificatory modalities – adhesive and introjective – that are present in the child's own internal world. In such a context, it is difficult for analysts to distinguish between access to the despair of early life, narcissistic depression (because of the physical changes at puberty that require the self to give up the omnipotent idea of belonging to both sexes at the same time), the depression involved in the Oedipal situation with the accusing superego, and genuine feelings of compassion arising from the pain of having damaged the object. Alvarez (1992: 127–137) discusses this problem, arguing that a distinction has to be made between "manic defence" and "manic position".

When the psychoanalysis of autistic children can be continued through adolescence, entry into adulthood, with its concomitant dimensions of sexuality and work experience, is a highly productive moment whose dynamics put us in touch with renewed aspects of emotional life. New reorganizations in the mind are still possible. In some cases, the thinking self can have access to new stages in processing the depressive position as dramatized in the Oedipal situation.

Laura, now 28, was a former autistic patient whose therapy began when she was four years old. She had just lost her father, with whom she had an extremely powerful Oedipal attachment. She was working in a centre for the disabled, and lived with her partner in their own accommodation. One of her aims in gaining her independence was to be able to continue her therapy with me on a private basis. Everything was called into question by her mother's severe depression after the death of her husband; she wanted Laura to move back in with her. Laura at first hesitated between sharing her mother's grief and triumphing over her in a manic way; then she experienced the pain of guilt with respect to both parents. After working through all this, she exclaimed: "I was never able to replace my dead sister, who died before I was born in a road accident. I won't be able to stay with my mother and replace my father. I have my own grief, and it's not the same as my mother's."

Alvarez uses her own counter-transference in the analytical field in order to understand how best to help the patient towards restoring links. This was particularly the case with Robbie, with whom she developed a whole range of meaningful emotions that enabled them to analyse the ritualistic behaviour of this adolescent as he moved towards adulthood. She was thereby able to experience with him how ideas developed throughout that period. Sharing her experience in this way with us was very helpful to me in my own work with these patients as they move through the adolescent process, in particular her detailed exploration of how they can get back in touch with new and precious possibilities buried within their formerly frozen selves.

Julia, a former autistic patient, saw herself in "a looking-glass" in "Las Vegas", as though the psychotherapy were a card game in which she was to have all the "aces" that would transform her into a boy – the "ace"[2] is the strongest card of all, for it can beat even the king and the queen. But two years later she was able to write "The snow dogs"... In her presentation of Robbie, Alvarez highlights the difference between denial of sadness and the elation felt on emerging from the internal prison and being able to make contact with one's own personal subjectivity in a relationship of reciprocity with the object. The same is true of the counter-transference. On the one hand, the analyst has to avoid being plunged into despair; on the other, acknowledging that levels of development exist, and having due regard for defensive organizations in the service of life, the analyst must also – when improvement is well under way – avoid falling into an illusion that would simply ignore the adolescent's destructiveness. It is only then that the therapist can experience true amazement at the sight of the patient's developing capacity for thinking and for loving, now that adhesive identification is a thing of the past as the adolescent progresses towards adulthood.

Gammill (1998), following Klein (1945) and Meltzer (1978), shows how working through the depressive position has to be gone through again and again, at each critical step in life. For post-autistic children, adolescence is a critical phase in which they may collapse into a psychotic breakdown, depression, acute delusional attack, or full-blown schizophrenia. I presented Julia's material to Meltzer in 1999, when these concerns were uppermost in my mind. In Meltzer's opinion, "in the revolution that is adolescence and puberty, Julia may well be able to do something creative with her autism", and in particular with her poetic talent. He spoke of "neglected artists enveloped by distress", and of the "terrible struggle that these adolescents undertake to climb back out of the holes they have fallen into". If they are not to fall back down into the amorphous experience of one-dimensionality, they will have to "reinvent in the first place the infrastructure of two-dimensionality, then that of three-dimensionality. It's hardly surprising that some autistic children just give up..."

Together with the "reinvention" of three-dimensionality that some former autistic patients must accomplish, they have also to process the depressive position through successive life crises. This is not simply a "re-edition" – each time is in fact a reinvention, and the analytical relationship (if it is still ongoing) can help reintegrate into personal space what had earlier been evacuated through projection. A genuine shared emotional experience can offer the hope of progressing beyond the necessary idealization (Alvarez

1992) to the joy of reclaiming one's identity and being able to make true reparation, motivated principally by love. The development of a more benevolent superego is proof that identification with the parental couple, with each parent recognized as distinct, has changed somewhat in the course of successive processing of the depressive position through these different stages in life (Gammill 1999).

Veronica's tale

The Bud

At the very back of its box
The bud keeps itself hidden.
In its too narrow prison
It yawns, yearning to breathe.
It hears singing,
The noise of wings fluttering.
It would like to know what's going on,
And burst its narrow, green, too-tight corset.
A sudden gesture and the corset's torn.
At last says the bud, I can breathe, I can live,
I am free. Good-morning!

(a poem Veronica dictated to me in 1996,
when she was twelve)

When I met Veronica for the first time, she was five and a half years old. At that time she was in a very autistic kind of withdrawal, emerging from her sleepy torpor only to spin round frantically or whirl other objects around; I could never have imagined that one day she would write poetry. Nor did I expect that, at adolescence, there would be such a thawing-out of her emotions.

Veronica's parents had themselves thought of infantile autism when she was just eighteen months old. She had been hospitalized in a paediatric unit, where the diagnosis was confirmed and remedial psycho-motor treatment prescribed. Later, she was admitted to a day hospital where she took part in various activities. The mother felt that this type of treatment approach was unsatisfactory, and was wondering about psychoanalytical psychotherapy.

Veronica is the youngest of three children; her brother was nine at that point, and her sister eight. Her father is a civil engineer, then fifty years old. He is a well-built man, uncommunicative and gloomy, though he did express a great deal of tenderness towards his daughter. He was always very cooperative as far as the analysis was concerned. He has an older daughter (then twenty-eight), born during an earlier marriage, who lives in Paris. Veronica did not have much to say about her. As regards her father,

Veronica told me, when she was fourteen, how unhappy she felt when she discovered his racist outlook on life. Her mother no longer went out to work. Very discreet, attentive towards her daughter – at times almost in a relationship of complete fusion with her, always anticipating what Veronica might want and leaving her no opportunity to take initiatives. Indeed, this attitude remained the same all the way through the therapy, and the end of the analysis, when Veronica was an adolescent, was very difficult. Both father and mother were faced with the death of important family members during the years that the therapy lasted; when Veronica's maternal grandmother died, this was a real ordeal for the mother. At puberty, Veronica told me that her grandmother had been a midwife; she used to be very controlling with her daughter, giving her regular enemas (right up until her wedding) to prevent any risk of intestinal obstruction.

The parents were looking forward to Veronica's birth. The pregnancy passed off well, and delivery was almost at term. However, at the birth, Mrs G was extremely anxious about not being able to control her body, and she had the physical sensation she was about to die. Since the gynaecologist was due to take his holidays in July, the delivery was induced. (Later, whenever the therapy was interrupted in mid-July – close to Veronica's birthday – she felt very anxious, though did not regress.) Mrs G was very disappointed by her initial relationship with her daughter. Veronica was born with both eyes open, and when she was placed on her mother's body Mrs G looked at her and exclaimed: "How wide-awake she looks." The baby was staring at her mother. When she was taken away to be examined, etc., Mrs G felt wonderful; but when she was brought back to her mother Veronica was asleep. What had happened? The baby she was so excited to have, whose gaze she was so keen to see, slept all the time. Mrs G felt as though her baby was dead. This was perhaps a projective identification prolonging the experience of the delivery, or a perception brought about by the baby's tremendous sleepiness. She would not even wake up for feeds.

The first bottle was taken well enough, but all the others were vomited up, spraying all over the place. The formula milk was changed several times, and X-rays were taken of the baby's digestive tract to see if she had pyloric stenosis. A week later, Veronica was no longer looking at her mother. Later still, she would look at bright lights and burst out laughing. Unmotivated laughter lasted until she was more than ten years old. Very early on, Veronica would have attacks of anxiety whenever lights were turned out or there was a power cut.

Later, in the analytical relationship with Veronica, I was able to understand in my counter-transference the mother's initial feelings of despair as she tried helplessly to make real contact with her daughter. I was reminded of the floppy limpness described by Alvarez (1992: 26–41). What had happened during the interactions at the very beginning of Veronica's life? Did she escape into sleep so as not to experience her mother's projections? Did

Mrs G, so disappointed by her daughter's incomprehensible responses, find herself facing the same anxiety about losing vitality as she had done during delivery? What kind of resonance was there with her internal maternal object and its possessive character? How was she dealing with her Oedipal guilt, reactivated by her feelings of failure at Veronica's birth? As for me, all through the analysis, and particularly as adolescence approached, I had to struggle hard against an almost irresistible tendency to fall asleep. The links I was able to make in my associations to these distressing experiences at the beginning of Veronica's life prevented me from feeling so excessively guilty that the quality of our communication in the sessions would have been radically altered.

Veronica's subsequent development was uneven. Hypotonic, she was not able to sit up before she was a year old. She was always sleepy. Babbling did not appear before eighteen months. This was the point at which the mother set in motion the process that would lead to Veronica's being diagnosed as autistic. Mrs G was alarmed too by her daughter's phobic reactions to vacuum cleaners and water draining away.

In our first meeting there was no hesitation in my mind about the diagnosis. She clung at first to her mother, paying no attention whatsoever to me. She spun round and round, fleeing any contact. She whirled objects around on my desk, in a mechanical way – but as though she were contemplating something internally. From time to time she would say things, incomprehensible utterances in words she invented or repeated in an echolalic way. Then suddenly, as I was trying to get her interested in a doll's house, I was surprised to hear her say in a very quiet but husky and determined voice: "'Fraid, 'fraid . . . Madness." I saw in her voice and in her eyes a call for help. I suggested psychotherapy in addition to the treatment she was having in the day hospital.

In our preliminary meetings, though the parents were very critical about the therapeutic approach of the day hospital team, they were also very ambivalent about agreeing to psychoanalytical therapy. Administrative obstacles meant that we had to wait a long time before it became possible to establish a proper setting. (The family lived some ten miles away from the clinic.)

A proper setting in fact had to wait until 1992, when Veronica was nine years of age. The parents finally reached a decision because of the terrible nightmares Veronica was having. We had three sessions a week, on the days she did not attend the day hospital. She was very rapidly able to attend primary school on the days she had her sessions. She adjusted well to school, had a great deal of pleasure in what took place there and came out of her depression.

The first session

Veronica did not look at me, nor at the contents of her personal drawer when I showed it to her. She laughed in an incomprehensible way. Her language was indecipherable, badly pronounced, without any sentences. I perceived her to be in great despair, her face was expressionless, as though it were frozen. She was bent over like a little old lady, and she walked with tiny little steps.

She finally took out of the drawer two lions that she placed opposite each other, as though ready for a fight, then took out the pigs – a sow and piglets. I said that she seemed to be unsure about what was going to happen in our meeting together – was it to be like the lions or the pigs? She then added other animals – a horse (I thought of my name[3]), slightly apart from the rest, and some fencing. Veronica was flaccid, as though not really motivated in her play, but she did brighten up for a moment when she made the animals smell each other, starting with the two lions – she gave me to understand they did not have a pleasant smell. Then the lions and the pigs smelled one another. I was surprised to hear her say the word "friend" – I commented that perhaps friendship was possible here between Veronica and me even if we were not to smell nice.

She then made the horse jump over the fences, and the pig joined in. I said that maybe the horse that was in Mme Lechevalier was joining up with Veronica-pig in order to be friends. But then a fight broke out between the lions, and they were wounded. I commented that even if we were friends, there was still a risk that the lions inside us might have a ferocious fight. The horse and the cow carried the lion. A shepherd arrived. I commented that now Veronica, wounded, was being helped by a human being. I heard her say "yes".

The problem now was – as she showed me in her play – that the cow would like to offer milk, but the lion did not know how to drink. I thought of the very early stages in Veronica's life as they were repeated in the transference and counter-transference. When I told her the session was over, she put the horse to one side and showed me that it seemed to be losing interest . . . "Just like you think I do, perhaps, when I tell you it's time to go", I said.

I was surprised by the fact that in this first session, once the setting was established, Veronica was so quickly able to make contact in such a meaningful way; there was no longer a feeling of emptiness or psychic death. The treatment in the day hospital had certainly been of benefit to her. Alvarez talks about the importance of the initial messages in the first session (1992: 12–25); though there were grounds for hope, Veronica was telling me also about the "fragile and slippery foundations on which [her] responsiveness was based".

In the second session, fences were set up between the animals and me. Out came a giant mad gorilla and a dangerous crocodile – the horse was kept some distance apart. The question was whether the animals were friends or not. I wondered about the fencing: were they protections against instinctual drive impulses, but thereby encouraging autistic withdrawal and imprisonment? The same play went on and on; I began to feel bored. After an interpretation about the fences that protected us, the horse jumped over the fence, and Veronica later took them down. I understood that, though the horse was now free, it might well get lost. I made an interpretation in terms of the anxiety we feel when we get too close or too far apart from each other. Veronica looked puzzled. She brought the shepherd back to rebuild the fences. The animals hurt themselves as they tried to jump over, and the lion carried them. I commented on the hurt we can feel when we meet. She showed me that it was hard work carrying the animals, but that we would manage to cure them.

The following Monday, after the weekend break, during the night – while the shepherd was asleep – the lions and crocodiles devoured the other animals, keeping their skin in their mouths. It was the shepherd's fault; he did not give them enough to eat. I noticed that Veronica's teeth and lips were moving. I made an interpretation in terms of the hunger for words about emotions, both in the sessions and in the interval between them; we ran the risk of having everything that was alive inside us being emptied out by these hungry and angry animals, when I went to sleep like the shepherd. The horse, who was asleep until that point, woke up, as did the shepherd; the horse blamed the shepherd for what had happened. The lions took care of the horse. Veronica said that the fight was similar to what went on in her dreams. When she put the animals away at the end of the session, she told me that they were all alive.

Later, during her adolescence, when I again felt like falling asleep at times when she appeared to be devoting herself entirely to repetitively obsessive actions devoid of affect, I remembered this session and her need for my "live company" – to stop the forces of destruction that threatened to overwhelm her if the fences came down and she did not have enough food for thought. I thought also that Veronica was showing me that it was the strength of her very much alive aggressiveness that enabled the "wounded horse" to be looked after when we were together.

In subsequent sessions, Veronica wanted to paint – but she was very clumsy; she hardly seemed able to handle water and paintbrush, and she wanted to use my hand to help her out. I helped her, and shapes appeared: *a red boat, a green wave some way off, two circles on the boat to represent the passengers, and a yellow sail attached to nothing in particular*. She started to sing and I recognized the tune of "There once was a little boat". I sang the words to her: "There once was a little boat/that had ne- ne- ne-ver sailed . . . It went on a long voyage . . . After five or six weeks, there was no more food . . . They drew straws to see who would be eaten . . . Fate chose the youngest of all, who had ne- ne- ne-ver sailed . . .' I interpreted this. Veronica commented:

"Yes, but what you don't know is that we weren't eaten up at the end of the story – Land ahoy!" She added *a blue shape and some green circles to her drawing, then did another: a red house on land, a house that contained not only the sailor who was not eaten up but also the others.* That was what kept my hopes alive during the long wilderness that adolescence brought in its wake...

Shortly before the Christmas holiday, I experienced the same theme in my counter-transference. At times I felt like falling asleep, at others that I would not be able to control my impulses. A crocodile went missing from her box and I wanted to replace it as a matter of urgency. I wanted to see if my car, which I had parked in a no-parking zone, had been impounded by the police. I felt lost, unable to get back home, alone in the cold. I wanted to call for help. Just then I heard Veronica say: "It's the last day." She drew a coffin in a cemetery. *A corpse was lying in the coffin, on which were placed a tombstone and a cross. Several concentric circles, containing other graves, went round the coffin.* Veronica said: "It's somebody bad who's been put in prison." I wondered aloud: could it be me, punished for not spending Christmas with her, leaving her all alone in the cold like a new-born baby? Did she feel dead, in a cemetery inside me, instead of a Christmas feeling of birth? Veronica replied: "The dead body isn't dead – it's alive." She drew *a wicked person with teeth and enormous hands that had claws. The eyes were terrifying. The person was alive.* I commented that this alive person with claws and teeth for hanging on was really quite frightening. Veronica said: "I'll draw a dead person again, the dead person's nice." She drew *another corpse lying in a coffin.* I commented: "Better to be a nice dead baby, who doesn't move, who sleeps all the time, than an alive person who moves about, demands things and frightens us because it's hungry and might eat us all up like a crocodile."

Veronica then drew *an alive person, very frightening, but this time with no arms or hands, and the mouth was shut.* Her voice became very deep and solemn. In her play, the animals found food inside a house. I no longer felt like a hungry crocodile constantly on the look-out for an inaudible and incomprehensible voice. In my desire to free the imprisoned crocodile, I had fallen into a trap, into anxiety and cold despair. But in the effort I had made to free myself I had also set free a hungry crocodile that was to come back time and again...

The theme of the "horse" that fell ill and had to be taken care of also returned subsequently. In one sequence, the horse ate the poison; the animals then removed it and thanked the horse for having taken it in, because it took a lot of strength not to die. I thought then of projective identification and counter-identification, of my struggle not to fall asleep – a struggle against a poison-induced psychic death.

In her play around March 1993, the cow-mummy was beginning to understand a foreign language, English. She came to England and was able to offer milk. It was not her fault if she did not understand before, because

English is a difficult language. But there was a problem with the animal next door, who did not ask her for milk "because it did not realize she could speak the language and give milk". But in the end they did manage to understand each other and they were both going to be happy, in spite of the freezing cold and their hunger, because they could talk over things together. I was able to work on this idea of sharing strangeness in the cold, thanks to the fact that I now had a better understanding of primitive anxiety ... after discussions in England(!) with colleagues there; this led us closer and closer to the thawing-out of her emotions – though there was still the desperate fear of some new catastrophe (being devoured, poisoned, drowning, etc.).

In the next few months, Oedipal issues and curiosity about the primal scene came more and more into her play material. She expressed anxiety about death involving her mother as the Oedipal rival. Simultaneous working on her splitting mechanisms gave rise to the question of how to keep alive inside Veronica both the hungry lion full of life and the gentle sleepy cow it could gobble up. A sheep allowed them to live together, telling them that in time they would fall in love with each other and have children. The lion's strength saved them from death. The shepherd helped them, but he could not do it all by himself. "The lion's strength is needed for getting out" – getting out of the prison of repeated despair.

In February 1994, Veronica left the day hospital and had full-time schooling in a class that had only a limited number of pupils. She learned to read and write soon afterwards.

The following year was that of pubertal transformation and the explosive thawing-out of her feelings of love in an apparently manic way that included sexual play with other adolescents. It is possible, however, that this was more of a "manic position" as Alvarez describes it, in terms of a phase distinct from what we usually refer to as "manic defence". Veronica was excited on the one hand by the discovery of her adolescent body and the new objects that she idealized (her schoolteacher, a boy in her class), and on the other by the awareness that inside her there were new feelings and a new capacity for tenderness and wonderment. In spite of the anxiety aroused by her first periods and the confusion between genital and anal zones, Veronica was delighted with the changes to her body. That was when she dictated to me the poem she called "The Bud".

Shortly before this, a paediatrician had asked Veronica's mother to stop giving her enemas whenever she became constipated (i.e. when she had her periods). Veronica's anxiety was that she would empty herself, and the mother responded in terms of her own fantasy of dying of intestinal obstruction and peritonitis ... As I mentioned above, this fear had been transmitted to her by her own mother.

During this phase, Veronica's slowness and obsessional defences again made me feel bored and tired almost to the point of falling asleep. In a discussion of post-autistic adolescent obsessionality, Meltzer (1999) pointed out that besides avoidance of anything unfamiliar "they constantly explore sensation-based nuances and minute differences".

Veronica was by now becoming more and more independent, and the quality of her capacity for insight stronger and stronger. But her periods of intense excitement with unmotivated laughing and talking to herself made it difficult to decide what was involved in the idea of being swallowed up by the object as opposed to what Alvarez (1992: 137) calls "a dangerous heady flight which may lead to a crash". Oedipal rivalry threatened to transform the pleasure of life emerging from the dark tunnel of death into triumphalism and manic defence. A dramatic event made the situation even more complex: Veronica's mother had an operation for breast cancer that at first was thought to be progressively worsening. Veronica appeared indifferent to all this, expressing her delight at replacing her mother at home with her father, doing the cooking, etc. (Her sister busied herself with her studies.) A dream enabled me to propose a transference interpretation. *Veronica is on top of a wall, in the sunlight, with her schoolteacher; I am on the ground, in the shade, and rain is falling on me.* I very gradually showed her the splitting mechanisms at work as regards our relationship: the idealization of my "schoolteacher" part (with whom she could climb up high), while another part was down on the ground, in the shade, and getting all the rain/depression – the sadness and tears Veronica was trying to get rid of.

I came back to these issues when her material indicated Oedipal triumphalism. This took us some time to work through, with the need to go back to the work we did at the beginning of the analysis on the splitting mechanisms that were then in operation. The powerful lion and the gentle cow could both live inside her and inside her parents, without the cow running the risk of being devoured by the lion – just the opposite, in fact: the lion's strength would help the cow to survive, like a mother gives her milk and her love without risking death.

One year later, Veronica was in a class (again with a limited number of pupils) preparing for secondary school. She fell passionately in love with a supervisor, a young Algerian woman. She told me of an anxiety-arousing and distressing dream she had had. In the dream, *Veronica wakes up to find herself covered in water. Her head was trapped in a block of ice that was beginning to melt; water was dripping all down her face and flooding her eyes. The supervisor, Nadia, was looking at her in sympathy. In the dream, Veronica felt very upset: she didn't want to inflict any more distress on Nadia, whose own pain – the dramatic events taking place in Algeria, the killings, the many dead – was so great. But Veronica couldn't stop the block of ice melting.* (As a baby, Veronica had never cried.)

In the transference and counter-transference, the supervisor represented me, as well as Veronica's mother who had had the operation for breast cancer. The thawing of her emotions now meant, I think, that she could approach the threshold of the depressive position at the heart of the Oedipal drama.

From the autistic ice age we had moved towards insight through otherness – the mental space of another person with his or her own emotional history. Veronica was suffering from the compassion of compassion. Later on, Nadia's pregnancy and delivery helped Veronica to acknowledge and accept the fertile couple Nadia and her partner formed, then to identify with them through the different aspects of what she projected into their relationship.

The analysis came to an end shortly after Veronica was accepted on a job-training scheme. The decision to end the analysis had been discussed over the final year, but I still felt puzzled. Veronica declared on 10 December that her last session would be in mid-January. Several recurrent dreams preceded her decision.

In one of these, *Veronica has "a kid in her tummy". She goes to her former school to see Nadia. She is no longer worried about Nadia's health, as she had been at first. But Nadia doesn't realize she has changed. Veronica tells her of the pleasure she is having in her life now – and she is making this visit on her own, without her mother.* (In her comments, she said that this meant she had her own car and driver's licence.) *Nadia drives her back home in her car.* "She shouldn't have done that," Veronica said, "it's as though she didn't know I had a car and could drive."

I said that perhaps I gave her the impression of not trusting her to make the right decision about ending the therapy; but perhaps all the same I used my counter-transference car to accompany the feeling of separation. As to the baby she was carrying, perhaps it was conceived in the analysis. Veronica agreed with my interpretations. In her associations, she told me she passed the "Road Safety" examination; she even managed to do exercises with "somersaults" without her old fear of falling and breaking coming back to haunt her. "*You* wouldn't be able to do that," she told me. Her question was to know who the baby's father was: could it be her own father? Was she going back to her parents or into her own accommodation?

On the day of her final session, she told me her dream had changed. Nadia said goodbye to her on the doorstep, Veronica left in her own car and went home to her own flat. "The baby I'm carrying in the dream, it's the baby I'll have later," she added. "Nadia trusted me, she let me go back on my own, back to my own flat."

Identity, mental growth and working through the depressive position

As a defence against separation anxiety, adhesiveness is an ever-present temptation for former autistic patients as they confront their developmental crises. They may adhere in a two-dimensional manner to an internal object of the mother – as perhaps was the case with Veronica and Laura. The lost object that the parent was unable to integrate through an adequate mourning process seems to re-emerge, mobilize feelings of guilt and make clinging to these guilt feelings all the easier. In the life crises that bring Oedipal guilt into play, the temptation is to have recourse to this adhesive pseudo-identity in order to defend the self against, on the one hand, the depression inherent in the separation anxiety involved in exploring the novelty of transformation and, on the other, that aroused by the Oedipal conflict. This results in the loss of personal mental space and identity. This space is necessary for working through the depressive position, with adequate differentiation between the complex feelings of guilt concerning the internal objects of the adolescent and of the parents; mental growth depends on it. The road that has to be travelled through analytical space (a shared space that belongs to each participant) is a long one until growth becomes possible – growth in which the adolescent no longer fears awakening the mother's depression, growth towards reciprocal feelings of compassion, growth towards a smile of wonderment at the beauty of life and its workings.

Notes

1 Translated by David Alcorn.
2 "*As*" in French, hence the assonance with "*Las Vegas*" and "looking-gl*ass*" (translator's note).
3 "The horse" in French is *le cheval*, the first part of Dr Lechevalier's name (translator's note).

References

Alvarez, A. (1992) *Live Company*, London: Routledge.
Bion, W.R. (1970) *Attention and Interpretation*, London: Tavistock Publications.
Gamill, J. (1998) *A partir de Melanie Klein*, Meyzieu: Césura, pp. 129–134.
Gamill, J. (1999) "Élaborations successives de la Position Dépressive", *Bulletin du G.E.R.P.E.N.* (Paris), 43.
Grinberg, L. (1963) "Psicopatologia de la identifacion y de la contraidentificacion proyectivas y de la contratransferencia", *Revista de Psicoanalisis*, 20.
Klein, M. (1945) "The Oedipus complex in the light of early anxieties", in *Love, Guilt and Reparation, The Work of Melanie Klein*, London: Hogarth Press (1975), Vol. 1, pp. 370–419.
Lechevalier, B. (1987) "Manifestations psychosomatiques liées au transfert dans les Psychanalyses de l'Enfant", *Journal de la psychanalyse de l'enfant*, 4, pp. 139–177.
Meltzer, D. (1978) *The Kleinian Development*, Perth: Clunie Press.
Meltzer, D. (1999) "Entretien sur l'évolution des enfants autistes à l'adolescence" *Bulletin du G.E.R.P.E.N.* (Paris), 41, pp. 50–53.
Resnik, S. (1999) *Temps des glaciations*, Toulouse: Erès.
Segal, H. (1981) *The Work of H. Segal*, New York: J. Aronson.
Tustin, F. (1986) *Autistic Barriers in Neurotic Patients*, London: Karnac.

Chapter 8

Deficits in the object and failures in containment

Maria Teresa Gallo

Introduction

Anne Alvarez's flexible and multidisciplinary approaches have been, for me, the most salient aspects of her work and thinking. Rather than limiting herself to one theoretical school, she has always sought to extend Kleinian theory by comparing it not only with other psychoanalytic schools of thought but also with research from developmental psychology, ethology and anthropology, thus considerably enriching our knowledge both of normal child development and of pathology, taking into account both the internal world of the child and the external environment.

This wide-ranging approach has resulted in a flexible attitude towards technique which is relevant to each child's particular situation at any time during their psychic life. Alvarez offers us proof of the way in which psychoanalytic understanding is helpful in the treatment of deprived and borderline children, as well as those with serious mental disorders such as autism, both in terms of initial understanding during assessment and in offering appropriate treatment.

When Anne Alvarez arrived at the Children's Neuropsychiatric Clinic in Turin, in 1982, the tendency was to apply the Kleinian model by trying from the outset to address the deepest pathological dynamics of a patient's internal world, without considering the level of ego development or the effect of environmental experiences.

At the time, I was working in the child guidance section of the Children's Neuropsychiatric Clinic, and found that the use of a highly sophisticated psychotherapeutic technique of verbal interpretation was not helpful with children incapable of communicating, hardly aware of themselves or the world around them, or children so seriously deprived because of deficiencies in the parental relationship that they had not been able to develop an adequate internal world.

In the 1980s, Alvarez's teaching and supervision helped me to work more flexibly with these children. In particular, she encouraged me to work with mother and child together, both in short consultative work and in longer treatments. Her ideas have helped me to understand and deal with situations of deficit in the containment function of the object (derived from the relationship with the external parents), which results in ego deficits and thus a deficit in the capacity of the internal object to contain distress.

I will illustrate this work with two cases, the first being the joint psychotherapeutic treatment of Alberto, an autistic child of three and a half, who had serious ego deficits and who was locked in a pathological relationship with his mother. During the course of the treatment, by helping the mother to make a distinction between herself and the child, he gradually became more aware of himself and his limits and the possibility of using his mind.

The second case illustrates the internal development of Giulio, an eight-year-old adopted child, who had suffered abuse, maltreatment and lack of containment during his infancy. This psychic loss had given rise to distress and frustration. When he began therapy he showed serious behavioural disturbances. Within the psychotherapeutic relationship, he was able to test how it was to feel that someone was thinking about him, and to feel appreciated and looked after without being used. Over time, he was able to develop a better internal relationship with a good object and thus decrease his acting out in the external world.

Deficits in the object

The experience of a newborn and small child of being alone in the presence of its mother is, according to Winnicott (1965), fundamental to the acquisition of mental autonomy and the capacity to be alone. Winnicott defines this type of experience, where the child's immature ego is balanced by the support from the mother's ego, as "ego relatedness". As time passes, the child introjects the mother, who supports the ego, and so attains the ability to be alone.

In British psychoanalytic literature, great attention has been paid to the dynamic of mother–infant relationships as a model for the patient–analyst relationship. Much has been written about attachment and separation, the resistance to and attacks on the relationship, and the fear of being alone, whilst there has been little reflection on the outcome of the therapeutic relationship for patient autonomy, with Winnicott being a notable exception. Alvarez has explored from a multidisciplinary perspective all the different interlocking ways in which the mother–infant relationship emerges and develops. It is thanks to her that the horizons of psychotherapeutic technique have been considerably broadened. Beginning with the technical problems posed by the treatment of children seriously deprived or damaged, either from external or internal causes, Alvarez suggests a psychotherapeutic technique which is flexible and active, highly attuned to the moment, which takes into account all possible aspects of the relationship in the consulting room, not only during its dyadic moments but also in terms of the results of this relationship on the patient's individuality.

When considering the mother–infant relationship, psychoanalysis has often referred to an abstract model which describes the relationship in rather crystallized terms, without taking sufficiently into account the way in which the mother plays an active role in modelling the relationship and promoting the infant's growth right from birth. Ethological research has shown that, in nature, the aim of nurture is to help the infant grow towards independent life:

> The amount of time an infant spent at the nipple each day decreased at a fairly steady rate from birth through weaning. Weaning is apparently accomplished not by the absolute denial of milk, but by a gradual shifting in the conditions under which the infant is granted the nipple.
>
> (Nicholson 1987: 330–1)

Brazelton *et al.* (1974: 65) write that when the sensitive mother is asked to interact with her own child of about a month old, she will first ensure that the child is in a comfortable position and has no physical needs. She will then position herself right in front of the child and communicate with him, actively seeking and holding his attention. Finally, she gives him the space to turn away and to digest and recover from the experience – in other words, the being alone with the mother, as described by Winnicott (1965). Alvarez (1980) has used the term "reclamation" to define the active psychother-apeutic technique she employs with children who do not even seem to know that they exist:

> I began to feel a need and urgency to be more active and more mobile than with other patients for whom the containment model had proved helpful ... this situation seemed to require an extension of the models of the analytic function ... I did not feel Robbie was projecting into me his need to be found, nor did I feel he was even waiting to be found ... it seemed to me that my function was to reclaim him as a member of the human family, because he no longer knew how to make his own claim ... but even more urgently to recall him to himself.
>
> (Alvarez 1992a: 54–5)

The use of countertransference – which is essential in the understanding of a patient's psychological processes – in the case of children who are so lost that they do not even know they exist, is necessary to be able to foster their need to exist mentally. Initially, this need can only be formulated in the mind of a therapist through active imagination, giving importance to small, faint signs in the patient's behaviour. These children can be compared to the newborn baby: born with a *predisposition* to communicate which the mother transforms into the *ability* to communicate. In the same way, the therapist must take an active role when such children do not, initially, participate in the communication.

Alberto

Alberto was three and a half when his mother asked for psychotherapy for her son, on the advice of a child neuropsychiatrist. At birth, Alberto was in good health but, from the start, he showed great difficulties in adaptation. He was very withdrawn, gazing into space, he cried at the slightest change, he did not want to be held, he did not establish a regular sleep pattern, and he developed eating problems. Alberto's parents reacted to his problems by complying with him completely. In order to avoid him crying, his mother had learned to substitute herself for him in everything, anticipating his every need so that he would not be frustrated. This of course meant that he had no chance of creating his own mental space. The child had never been able to speak or communicate with actions or looks.

During the first observation, in the presence of both parents, the child was completely managed by the mother who took his coat off, settled him and gave him a drink with precise, mechanical gestures but without affection. Alberto was passive with respect to his mother's actions, as if he did not realize they came from another person. When the mother was not handling him, Alberto walked on tiptoes, waving his arms in circular movements, or he sat on the floor spinning the wheels of an upturned car. He was a good-looking, dark-haired boy, but his face had no expression and his mechanical gestures reminded one of a robot. The father, seated in a corner of the room, watched his son, without moving. He wept softly, but he never intervened.

The mother created a magnetic barrier, like an anti-theft device, which separated her and her son from the rest of the world. The child's condition was very serious in terms of how lost he was to himself and how trapped with his mother in a web of madness; he had no way of escape. Seeing Alberto on tiptoes, compulsively moving his arms as if in take-off, or turning the wheels of the upturned cars, I thought of failed escape: Alberto was like a fly trapped in a spider's web, trying to save himself. My countertransference, a sensation of terrible, suffocating claustrophobia from which I had to escape as soon as possible, acted as a counterpoint to these stereotypical gestures. From the phenomenology of the child's symptoms, he could be defined as autistic according to DSM IV. I agree with Alvarez (1992b) that a psychiatric-phe-nomenological-type diagnosis is not exhaustive, in that only observation from an interactional perspective offers a real picture of the child and informs the possibility of treatment. Such observation allows one to go beyond the phenomenology of the symptoms to an understanding of the underlying emotional situation, and its impact on the relationship.

The child's fixed gaze and face, although no longer communicating any emotion, seemed fixed on stupefied discomfort. Alberto did not send signals of unease – you can send signals only if you can communicate – he just left traces of something that had been faintly signalled. The rotating of his arms and the wheels turning in space presented a dramatic image of the fight this child had had to survive and at what point he had shut himself in. Alberto's mother treated her son as if he were only a few days old. Both were stuck in that moment of time, perhaps because there had been a hiccup in their relationship in the first week of life and, from then on, they both needed help. It was not only Alberto who needed active help but also his mother, because both were trapped in a web of madness that was stopping them from living.

I began working with Alberto and his mother at a rate of three sessions a week. In cases of serious communicational disorders, the aim of joint therapy (Fraiberg 1980; Gallo 1997a) is that of helping the mother and child to communicate by learning a more harmonious and regulated interactional reciprocity. In other words, to bring back to life a relationship which is static and crystallized in a pathological pattern which prevents the child from growing mentally. The hypothesis behind the therapy is that the functions of the ego are deficient – not only in the child but also in the mother. To the extent to which the mother is able to understand the meaning of the child's behaviour and begin responding to his needs, the child can begin his mental growth from where he left off and catch up according to his own capacity.

In my treatment strategy, I decided to steer clear of the spider's web as neither the spider nor the fly were suitable roles for me. They needed, rather, to be driven from the web so I saw myself more as having to work like a powerful magnet. I adopted a very firm mental position during the sessions: mother and son each had their own space which was not interchangeable, and I forced myself to think in a very fluid way and to be careful not to become repetitive. This was the most difficult aspect, because the web woven by Alberto's mother tried to encompass everything and paralyse any kind of mental life.

The sessions during the first year were extremely boring, marked by the mother's rituals which flattened my attempts to revitalise communication. She arrived holding the child's hand as if it were an extension of herself, always saying "Here we are, we've arrived" and going through the same routine of taking coats off, sitting down, looking around and looking disappointed if something had changed. I would greet them separately, looking first at one and then at the other, saying something different to each one. During the sessions, the mother would speak for her son, opening each phrase with "we", and she was constantly handling him in order to settle him or give him something, which he either let her do or went up and down on tiptoes waving his arms around.

I soon thought I could see a connection between the rhythm of Alberto's movements and his mother's actions. After she had handled him, he began to go up and down the room waving his arms more frenetically, as if responding to the claustrophobic contact, whereas when his mother was busy with something else his movements were less agitated. Initially, I gave the mother a lot of space in order to reassure her that I did not want to be in competition with her over her son. However, I also made sure that Alberto felt he had his own space: he had his chair, his table, his toys and my availability for him. I have purposely used the word availability and not attention because Alberto had had an overdose of attention. He was a child who had been so intruded on with looks, words and handling that, in order to survive such an impact, he had become a statue. The hypothesis I used in my work was that inside the statue there was something mentally alive which could be revealed, if the external pressure was released. For this reason, during the initial phase of treatment, I was careful to leave Alberto some space, to avoid looking at him closely, not to comment on everything he did and, most importantly of all, to give the mother some space in order to detach her from her son.

During the joint psychotherapeutic treatment, which lasted three years at a frequency of three sessions a week, there were never any amazing events but rather near-imperceptible movements, small signs of change which were consolidated over time. After a few months, Alberto's gaze began, minutely, to thaw and take on some life; it was not that he really looked at me, but I felt he was more present. That was followed by his giving quick glances at the things on the table, then he would sit down and touch the car – not just move its wheels – when his mother was busy talking to me. With another child I would have immediately commented on the progress made during the session, in order to encourage him, but with Alberto this was not productive. Not only would it have set off destructive reactions from his mother but, when he noticed he was being observed, he would go back to being repetitive and retire into his shell. What did help him was to have physical and mental space just for himself. Having previously been poisoned by toxic attention, he now needed detoxifying. This is what helped the child gradually to reanimate himself.

Alberto's mother also slowly changed. During the sessions, apart from the usual "we" with which she sealed the symbiosis with her son, she began talking about herself, the accountancy job she had left, and everyday things. In this way, her control over her son loosened because there was more space in her mind for other thoughts which she could share with me. One day, after about a year, she used one of her usual phrases beginning with we: "We didn't want to eat." I pointedly asked her what had happened to her and she replied: "Nothing happened to me, it was him who didn't want to eat." She said this very calmly, as though it was obvious that she and her son were two separate people. This was the first signal that the process of mother–son separation had begun. In the ensuing months, this separation became a known fact for the mother. As the mother now had other things in her mind to think of, she no longer needed to possess Alberto mentally, and she let him go very easily. This allowed me to interact with him. The web was broken.

Unfortunately, it was not possible to help Alberto's mother to begin carrying out the appropriate maternal function of mental containment. She was ready to help, during sessions and at home, with her son's upbringing and his educational development, but she never showed herself capable of noticing and understanding Alberto's feelings because she was not even capable of recognising her own. When I started describing the behaviour and feelings of Alberto during the sessions, she either laughed, got irritated or busied herself with something else. She let me work but never helped. This seriously limited the joint treatment in that Alberto made rapid progress in his cognitive development but remained blocked emotionally for a good deal longer. He still has great difficulty with this because he has never received much support from his family. When the web was deactivated, Alberto became more aware of himself and started taking the first steps towards equipping his mind. His use of language was preceded by mental developments.

Alberto, who now spent a long time sitting at the table handling the toys, began by putting plasticine on the toys and then became more selective, choosing brown plasticine, as though it were faeces, and putting it on the heads of the toy people and animals, and then on the top of the trees, and on the roofs of the houses and cars. A few weeks passed during which these faeces seemed inexorably to paralyse everything. Alberto systematically passed his time in the sessions by filling in every orifice of the toys with brown plasticine, whilst the mother huffed and went on suggesting I throw away everything to do with plasticine, as she had done at home. I did not give up, because I felt this was something important. Then Alberto began cleaning off part of the faeces from the toys' faces and from the car doors, to make them work. When I described what he was doing, he said: "Poo . . . no poo." It is true that when "poo" is blocking your mouth, you cannot speak.

During the next session, he was by the window moving his arms wildly. It seemed that he was using his old gestures to express something new, but I did not understand what. Then, I noticed that he was looking at a car on the other side of the room. It seemed as though he was trying to get the car to come to him by moving his arms. I suggested that this was what he was doing and explained that the car would not go to him but that he would have to go and get it. As he continued making a huge effort with his arms, while his mother laughed, I went with him to get the car. Then his mother helped him until, finally, he was able to do it by himself. He then learned to make the car move by using its wheels, whereas before he had simply scraped the roof on the floor. He learned to use a ball, first carrying it to me and then to the mother, and finally throwing it. At this stage, the child's sense of himself, his language and his ability to communicate properly, orienting himself in the external environment, became more consistent.

As we have seen, the child revealed the obstacles to be overcome before he could begin to communicate: first, the poo which suffocated and paralysed him, making him unable to move autonomously; and then, his confusion between himself and the world around him.

After the joint psychotherapy Alberto began individual therapy, which is still ongoing. He has developed his intelligence satisfactorily, he speaks correctly, and follows the school curriculum, but his thought processes are still too obsessive, and he has a difficulty in coping with change. Furthermore, he is still inhibited from the emotional point of view, and does not tend to socialize. Alberto's first years in isolation have left their mark; over the years this is fading, but does not show signs of disappearing. This is also due to his home environment which is characterized by obsessiveness, an intolerance of change and emotional withdrawal.

Failures in containment

A common theme in the psychotherapeutic treatment of deprived, mistreated and abused children is that these children should be helped to recover the traumatic memories of their past experiences in order for these to be worked through. However, the type of memory on which the psychotherapist should work is different: it should be the memory of the history and geography of the internal world of the patient and the emotional colours of these memories, rather than memory of the historical facts.

Not all traumas are the same: there are the traumas resulting from isolated incidents of violence or abuse, and those of ongoing maltreatment and abuse which are so long-term that they become a way of life for the child. The child's physical and psychological experiences can vary, so that every case must be evaluated and handled with discernment, keeping in mind the child's needs and experiences. As Alvarez said (1992a), forgetting and remembering are two indissoluble aspects of the working of the mind. Children, like adults, may need to be able to forget just as they may need to remember. The patient's internal needs must be respected, without forcing him to premature remembering.

> What the abuse has meant for the child and means to him now may be very different from its meaning for us. He may, for example, be too emotionally and cognitively blunted for anything much to have any meaning at all. Or he may have been corrupted himself and have become fascinated with abuse or an abuser himself. He may fear the abuser far more than he fears the abuse. Or he may feel deep love for the abusing figure and this love may be stronger than fear or distaste for the abuse. Or he may have all of these difficulties.
>
> (Alvarez 1992a: 152)

When dealing with a case of sexual abuse, just as with any other case of maltreatment or deprivation involving a child, it is therefore important to know about the experiences and the particular dynamics of the child's internal world. These may then be expressed and processed in the context of a therapeutic relationship which allows him to test emotional containment from an external object which is prepared to be responsible for his need for growth without premature forcing.

Giulio

Giulio, who was born in a non-EU country, was adopted at the age of eight by an entrepreneurial couple in their late forties. The child had been abandoned by his mother at birth. His father, who could not take care of him, had taken him to a children's home with the intention of leaving him there for a short period. But then he had abandoned Giulio and it was subsequently declared that he could be adopted.

A few months after Giulio joined the Italian family, his adoptive parents contacted a Neuropsychiatric Centre about difficulties in their relationship with the child. Individual psychotherapy was prescribed following the diagnosis of: "symptoms of sexual abuse and thought processes compatible with exposure to sexual abuse, which has left him with devastating memories".

At the first meeting with the child's parents, I found myself in front of two simple people, good folk, but with much prejudice and confusion. They complained about Giulio, saying, however, "Poor thing, it's not his fault given what they've done to him" – meaning the sexual abuse – but he behaved intolerably, continually putting them into a difficult position. He was a rebel, aggressive, and in addition he was "always touching himself" and had erotized habits, including always wanting to be cuddled, kissed, caressed and held, and to sleep in his parents' bed. The psychologist from the centre, to whom it seems that Giulio had talked during his assessment of sexual abuse at the children's home at the hands of older companions, explained to the parents that Giulio behaved in an antisocial manner and was in this way seeking physical contact due to the sexual abuse, so that physical contact should be avoided. The parents followed the psychologist's advice "to the letter", "for the good of the child". At school, the teachers complained about Giulio because, although he showed a good aptitude for learning, he was always starting "things that disrupted the class".

I was perplexed as to the emphasis the parents placed on the sexual abuse. I have often noted that the idea of sexual abuse of a child stirs up many emotional feelings, and that the people involved become confused and tend to blame all the negative things that are thought to have been or to be outside or inside the child's mind on the abuse (Gallo 1997b). In Giulio's case, the parents, using the screen of sexual abuse, avoided questioning their own actions and did not realise that they, in turn, were being prevaricators and abusers *vis-à-vis* their son, incapable of empathy, affection, or true giving. They felt that the child would be "all right" once the problems caused by the trauma were resolved, and that he would adapt to their lifestyle and their idea of a son. In the psychologist's opinion, it would be enough to "eradicate the roots of the trauma and everything would sort itself out", as she put it during a telephone call.

When observing Giulio, I realised that he was different from the child described to me by his parents and the psychologist. Instead of the mixture of symptoms caused by sexual abuse, I saw a suffering and problematic child who, at the same time, was rich in internal resources, despite the painful experiences of abandonment and neglect that he had suffered. Even though he was an intelligent child, he could not manage to do anything with the toys other than touch them, sometimes even in an aggressive way, and move them from one place to another as if they did not have their proper place. There did not seem to be a proper place for him either, so he was continually on the move. Confusion and ambivalence, as well as a certain inclination to perversion, were the most salient characteristics of the way he used his mind and interacted with the external environment. His internal references appeared unstable and surrounded by great confusion caused by a lack of discrimination between affection and sexuality – the most obvious outcome of the sexualized conduct to which he had been exposed. Nonetheless, Giulio was not a child suffering from "devastating memories" of sexual abuse which upset his mind. During the sessions, it was more the trauma of being abandoned at an early age that was revealed through his not knowing where to sit, never finding a place for himself or for his toys, which he often destroyed. This all showed a devastating internal poverty and emptiness.

Initially, I wondered what had helped this child not to lose his mind. It was soon obvious from the material during the sessions: the relationships that Giulio had had with his older companions at the children's home, even though they were contaminated to a greater or lesser extent by sexuality, had been the only relationships in which he had felt he had been taken into consideration, loved and confirmed as a person. He had, therefore, been able to develop his own identity. If I had focused the psychotherapy exclusively on the trauma of sexual abuse to help Giulio dwell on a solely negative experience, I would have committed a serious technical mistake resulting in the continuation of his confusion and further deprivation. Giulio had experienced the so-called sexual abuse not as "a horrible thing", as the mother put it, but as an affectionate and gratifying relationship which he remembered nostalgically and wanted to reproduce in his current interpersonal relationships. Giulio only knew how to express affection in a sexualized way. During the sessions, I tried to help him separate the two spheres (affection and sexuality), not colluding with him, not making negative judgements, but always trying to offer him an alternative within the sphere of the therapeutic relationship.

When Giulio began playing with the toys, for a long time he would play out the adventures of two groups of male animals which fought each other for the possession of territory. Their parents had been killed and they lived in a pack, all doing the same things, as there were no differences between them and their roles were interchangeable. Within each of the two groups, Giulio had formed more or less stable couples who, in the evening, "made love because it was beautiful, they were free and they loved each other". During a session a few months later, Giulio kept apart a baby squirrel that was very small and could not stand up. He made as if to throw it away, smiling with cynical indifference saying, "that's useless", but then he caught my gaze and stopped, confused. Then he asked me if I thought he could keep it. This was a very touching moment, when the memory of his need for care when he had been, in fact, thrown away as a young child, was slowly returning from a long way back. This is the kind of memory that it is very important to recover during psychotherapeutic treatment, a memory to do with the history of the internal world, and which is therefore significant in understanding what the patient has experienced. I spoke to him about how fragile the baby squirrel was, of how important it was to find him a place where he could grow with someone to care for him, and then compared it all to Giulio's relationship with me. A thoughtful Giulio put the baby squirrel in the toy box. Next time, he brought a tiny box with him where he could put the squirrel apart from the others so it would not get squashed. He then even "repaired" the squirrel with a file so that it could stand up. Just as I was looking after Giulio, he could look after the squirrel, getting better and better at it. At first, he gave it any old thing to eat, even rubbish, like the other animals did, pretending it was good. Giulio also had a habit of stuffing himself with any sort of food, all day. He always said he was starving, that he never had enough to eat and accused his parents of being mean.

The child's parents were not generous towards him, putting limits on everything, including food and the number of the sessions (only one a week), making him even more demanding. Giulio was insatiable regarding every-thing for a long time, not only because of his parents but because he had to battle with his experience of unfillable internal emptiness. He was even very demanding with me, at first: the sessions were not long enough, there were not enough toys. He got cross with the limits imposed on him. The defined framework and security of the setting, the way I was firm but open to contain his emotion and look after him, and thinking of him during our separations, were the things that helped Giulio most in reorganizing his internal world and overcoming the disorder and confusion. The fact of having experienced his primary needs being understood, and taken into consideration after they had been disregarded for so long, was the main pivotal point and guiding thread of this treatment. Once Giulio had experienced that little ones can grow in a protected place with the care of an adult who understands their needs and does not use it to their own advantage, it was possible for him to find a new way of understanding interpersonal relationships. So, in the pack of animals where there had been confusion for so long, parents appeared, to put everything in order and take care of their children. Once Giulio realized

that things that were in a mess could be put right, it helped him to drop his
seductive ways and be capable of sincere shows of affection which were not
mixed up with sexuality. "Yesterday, I saw my aunt in the street and I hugged
her for real, it's true." The negative effects of the sexual abuse he had
previously experienced were lessened by the fact that Giulio was able to
experience an interpersonal relationship, in a psychotherapeutic setting,
which had fulfilled the deficit which he had previously suffered due to the
lack of containment by the external object. He had thus been able to have
more stable internal references, and feel richer and safer in his internal world.
Giulio's psychotherapy lasted five years. The last three were the most useful
as the mother, for health reasons, had left the care of her son to her sister who
was much more affectionate and open, so supporting the psychotherapeutic
work from the outside too.

During one of the sessions in the final year, Giulio spoke to me about a
school friend he liked because she seemed very sensible. He would like to
marry someone like that whom he would love for the rest of his life. Another
time, he told me that when he grew up he wanted to be an engineer and earn a
lot of money so that he could give his children the best of everything: good
food, nice clothes and good schools. If he had a handicapped, "defective"
child, he would not abandon him but keep him and look after him.

Conclusion

Both the joint and individual treatments described above show how the
extension of the psychotherapeutic technique suggested by Alvarez is indispensable when working in situations where the patient needs intensive care to
help mobilize previously paralysed mental functions and begin to repair deep
internal damage.

Alberto presented with a block in his mental development, he was lost to
himself and imprisoned with his mother in a web of madness. The idea of the
joint treatment was to deactivate the control the mother had over her son by
offering her an alternative relationship in which she found new interests in
life. This allowed the child to become more alive mentally. When the web had
been deactivated, Alberto could be helped to develop his own mind.

Giulio, who was already suffering from experiences he had had before
being adopted, found himself in the dramatic situation of being intruded on
mentally, deprived of affection and of having his own internal difficulties
misunderstood. Having experienced containment, during his psychotherapeutic treatment, from an external object that was respectful of his needs,
the child was able to reorganize his internal world in a more satisfactory way,
so overcoming the confusion and sense of emptiness that tormented him.
Moreover, Giulio had been able to forget – in the sense of putting to one side
– a way of being with himself and with others that was of little help.

In both cases, it was possible to help by beginning with a close observation of the patient's behaviour, recovering their memories of their disregarded needs and becoming responsible for them through a therapeutic undertaking to foster mental growth where the child would feel welcome, and emotionally contained but not intruded on.

References

Alvarez, A. (1980) "Two regenerative situations in autism: reclamation and becoming vertebrate", *J. Child Psychotherapy* 6.
—— (1992a) *Live Company: Psychoanalytic Psychotherapy with Autistic, Borderline, Deprived and Abused Children*, London and New York: Routledge.
—— (1992b) "Observation of a therapeutic precondition in the treatment of autistic children", in *Il disagio emozionale*, Torino: Edizioni Minerva Medica.
Brazelton, T.B., Koslowki, B. and Main, M. (1974) "The origins of reciprocity: the early mother–infant interaction", in M. Lewis and L.A. Rosenblum (eds) *The Effect of the Infant on its Caregivers*, London: Wiley Interscience.
Fraiberg, S. (1980) *Clinical Studies in Infant Mental Health: The First Year of Life*, London: Tavistock.
Gallo, M.T. (1997a) "The little alien: links between mind and body in parent–infant psychotherapy", *J. Child Psychotherapy* 23: 2.
—— (1997b) "Le interazioni affettive nelle situazioni di abuso psichico o fisico", in *Le vittime e gli attori della violenza*, Torino: C.C.I.
Nicolson, N.A. (1987) "Infants, mothers and other females", in B.B. Smuts *et al.* (eds) *Primate Societies*, Chicago: The University Press.
Winnicott, D.W. (1965) *The Maturational Processes and the Facilitating Environment. Studies in the Theory of Emotional Development*, London: Hogarth Press.

Chapter 9

Thoughts about the concepts of cognitive development, reparation and the "manic position"

Two clinical examples

Gabriella Pansini

I remember a conference given by Anne Alvarez in the Clinic for Child Neuropsychiatry in Turin several years ago entitled "Modern Developments in Psychoanalytic Psychotherapy with Children". On that occasion she spoke, as she had done many other times, about mental growth and development and about the growth and development of psychoanalytic understanding. In all her work, over the years, the passionate attention she paid to the mind, and to the birth and development of psychic activity in the person has always been, in my opinion, a very strong stimulus in her research and clinical work. From her evolutionary point of view she urges us to consider, more than ever before, the potential impulse of the psyche to evolve "towards" and "beyond" something, rather than insist on regressive, defensive and destructive aspects which, while really existing, would be sometimes like selling arms to the enemy.

Alvarez has found the spiral model expressive as a way of representing the creative development of the mind, because it is able to condense a non-linear idea of time with an upwards tendency and an aspect of continuous spatial enlargement of mental action. Her work is characterized by her natural psychoanalytic curiosity about humanity in its most varied expressions and by an unprejudiced interest in other disciplines, from mathematics to genetics, from literature to music and cinema: creativity, science, thought. Her interest also turned naturally to the experimental research of cognitive psychologists on the development of intelligence and babies' early behaviour. All of this, together with her personal clinical experience, has produced a body of very interesting ideas that is modifying the understanding of the meaning of some of the key concepts of psychoanalytic theory and is stimulating the tendency started by Bion (1961, 1962) to think psychoanalytically about thought.

The cognitive part of the mind, from a psychoanalytic point of view, consists of the set of concepts that can be used to think about the external and internal world. Alvarez has paid great attention to the interaction between presences or lacks in mental grammar and the structure of thought and behaviour. She has shown how the lack of a word, a concept, or even a grammatical or syntactical structure related to a thought, can correspond to the lack of an experience and even to the impossibility to imagine, project and insert something into the field of possibilities; as a result, the world can become smaller and poorer. Vice versa, a new word, and in particular new possible organizations within verbal structures, can enrich the internal image of the world and of oneself and can increase the possibility of movement in the world of ideas and in life.

The language of the mind and psychic development

The development of verbal thought and communication implies following a difficult evolutionary path, which in large part is still mysterious. It forces us to notice the strength of vitality and creative capacity people have from the time they are very small babies. The dynamic path of emotional relations to life's first objects, as Melanie Klein referred to them, with their complex passages across paranoid–schizoid and depressive positions and the incessant projective and introjective activities involved, produces a great psycho-physical ferment. If favourable conditions can be established, the person emerges with a new mental ability to evoke the missing object and to develop symbolic functioning.

From a non-psychoanalytic point of view, Piaget, an epistemologist and researcher into the origin of intelligence, also strongly emphasized the child's creative activity as a condition for development, which he considers to be the result of continuous integrated movements from physical to symbolic intelligence. The movements are stimulated by a process of assimilation of new experiences and adaptation of the previous cognitive structures, which as a result are amplified and enriched. The most interesting thing is that the operations of assimilation and adaptation, which begin immediately after birth, since they occur simultaneously, turn out to be a process of construction of the object in the first stages until, in a later period (which Piaget, 1936, places after approximately 18 months of age), a real inventive power appears which is the essential characteristic of mental intelligence. This is something that recalls the "birth of a new idea", which Alvarez discusses amply in a chapter of her book, *Live Company* (1992), dedicated to disorders of thought and behaviour as a form of cognitive deficit.[1]

Piaget distinguishes between physical experience, and physical perception, in that the former is the result of active structuring by the subject, while the latter is more passive. What counts in the construction of thought is the action, the capacity to coordinate mental activities at levels that get wider and richer throughout life. Stern (1985) states that despite possible reservations about the constructivist position, "there is no doubt that children not only perceive relations directly but also construct them". He develops this concept further with the idea that children can also build relations between external perceptions and their own internal states, producing an experience that includes reality combined with the emerging self.

I have been working with a child who had been raised almost exclusively according to the rules of polite behaviour. The concept of a "thinking child" was truly lacking in the parents, and he was, for a long time, a good little robot until he started school; then, problems began to appear because he was unable to learn. When the child stopped being a robot, he became psychotic because he had enormous problems with his own identity and with identifying his feelings: he really did not know how to think about his emotions, he did not know the right words for this, and consequently he used to act and dramatize what he felt in a confused way. Often his acting in and out were extremely dangerous. Later, after he became an adolescent, we still kept his old box in the sessions, filled with broken and useless things. He thought that he could not do without it, and I did too, since he was unable to formulate coherent verbal communication. I finally realized that no one could imagine that he might have a mind, so I began to demand that he remain seated in his chair and that he talk to me instead of spending the whole time doing some kind of physical activity. Little by little he managed to limit his motor exuberance and to talk more, sometimes throughout the whole session. I am still working with him and I think that he is experimenting with the possibility of human communication, and the fact that his periods of coherent communication are lengthening makes me believe that he is really building them. While he is not too busy evacuating confusion, his chances of introjective activity increase.

For another little girl with a serious borderline structure and a bi-dimensional thinking capacity, where a flat view of the world and a non-three-dimensional mental space for thinking in an abstract symbolic way impedes development, the introduction of a word (and of the corresponding idea) showed very clearly how cognitive enrichment can have repercussions on both the psyche and the body. During a session she was lying on the couch and something was bothering her, maybe something that could not be processed mentally. She told me that she had a pain on her stomach and wanted to go to the bathroom. I asked her "on your stomach?" stressing the word "on". She corrected herself, saying "in my stomach", and then told me that she no longer needed to go to the bathroom. Not only did her stomach become three-dimensional, but also her mind began to function like a container because the physical disturbance disappeared.[2] Naturally, these little miracles are not part of our daily experience as psychotherapists, but, when they happen, they are like reflectors that, at least for an instant, light up very clearly the intertwining relations that exist between the different competencies of the mind and the resulting consequences at all levels.

New evolutionary ideas

Alvarez insists on the importance of people's vital, constructive tendencies, the ability to form links as a principal instrument of mental progress, and the strong connection between this activity and object relations. Thus, there emerges a more strenuous effort in terms of technique to capture the constructive impulses, even when the internal space is overrun by destructiveness and persecution. Alvarez (1992) says that it is possible that links that could be attacked or broken may never have been able to be formed, and that it could be essential to help our young patients to build objects they have never had. She believes it is essential to take into consideration even the virtual movements towards new possibilities so as not to destroy the first signs of hope that could take root in them.

As a result she introduced the ideas of "primary lack", "object deficit" and "evolutionary interpretation", which is a technical consequence of the primary lack. She emphasizes the need to distinguish between mental states, differentiating "manic defences" and "manic position"[3] from a "need" which corresponds more to the impulse to overcome depression and emptiness than to triumph over an object in order to deny loss and separation.

These concepts are extremely useful, and it is not a coincidence that they should appear at this moment in history, when the development of psychoanalytic theory and social pressures lead us more and more often to deal with children with very serious disorders, with histories of violence, abuse, neglect or serious traumas. Greater attention is being given to children suffering from serious lacks, because there are more of them and their plight is more visible. Migratory movements from very poor, traumatized countries to much wealthier nations, the lowering of the birth rate in the rich countries and the increase in the demand for adoptions, the global distribution of information via the media, stress caused by either an excess or a lack of work: all these factors and many others are making psychotherapists face the demand to help very ill children who cannot be clearly pigeonholed into the classical pathological categories of psychoses or borderline structures, except as exclusively descriptive instruments.

Clinical examples

I would like to present two clinical contributions which seem pertinent to Alvarez's ideas about the vital strength that is intrinsic to the nature of mental life. Elena is a girl who went through serious deprivations in her childhood and who, in spite of everything, is managing to overcome her internal devastation thanks to the help of her social worker, analysis, and her own confused attempt to find the road to salvation. Alessandra is a heroic little girl who, although only two years old, has sucked up all the strength she has found in her family environment and in herself in order to overcome an external and internal condition that could have seriously damaged her.

Elena

When Elena was sent to me for analysis she was thirteen years old. She had a history of total emotional deprivation: born of a schizophrenic mother, Elena was taken away from her mother and placed in her father's custody following an intervention by the social services. By the age of three, she had already suffered repeated oral sexual abuse, first by her father and then by her older brother. As a result, she was taken away from her original family and placed in children's homes, and twice in families, but every time she began to fabricate malicious stories and consequently lost her place there.

She was not psychotic; she managed to progress in school, although with difficulty. She was still incontinent and had autistic-like behaviour: she often isolated herself, held her head in her arms, all huddled up, and would sometimes beat her head on her table. She suffered from eczema, especially on her head, face and arms, and this caused her classmates to reject her, treat her with disgust and call her a leper. It is hard to imagine the enormous amount of suffering this girl must have had to put up with, but during therapy she did all she could to give me a concrete idea of what she had been through. The hardest part for me was in containing so much refusal, disgust, scorn and blame. Her terribly destructive attacks were due, above all, I think, to envy of normal families. However, I was never able simply to think of her as wreaking vengeance on the world and conquering me with her permanent contempt. I felt that her first need was to be able to evacuate part of her powerful experiences into someone, and that her body would then stop putting out dirty "beta" elements in the form of festering sores. I received my first encouragement about my decision not to make her feel even more strongly that she was a filthy person by avoiding interpretation of her mania and triumph when, after a year of analysis, the eczema disappeared, and she began to become prettier and tidier. In one of the first sessions, at the very beginning of the therapy, she built a little box with a piece of paper, but told me that it was not for holding anything. The presence of a container, however, gave me hope.

Now I knew that for her a clean container could be nothing but an empty container. Especially at the beginning, she refused almost all my interpretations about her feelings because any attempt to talk to her about what was happening inside her mind was perceived as an abusive intrusion into her inner space similar to that received from her father and brother. Later, when a therapeutic relationship was more established between us, she could not only push all her anger into me, but she became able to have some less aggressive verbal exchanges with me when I caught and emphasized more depressive feelings: her worries for her brother, for example, who, like her, got kicked out of families that took him in. This made me understand how much she needed to have something good seen in her.

I would like to describe one brief vignette which shows the presence of some reparative searching, even in an overall climate of great aggression. One characteristic of this girl's lack of mind was that it was impossible for her to remember the times and days of her therapy sessions. For this reason the job of bringing her to me was totally delegated to the workers who ran the Institute in which she lived. This fact was used by her as proof of her total disinterest in her therapy, and she used it to project this lack of importance into me.

One day something else happened: she was shouting that I would never be able to help her because I would not be able to give her the family she had not had – the father and mother she had never had. I told her that perhaps, by forgetting her appointments, she was trying to get back something of what she had never had and become like a little child who has parents who know what the child has to do. She replied that I was completely crazy, but that same day when she left she said goodbye to me, which was very unusual and which I considered a sign of recognition of my existence and presence.

Elena's "manic position" was held principally by me, and by her social worker, while she spent a long time in analysis completely caught up in a "manic need" to face her persecution, aggressiveness, and guilt. The events of the paranoid–schizoid position, which she could only reproduce again and again in her life, were not the result of the presence of an inborn destructive force that was too strong, but rather the result of the real lack of repairable objects in her first experiences. Her bad objects were *really* bad objects and in her mind there was no other way to deal with them than to destroy them. Her best object was "no object", as she made me understand when she insisted that I should not be there, I should be "no-one" for her. In her own way it was a strange attempt to save me, linked with an attempt to pass on to me those experiences of her history when she really must have felt she was no one while her father and brother were raping her. Perhaps it is better to feel you are no one while your body is being abused.

My work with her is ongoing and her projection of atrocious suffering is a constant element in our relationship. However, in some way, she has been able to use her relationship with me in a manner that was secretly positive: although she may still scream that my suggestions are stupid ideas that I get from books, she has begun to read novels, and while she may make fun of me because I think before saying something to her, she has begun to build up some mental space which allows her to stop exploding in the children's home where she lives every time something does not go her way. She no longer attacks herself physically, hitting her head against tables, and sometimes she is able to sit and study for a long while.

Alessandra

When I met Alessandra, she had just turned two, but she had already had a very complicated life. Her parents had been separated for about six months and she was brought to me for an assessment by her father and her paternal grandmother because of some symptoms that she had begun to show after spending two weeks during the Christmas holidays with her mother: she stammered, refused to go to bed, was afraid of the dark, and even seemed to hallucinate a man hidden behind an armchair. She burst into heart-rending cries of anguish when she had to leave her father's family to go to see her mother.

This child's history shows evidence of a primary deficit that goes back to before her birth and is connected to her mother and father's personal history. The life of Alessandra's father, whom I shall refer to as Adam, was full of loss and death. His mother died when he was still a small child and he spent his days with relatives or friends because his father had a job that obliged him to travel and stay away from home for long periods of time. Two years after his wife's death, Adam's father got married again to a woman who loved children very much and the little boy once again received maternal care; but Adam felt, almost concretely, the presence of a negative force acting inside him. In fact, when he was fourteen a very good friend of his, who was riding behind him on his motorbike, was killed in an accident caused by his carelessness. A few years later, he had another serious motorbike accident in which he lost the use of his legs.

After the accident that destroyed Adam physically and morally, he underwent years of long, painful, humiliating rehabilitation, supported constantly by his step-mother, and thanks to this care he regained a large degree of autonomy and learned to live almost completely independently. The presence of a strong vital force in both the father and the grandmother must have played an important role in forming qualities in her internal world, and in the personal capacities that Alessandra later developed in order to overcome the difficult situations in which she found herself.

Introjective identification with new objects enables nourishment to be offered to the deprived parts of the personality, in order to repair those that have been damaged by bad objects and so to sustain the healthy parts. This is an event of great therapeutic importance both in life and in the analytic relationship. On this subject I recall a comment by Alvarez that I have never forgotten and which must – I hope – have had a strong influence on my later work. Many years ago, I started treating a schizophrenic boy, and when I presented the first sessions to her, she immediately said, "You are going to be his bad object for years to come." Then she stopped to think for a second and corrected herself: "No! you must be his good object."

Adam married a very beautiful young girl who worked as a nightclub dancer. She was from a distant country and felt lonely, depressed and persecuted in Italy. There followed a period in which the couple felt very happy, but this time was a kind of dizziness, like a return to that exciting sense of limitless power that could cause a boy on a motorcycle to forget about the existence of traffic lights. There was a kind of uncontrolled need to enjoy life, no matter what: Adam spent his day working and his night watching her wife dancing in night clubs.

It is difficult to say what produced this slide into pathological excess: the separation from his step-mother and his union with a fragile child-woman who was also in need of help must have been too much for Adam's still-convalescent mental condition. The vain desire to recover the long period of his adolescence that was lost forever must have also played its part, and this is part of the concept of "false reparation" or "manic reparation", mentioned by Klein and recalled by Alvarez,[4] which consists of the omnipotent fantasy of reproducing an object identical to the damaged one. So, when Alessandra was born, her parents had no place for a real child because they were so busy using all their strength to regain joy and vitality in a narcissistic way.

Alessandra was breast-fed for about six months, during which she was also kept in continuous close physical contact with her mother's body, the nipple always in her mouth, melded with her mother and not yet really born. This period ended when the parents began to want to live again as they had before Alessandra's birth and, to do that, they set up a complicated programme. The mother would put the baby to sleep, then take her to some friend's house, and pick her up before she woke up, being absolutely sure that the baby would not notice anything. "I was the last person she saw before falling asleep and the first she saw as soon as she woke up", her mother told me with conviction. I found illuminating a small conversation that took place while I was observing the mother playing with the child during a session. The mother said, "Good morning!", opening the window of a little house; Alessandra replied, "Good night" and, vice versa – if her mother said "Good night!", Alessandra would reply "Good morning!". She had such a satisfied expression that it made me think about how fundamental it was for the little girl finally to face the subject with her mother in a game, but also how much she had developed her awareness of the reality of her own experience and her ability to bring the question out into the open, as soon as she was given the chance to do so, and so to begin a symbolic process in a transitional area, as Winnicott ([1951] 1958) called it. In real life, after her "good morning" came her mother's "good night", because she fell asleep leaving the baby in her bed (sometimes she fell off it) or in her box. The game represented reality symbolically and what fell from balconies, windows, or down the stairs of the house were dolls, not real children. At a deeper level, the child was expressing the feeling that she and her mother could not exist at the same time, but what was really important was that at that moment of verbal exchange they *were* living at the same time!

I was greatly struck by the contrast between such a traumatic, deficient early experience and the child's clear intellectual, communicative, and representational resources. Bion (1967) says that primitive proto-thoughts are all bad objects, because they are born when the object one needs is not there and thus becomes a bad object. Later on, the repeated experience of finding the mother again, as well as experiencing her containment and reverie, will enable the child to evoke the missing object, and thus to start an imaginative process followed by a symbolic one. In Alessandra's primary experience she had no physical frustrations, but she had a psychic lack due to her mother's inability to allow her to have an independent mental life. And yet her motor and cognitive development were precocious. In the same box where she spent so many hours all alone, with her mother sleeping, she also began to pull herself up and tried to take her first steps without help when she was only five months old. At nine months, she began to walk. In our sessions her intelligence was evident, as was her capacity for symbolic expression and her muscular strength. On the other hand, when the development of a game in a session caused her anguish, she would begin to stammer, her words became incomprehensible, and her infantile fragility emerged for a few seconds, blocking off her cognitive acquisitions and eating away at her language.

Just one week after her birth, Alessandra had to be hospitalized due to a symptom that was very worrying for her family: she would become rigid and seemed to stop breathing. This symptom is known to psychiatrists in Italy as "emotional spasm", and is connected with anger. The very way in which she reacted was the first sign that the baby had perceived a lack of containment very soon after her birth, so she produced a sort of muscular self-containment in order to hold herself together in some way and held inside her muscles and nerves all the aggression she felt she could not release into the family environment around her. After that time, Alessandra grew up almost by herself and also very quickly, without causing any problems until the breakdown of the equilibrium which led to my involvement in her case. This must have happened as a result of internal emotional stimuli that were too strong to be held in by the psycho-muscular shell, already developed after birth, and reinforced by two years of practice. Then came the parents' separation, and Alessandra stayed with her mother for a period of time after which she was again separated. This probably created a cumulative effect which, combined with her previous experience of loss, provoked the outbreak of her symptoms. My opinion is that at least three things happened at the same time at different levels: her shell of self-containment broke, her frustrating, bad maternal object was attacked, while a healthy call for help was sent to the absent parts of her parents' personality.[5]

In the sessions I saw the father unconsciously let words "fall out" of his ears if they caused him too much pain, and he would not see images that might have produced the same effect. I also saw the mother go blank mentally on occasions, or just concentrate on her tights, for example, right in the middle of a game with her daughter. I saw her sit listlessly in a chair like a rag doll after I told her that the session was over. I saw Alessandra put out her hand and determinedly pull her up (but without any superiority or disdain) and say, "Up, let's go."

I would like to give a few excerpts from the first session with Alessandra and her grandmother in order to give an idea of her vitality: "Up, let's go", she told herself when she met me for the first time and felt frightened and anxious. At first she did not respond to my greeting, then she grabbed the baby bottle handed to her by the grandmother and took a long drink of water. After that she seemed ready to start. This made me think of Popeye when he devours a can of spinach to become strong and muscular.

In the playroom Alessandra began a dynamic interactive activity which included her grandmother, myself and the toys. Alessandra demonstrated that she could deal with objects that called out to her as well as objects which abandon her mentally and physically. For example, she pacified her grandmother who tried to attract her attention, but then she used the space to play as she liked. She gave me one of the toys and this reassured her enough to be able to use the others for herself. I believe that since she was a very young child she has been able to transform "remaining alone" into "having space for herself".

She set up a symbolic personal process centred particularly on the problem of internal space, in terms of her relationship to internal objects. The process focused on security and mobility, inside and outside, the ability to enter and leave, go away and come back. She used a farmhouse to study all the entrances with a scientist's zeal – doors, windows, balconies for all sizes and shapes of living creatures (she used all the animals and the people from the toy-village), and all the possible ways out – from the door, going down the stairs or flying down from the balcony. After that she put all the little animals and children into the house, then lifted it up and laughed when she found them again. She picked up the animals again, and when she tried to make a little hen that was always falling over stand up her grandmother said it was like daddy who could not stand up because he was not well. The child took the rooster, said it could not stand up because "it's not well either", and then put the rooster in front of the hen and stated that "they have to talk to each other".

There were more ideas in her head than she had words for, and she showed a great appreciation for verbal communication. In the session the grandmother taught Alessandra the names of all the new things she found, both animals and objects. I was struck by how naturally the grandmother spoke about the father's disability, and built a symbolic link between the game and reality. Alessandra, at the same time, did not miss the opportunity to develop the idea of emotional suffering communicated within a two-person relationship, thinking of a reparative move based on symbolic verbal communication. This was a significant jump in both her cognitive and pyschological development.

By this time Alessandra's symptoms had already disappeared, along with a change of attitude in the grandmother and the mother. Instead of quarrelling as soon as the mother went to the grandmother's house to pick up the child, they began to talk to each other. Little by little, the grandmother invited the mother inside and encouraged her to play with Alessandra before taking her away. This ended Alessandra's anguished refusal; now she was able to go away with her mother with just a normal sad pout.

Concluding observations

Not all such young children could rely on the resources necessary to sustain and hold themselves up in a context of deprivation of attention like that experienced by Alessandra. I do not believe it is yet possible to find complete explanations why some children suffer serious disturbances for much less serious reasons, and others, instead, manage to develop and strengthen themselves. There is an initial disposition and certain imperceptible qualities in terms of relating that can make all the difference. As far as Alessandra is concerned I think that the presence of an extended family and willing friends around her parents was of great importance, in addition to her own inner strength. The sessions with her and her relatives led me to suppose that a part of this strength developed on the basis of a relationship with the depressive aspects of her objects and the will to live contained in the manic activities they had organized. Inside Alessandra, the libidinal strength and aggression "talking to each other", produced self-confidence and faith in her own internal good objects. Even the omnipotent fantasies from Alessandra's "nipple-always-in-the-mouth" phase, could become a precious source of capacity and power when needed.

Elena, by contrast, started out from an internal situation that was much too contaminated and had to go through a long "cleaning" phase simply in order to reach a detoxified empty space. Her inability to accept the relationship between facts and emotional meanings is also compromised by the need to squeeze her internal space in order to expel the malign experiences and projections. I do not know whether time and therapy will permit her to imagine not just a three-dimensional space, but also clean thoughts that can be manipulated mentally in order to play with ideas creatively. Nevertheless, she is busy building a stronger sense of self that can finally say "no", and spit out what it feels is bad, on the way towards the contruction of "Me".

I do not believe that I could stand working with her without the help of Anne Alvarez's positive concepts.

Notes

1 "Il problema della nuova idea: disturbi del pensiero del pensiero e del comportamento come forme di deficit cognitivo". Ed.it. pp. 100–114. ("The problem of the new idea: thought and behavioural disorders as a form of cognitive deficit".)
2 Pansini (1997).
3 The concept of "manic position" has already been used by Melanie Klein, but Alvarez stresses the importance of recognizing this state of mind as a useful one.
4 Conference on "Reparation" given by Anne Alvarez in Turin on 30 March 1985.
5 Bion's theory (1997) about the psychotic and non-psychotic parts of the personality helps us imagine how different mental things can happen at the same time. Even if Bion's idea is actually to distinguish between these parts, it is precisely this complexity and this need to distinguish, considered from the opposite point of view, that authorizes the formulation of the hypothesis that dynamic lines can move from different starting points and meet in a psychic area to build a kind of behaviour that represents all of them.

References

Alvarez, A. (1992) *Live Company: Psychoanalytic Psychotherapy with Autistic, Borderline, Deprived and Abused Children*. London and New York: Tavistock/Routledge.

Alvarez, A. (1997) *La riconoscenza del clinico nei confronti di Winnicott*. Richard and Piggle, 2/97. Roma: Il Pensiero Scientifico Editore.

Bion, W.R. (1961) *Experiences in Groups and Other Papers*. London: Tavistock Publications Ltd.

Bion, W.R.T. (1962) *Learning from Experience*. London: Heinemann.

Bion, W.R. (1967) *Second Thoughts*. London: Heinemann.

Bonassi, E. (1999) *Il periodo ipotetico di 4° tipo: uno sviluppo nella grammatica degli affetti*. Richard and Piggle, 1/99. Roma: Il Pensiero Scientifico Editore.

Bruner, J.S. (1983) *Savoir faire, savoir dire. Le developpement de l'enfant*. Paris: Presse Universitaire de France.

Di Cagno, L., Lazzarini, A., Rissone, A. and Randaccio, S. (1984) *Il neonato e il suo mondo relazionale*. Roma: Borla.

Fattori, L. and Benincasa, G. (1996) *Psicoterapia psicoanalitica e deficit cognitivo*. Milano: Cortina.

Goretti, G. (1997) L'incendio della Fenice. *Rivista di Psicoanalisi*, vol. XLIII-1-gennaio-marzo.

Joseph, B. (1989) *Psychic Equilibrium and Psychic Change*, London: Routledge.

Klein, M. (1921–1958) *Contributions to Psycho-Analysis 1921–1945*. London: Hogarth Press.

Klein, M. (1952) *Developments in Psycho-Analysis*, London: Hogarth Press.

Klein, M. (1978) *Scritti 1921–1958*, Torino: Boringhieri.

Piaget, J. (1936) *La naissance de l'intelligence chez l'enfant*. Neuchâtel and Paris: Delachaux et Nestlé.

Piaget, J. (1967) *Biologie et Connaissance. Essai sur les relations entre les regulation organique et les processus cognitif*. Paris: Gallimard.

Piaget, J. (1970) *L'épistémologie génétique*. Paris: PUF.

Spitz, R.A. (1965) *The First Year of Life. A Psychoanalytic Study of Normal and*

Deviant Development of Object Relations, New York: International Universities Press, Inc.

Stern, D.N. (1985) *The Interpersonal World of the Infant*. New York: Basic Books.

Winnicott, D.W. ([1951] 1958) Transitional objects and transitional phenomena. In *Collected Papers: Through Paediatrics to Psycho-Analysis*. London: Tavistock.

Chapter 10

The sense of abundance in relation to technique

Maria Rhode

In a paper written with Piera Furgiuele, Anne Alvarez pinpoints three main aspects of a mother's mental equipment which have a particular bearing on her baby's developing sense of identity, on his emotional security and on his cognitive capacities (Alvarez and Furgiuele 1997). These three aspects of the mother's equipment are her ability to give her baby her full attention and to respond appropriately to his initiatives; her ability to keep him in mind while attending to something else; and her ability to wait quietly and with interest while his own interest is deployed elsewhere. Paul, one of the babies Alvarez describes, had a mother whose capacity for attention was impaired in all these respects. Her sense of personal inadequacy was easily stirred, and quickly led her to attack and undermine the baby whom she had come to experience as her accuser. Paul's decline into apathy and despair is documented in heart-rending detail. Such moments of hope as did arise tended to occur when his father or grandparents interacted lovingly with him, and his mother could be "a not unfriendly witness". Not surprisingly, it was not only his sense of having a good identity and a sense of agency that were being undermined. His milestones were delayed; he bit his hand and beat himself; and his play became "ominously repetitive" rather than joyful and creative.

Alvarez contrasts Paul's plight with the situation enjoyed by two baby girls, Alice and Angela. Their mothers were both remarkably able to give them their full attention, to "read" their initiatives correctly, and to respond in a way that gave the babies many opportunities to "delight in being the cause" (Broucek 1979). Their sense of having a good identity flourished; so did their expectation that their attempts at self-assertion would be welcomed and would lead to a good outcome. Alvarez cites observational material to illustrate the importance of the mother's ability to keep the baby in mind while attending to something else. In one instance, Alice's mother showed that she knew exactly what her daughter was looking for, even though she had been talking to her husband. In perfect parallel, Alice was able to remember without looking where she had put down her cup while she was watching her brother. Alvarez links this to Bruner's discussion of the cognitive capacity to "think in parentheses" and to "placehold", with all that this implies for the capacity to think laterally and to relate thoughts to each other (Bruner 1968).

The other little girl, Angela, had a mother who could wait with interest, and without feeling too rejected, when her daughter's interest turned to someone or something else. Alvarez discusses the importance of this mother's attitude for her daughter's capacity to experience the world as a place full of objects of interest which she could explore without feeling that she was turning away from her mother, and with the assurance that her mother would be waiting to welcome her. In Alvarez's view, this assurance extends to Angela's relation to her own thoughts: she should be able to pursue a new thought, confident that previous thoughts would "wait patiently" at the back of her mind for her to pick them up again. In such a situation the child experiences what Alvarez calls a "sense of abundance": a sense of people who are rich in loving relationships and of a world of thought that is rich in exciting possibilities which his parents encourage him to discover. This sense of abundance was tragically negated for baby Paul, in terms of the capacity for thought as well as personal relationships.

My aim in this chapter is to discuss Alvarez's formulations in relation to children with autism, whose personal relationships and cognitive capacities are characteristically so severely restricted. I shall present material from a child who became able to take turns once he began to conceive of someone's attention that could encompass him along with another person. His steps forward were marked by a heightened capacity for communicative, symbolic speech. I shall argue that the implications of the "sense of abundance" make it possible to extend Alvarez's conceptualisation of those technical issues which arise when children experience words concretely and therefore misunderstand interpretations (Alvarez 1992: 115; 1997). Finally, I shall suggest that some technical modifications which can be useful in making contact with children who are functioning on a concrete level may be theorised in terms of the establishment or re-establishment of an Oedipal triangle, without which neither self-reflection (Britton 1989; Fonagy et al., 1991) nor Alvarez's sense of abundance can develop.

Clinical illustration

Six-year-old Anthony was referred as a matter of urgency by his school when his mother was expecting another child. His parents and teacher were worried that he might hurt the baby, since he habitually attacked his classmates and siblings whenever he was upset. He was a child with moderate to severe autism, well-built and dark-haired, with a set, wary expression. He did not make eye contact or speak communicatively, though he made good use of the computer at school and was described as highly intelligent. His parents said that if they took their eyes off him for a second, he smashed up the house. During the assessment he sat between them with his head tilted to one side, looking as though he were totally involved in watching or participating in a performance invisible to the rest of us. His parents described his smile as happy, though to my colleague and me it seemed to be strongly tinged with cruelty. We were encouraged by his moving closer to us and beginning some rudimentary play after we pointed out the importance of distinguishing genuine happiness from a deceptive appearance.

In individual assessment sessions, Anthony expressed dramatically his terror of falling. Again and again he let himself drop over the edge of the desk, clutching at the drawstring of his tracksuit bottoms as though that could keep him safe, his mouth twisted into a tortured grimace. At other times, he growled "Fee, Fie, Fo, Fum", like the man-eating Giant in *Jack and the Beanstalk*. His expression became implacably cruel as he stood on the furniture towering above me, though his footing was in fact unsteady and I had to pay careful attention to make sure he did not fall. There appeared to be no connection between these two extreme states, and, what was more, Anthony took no notice of any offer of help, whether I expressed it in words or in gestures: he seemed determined to refuse any possibility of connection with me. This attitude was understandable if, for him, human relationships meant laying himself open to the danger of helplessly falling; but it did not encourage me to expect that therapy was likely to be helpful. I began once-weekly work with considerable misgivings and on a short-term basis when Anthony's mother had her baby, with the limited objective of providing some containment and possibly defusing some of the expected violence.

Getting started

To begin with, it seemed I might as well not have been in the room: Anthony did not respond to anything I said or did. However, he repeatedly sang the beginning of the theme song of a children's television programme, *Postman Pat*. The words soon faded out into incomprehensibility, but still aroused powerful feelings in me. The last line of the song is "Postman Pat's a very happy man"; and although Anthony did not sing those words, what he did sing conveyed a yearning for the sense of order and simplicity and happiness in everyday events which, at their best, children's television programmes can conjure up. Feelings such as these can be difficult to describe without sounding self-idealising or sentimental, particularly where love and hate are so unintegrated, as they are for many children with autism; but I believe it is vital to attend to them, or we risk perpetuating the dominance of the visible unresponsive part of the child's personality. Of course there was no way of knowing whether this was a tentative communication, or simply associations of my own; and when I spoke about Postman Pat, Anthony completely ignored me in a way that crushed hope.

By chance, some time later, I came across a little toy van with Postman Pat and his cat, and I decided to add it to Anthony's toybox. He gave no sign of noticing it; he didn't even sing about Postman Pat anymore, so there was no opportunity to link the toy to the song. I felt I might as well not have bothered. But whether it was accumulated disappointment and exasperation when for the hundredth time he tipped out the contents of his box as though it were rubbish, or an obscure feeling that the brutal, contemptuous Giant needed standing up to, I found myself not talking as I normally did about how the toys should get out of the way; what rubbish they were; what rubbish I was; how powerful the Giant was. "Look," I said to Anthony, "here's Postman Pat. You used to sing a song about him, do you remember?" – and I sang some of the song before talking about Postman Pat who was a happy man, and how much perhaps Anthony wanted to be that himself, one day. Anthony came over, looked at the Postman Pat toy, and began to play with it, pushing it along the desk. I wondered aloud where Postman Pat was going with his black and white cat; whom he was delivering letters and parcels to. The moment did not last long. Anthony soon moved back to the familiar position of being the Giant, standing far above me on the table. It would not even really be accurate to say that this had been a moment of shared attention; but it had been a moment in which the two of us had paid attention to the same thing.

The next development was also mediated by a song, and was just a bit easier: I did not have to provide a concrete realisation of something that Anthony had been referring to, or assert myself and my viewpoint. This time the song was "Pat-a-Cake", and again he sang the tune with only a few of the words, which soon tailed off into jargon. When I joined in, he sang the first stanza clearly, ending with: "and put it in the oven for Baby and me". I responded with the next stanza: "and put it in the oven for Anthony and me." Later in treatment, Anthony introduced variations, singing "Mr Rhode" instead of "Baby", whereas my part was always to sing about "Anthony and me". "Pat-a-Cake" became a significant point of reference, so much so that when Anthony was at his worst and most unreachable, it was often enough to ask, "Do you want to sing Pat-a-Cake?" to re-establish contact.

Alvarez (1980) has written about the need for the therapist actively to "reclaim" a child with autism. That was certainly the case with Anthony, though perhaps with him it was less a matter of going in search of someone who needed to be found, and more a matter of holding onto my belief in the memory of someone who had given indications, however fleeting, of being present. In Frances Tustin's opinion (personal communication, 1992) the ease with which children with autism can undermine their mothers' self-confidence makes it essential for the therapist to be able to stand up for her own viewpoint when necessary.

It is important, I think, that communication with Anthony first got going in connection with an object "out there", not directly between him and me. Postman Pat's van was concretely tangible; the songs were not, but they too were a shared reference. Bardishevsky (1998), who describes the gradual recovery of Serioja, a toddler with autistic features in a Russian orphanage, makes the point that the successive stages of his development were significantly different from those seen in normal children. A normal baby will progress from two-person intimacy with his mother (primary intersubjectivity) to joint attention (secondary intersubjectivity) (Trevarthen and Hubley 1978). In Serioja's case, this sequence was reversed: adults had to work patiently towards a one-to-one relationship via joint attention to objects or events, just as I had to do with Anthony. It is as though the threesome of joint attention had to be securely established before the child could dare to attempt a direct, "you and me" relationship with one other person. (Indeed, the words of "Pat-a-Cake" are about turn-taking in a group of at least three people.) This resembles the way in which parents, teachers and therapists will intuitively talk about a child with autism in the third person, and not attempt to address him as "you" unless they sense that he is in a state to manage this.

There could, of course, be a whole range of reasons for the child's inability to engage directly in a face-to-face relationship. Ellen Stockdale-Wolfe (1993), an adult with autism, mentions "fear of fusion" and of losing her identity. Other reasons could include the fear of being projected into or of catastrophic experiences of dependency; or indeed simply the inability to know how to relate to another human being, which would make it preferable to relate in terms of a "thing out there". Anthony, like other children with autism I have seen (Rhode 1997a, 1997b), seemed to be afraid that he and I were in competition for what Tustin ([1981] 1992) has called "the extra bodily bit" that ensures survival. We were to spend much time working on how important it was for him to be able to feel that he and I could both be all right when we were separate people, instead of one of us being all right at the other's expense. For example, before a holiday he was concerned that I was hurt. Looking at water leaking through the gashes he had once cut in a plastic beaker, he commented, "lady crying". It seemed to reassure him when he could assign a full, intact beaker of water to each of us: he was better able to speak and to make use of his intellectual capacities. When I described the beakers, "One for Anthony, one for Mrs Rhode", he was able to generalise this to describe the colours we used on the holiday chart: "Red for clinic, green for holiday" (Rhode 1999).

Like Tustin (1972), whose patient David built up his identity by snipping bodily bits off his father, Alvarez (1999b) has stressed the problems children with autism have with introjection. If growth is felt to be a matter of physically despoiling someone else (Tustin 1972; Rhode 1997b), then relating by means of joint attention to a third object would serve as a reassurance against this. I believe that this is one of the reasons that children with autism so often communicate by means of stories, songs or videos (though this can easily degenerate into defensive meaninglessness). The fact that the therapist knows the song or video makes it safe for the child to know it too. Anthony's words became clearer when I showed that I knew the "Postman Pat" song and "Pat-a-Cake". Technically, therefore, I feel it can be important for the therapist to show her knowledge of well-known songs and videos, in a way that she would not do with a neurotic child. This also provides an opportunity to help the child to differentiate between songs and videos that are part of the culture and that everybody knows, and others which no one could know about unless they had been present in a specific situation. The child gets a chance to practise seeing things from the therapist's point of view: to move towards developing a theory of mind (Leslie 1991; Baron-Cohen 1995).

Another way of conceptualising joint attention, as Burhouse (1999) has pointed out, is in terms of Britton's Oedipal triangular space. Britton (1989) links the "closure of the oedipal triangle" to the ability to observe and think about relationships that we are not part of. By internalising the parental capacity to observe and think about us, we learn to "reflect on ourselves while being ourselves". Many children with autism, I believe, have virtually no belief that they can be reflected upon unless they physically displace a father or sibling (Rhode 2000); as though they had no notion of there being a good place for themselves that was not the same as "Daddy's place". This state of mind is the quintessential opposite of a sense of abundance.

Mirror images and images in the mirror

In discussing which words to choose when children cannot experience them symbolically, Alvarez (1997) describes a patient whose cruelty to small animals was inflamed when she interpreted his murderous jealousy. She stresses the importance, in cases like this, of interpreting instead the child's legitimate need for a place of his own. It was in this sense that I understood Anthony's pre-occupation with his own reflection in the mirror. Since witnessing another autistic boy's creative use of a tiny dolls' house mirror, I now provide a larger mirror for children with autistic spectrum disorder. Many use it to work on issues of identity and of being seen at a stage when, for reasons like those I have discussed above, they are still unable to make use of the therapist's eyes.

Anthony seemed to derive a fundamental sense of having his existence confirmed from seeing his face in the mirror – the kind of confirmation which, as Winnicott ([1967] 1971) has described, would normally be provided by the mother's face and the love in her eyes. Anthony did not appear to feel that such direct confirmation could be for him: instead, it was as though the parental couple provided it for each other by being each other's mirror image. For example, he tipped the cow forward so that it was standing with its muzzle touching the mirror, as though looking at its own reflection, and said, "Mummy and Daddy". It was as though exclusion from this mutually adoring couple with eyes only for each other left him without a sense of being visible.

I hoped it might be possible to use the mirror as a third object that could reassure Anthony about making eye contact, so I tried to play at "finding" him by catching his eye in the mirror. Usually this did not work: it seemed that Anthony felt too insecure to tolerate my reflection in the mirror alongside his. It was as though he himself, together with his reflection, had to constitute the mutually adoring, twin-like, mirror-image parental couple, whose preoccupation with each other left no room for my existence to be recognised. He may well have expected any intruding third person to be hostile and dangerous. However, one day when he was feeling more robust, he did allow me to catch his eye in the mirror. Smiling with pleasure, he said, "Hullo mirror." Tolerating the appearance in the mirror of someone else's face freed him for a moment from his imprisonment in sterile narcissism, and he found his voice to speak to the mirror as though it had human qualities.

At that moment, Anthony was able to show his pleasure in Alvarez's "sense of abundance". Instead of being threatened by my reflection in the mirror, he seemed to feel that it contributed to the vitality of the object that reflected him. As Alvarez (1992) has stressed, genuine mirroring involves a vital transformation rather than a mechanical process of reflection. This links with Melanie Klein's formulations on the way small children can experience their mothers' qualities; that is, not so much in terms of her own qualities as in terms of the qualities of her supposed internal occupants. For example, in the *Narrative of a Child Analysis*, Klein's patient Richard wanted to turn off the glowing bar of an electric heater which had previously been understood in terms of the father's presence inside the mother. Once he had done so, the playroom felt dead to him (Klein [1961] 1975: 46–9). When Anthony felt sufficiently secure so that he did not need to be the only person in the mirror, the presence of another human being seemed to endow the mirror with humanity – the very opposite of the situation characteristic of children with autism in which human beings are treated as though they were things.

When babies are developing well, they are much more interested in another child than in their own reflection, once the novelty of recognising themselves in the mirror has worn off. Maiello (1997) has described an infant observation in which baby Lina's mother, under considerable strain through being separated from her family of origin, had little to spare for her daughter in the way of emotional resources, and tried to fob her off instead with her own reflection in the mirror. In fact, Lina was hardly interested in her reflection – "her little friend", as the mother called it. Instead she used the mirror to catch the observer's eye, and would then look back and forth between the observer and the observer's reflection. In his better moments, Anthony could enjoy it when I took the first step for him by catching his eye in the mirror; the second step, of looking from my reflection to me, was still beyond him.

One could speculate that this was because Anthony was as yet imperfectly able to experience people as people. Instead, he experienced them as functions. Instead of saying "Hullo" to me in the mirror, he said "Hullo" to the mirror which had become enlivened by my presence in it. This would seem to imply that he experienced me at that point as a father or sibling whom the mirror-mother could encompass together with him, rather than as a mother figure. To put it another way, he, the mirror and I did not really constitute the kind of three-person relationship within which Anthony could have made eye-contact with me while still trusting, as Alvarez describes baby Angela being able to do, that the vital reflective function of the mirror-mother would wait for him.

Taking turns

Gradually, Anthony began to be able to use the mirror for what it was meant for: to provide information about himself rather than to confirm his existence. One of the things that most held his attention was moving the mirror away from his face and back closer to it while making terrifying grimaces. He seemed to be experimenting with getting the right distance to a monstrous part of himself, and trying to establish where it was located.

In the last session before a Christmas holiday, lying on the floor, he studied his mouth in the mirror when his index finger was in it, and then when he moved his index finger away. He repeated this many times. I spoke about how the mirror showed him that his mouth was still all right even when he could no longer feel his finger in it; that his finger remained part of his body, and that he could bring it back. I added how important it was to feel he could bring me back after the holiday, even if I was not the same as his finger or part of his mouth (Tustin 1972). Anthony began to sing "Silent Night"; when he had sung the first line, he waited for me to sing the next. In this way, line by line, we went through the song.

I think that at this juncture the mirror provided another "viewpoint", beyond his or mine, that made it possible for him to listen to what I said and then to take turns with me, instead of feeling that it was him or me, as so easily happened when we were face to face with each other. (It probably helped that I took care not to let my face intrude into the mirror.) One aspect of this other viewpoint was that it provided him with visual information about his body, so that he no longer depended exclusively on the tactile sensations provided by the finger in his mouth (Tustin 1972). Authors including Tustin ([1981] 1992), Meltzer (1975: 25) and Haag (1991) have written about the interplay of different sensory modalities in children with autism, but for the purposes of this discussion, what I wish to emphasise is the congruence between the "binocular vision" (Bion [1950] 1967) afforded by the two senses of touch and vision working together, and Anthony's new-found capacity to take turns with another person. In this reciprocal relationship, each of us contributed something different to the whole: we could each have our own voice, just as earlier Anthony had given each of us an intact beaker and had generalised my comment "One for Anthony, one for Mrs Rhode' to "Red for clinic, green for holiday".

Discussion

Anthony's one-to-one relationships at the beginning of treatment were characterised by life-or-death rivalries. These could be rivalries for attention (as when he could not tolerate my reflection next to his in the mirror) or for Tustin's "hard extra bit" that ensures survival (his finger in his mouth before the Christmas holiday). In the absence of mirroring or of his finger, he easily felt vulnerable to terrors of falling. Equally, he often experienced me as fragile and vulnerable when he attempted to get through by such violent means as cutting gashes into a plastic beaker ("Lady crying"). The possibility that we could each be all right – each have a beaker of our own – was a fundamental step, and one which was facilitated by the introduction of a third object which we could each relate to. Postman Pat's van was a concrete realisation of a reference which Anthony himself had introduced. In retrospect, I feel that this demonstrated that room would be made in the therapy for what mattered to him (Milner 1955).

In fact, each of Anthony's steps forward that I have described was mediated by the establishment of a three-party relationship: between him, me and the Postman Pat toy; between him, me and the "Pat-a-Cake" song, which itself refers to harmonious threesomes; between him, me and the mirror; between his mouth, his finger and the mirror; and between him, me and "Silent Night". Beginning with the side-by-side, not quite joint attention to Postman Pat's van (rather as though there were "one-link-with-the-van for Anthony, one for Mrs Rhode"), he progressed to greeting the mirror that included us both. He could move on to taking turns with me in a reciprocal relationship when the visual evidence provided by the mirror reassured him that the integrity of his mouth and body did not depend on my physical presence (Tustin 1972). In Alvarez's terms, having welcomed the sense of abundance associated with an object (the mirror) that was capable of encompassing two people, he could feel sufficiently sure of his and my separate and individual identities to be able to take turns singing "Silent Night". At that moment, he was able to believe that he and I could each have a voice, and to wait with confidence for his turn. The presence of another person was enriching rather than threatening.

The capacity to take turns is one of the characteristics of Trevarthen's secondary intersubjectivity, which in normal development follows on from the primary intersubjectivity and attunement between mother and baby (Trevarthen and Hubley 1978). Before the secondary intersubjectivity of joint attention is achieved, the baby goes through a stage of not tolerating the intrusion of another person when he is exploring an object. In Anthony's case, this developmental sequence was preceded by a stage of not-quite-joint attention in which relating through objects modified the terrors he associated with one-to-one encounters.

The degree of Anthony's autism is quite severe, and the achievements I have described very easily get lost. Partly, I think, this is to do with the world of extremes in which he lives. Any interruption tends to feel like banishment to a state of falling helplessly, against which he protects himself by being a psychopathic Giant; and he tends to ascribe any gratification to the Giant's power to bully me. For instance, greatly to his annoyance Anthony had to share a much-loved escort with another child. When the other boy stopped coming, Anthony regressed for weeks, withdrawing from contact with me and holding his head on one side as though he were a Siamese twin who had lost half of himself. He had a similar reaction when I increased his sessions to twice a week. This seems to be another example of Anthony's fear that there could not be room enough for two, so that having more of a good relationship became confused with eliminating real or imaginary rivals.

Indeed, it was as though the fear that there could not be room for two extended to the two contrasting aspects of Anthony's personality – the helpless baby and the psychopathic Giant. Alvarez (1999a) has differentiated actively *with*drawn children with autism from those who are passively *un*drawn. It was as though Anthony's personality comprised both these aspects, jostling for attention without co-existing for long enough to permit integration: the Giant who was actively withdrawing and *with*drawn, allowing little scope for the helpless baby to develop beyond an *un*drawn state (Meltzer 1975: 29). Anthony's autism could thus be thought of as resembling a pathological organisation, which can appear to offer a refuge from chaos and fragmentation (Steiner [1987] 1988). Technically, I found it useful to name these two characters and to show that I recognised them as they appeared in turn ("Anthony's here now" ; or "Oh, there's tricky Giant-Anthony"), besides talking about there being room for both of them. After some four years, Anthony began to be able to enjoy games of peek-a-boo, in which I never knew whether it would be Anthony or Giant-Anthony who reappeared from hiding.

Along with an intolerance of the frustrations which for him seem so catastrophic, this absence of integration has, I believe, been an important factor in the ease with which Anthony's achievements can get lost. On the one hand, he can retreat guiltily from improvements which can feel like the fruits of the Giant's destructiveness. On the other hand, each step forward can feel as though it were achieved in the face of the Giant's powerful obstruction.

This impression is reinforced if one compares Anthony's use of the mirror with that of Jasper, a disturbed but non-autistic three-year-old treated by Lore Schacht (1981). She describes an early session in which Jasper began by using the clasp of her handbag as a mirror, but quickly progressed to asking whether she could see him. As she put it, he made the move described by Winnicott ([1967] 1971) from the mirror to the analyst's face: "he discovers that my looking at him is the real mirror" (p. 82). A few months later, he and she caught each other's eye in the mirror. This time, instead of asking whether she could see him, he asked, "Can you see yourself?" He had moved forward from feeling that his therapist recognised and validated his identity to asking a question that implies a theory of mind.

The speed of this move suggests a process ready to unfold naturally once it had been triggered. Anthony has at times been able to enjoy the sense of abundance and the associated capacity to take turns; but every moment of eye-contact has had to be fought for, and a question like "can you see yourself?" remains well out of reach. Paradoxically, this may be through an excess of empathy rather than an inborn deficit: his own sense of identity is not as yet sufficiently well-founded for him to be able to enter into the experience of a "lady" who might turn out to be "crying".

Finally, I wish to highlight Anthony's appropriate use of words at both the significant moments I have discussed – when he volunteered "Hullo, mirror", and again when he sang "Silent Night" with me. This was very unusual: such language as he produced was usually spoken in someone else's voice. Partly, I believe, his communicative speech was linked to his feeling at these moments that he could have an identity, and a voice, without despoiling someone else (Rhode 1999). However, another aspect concerns the capacity to use words symbolically. As Alvarez has highlighted (1992: 115; 1997), this capacity is linked with being able to see that a statement implies its opposite; that a sentence like "You're worried you might fall" implies "But you might not need to worry about that." In contrast, children with autism, like others who are not functioning symbolically, will hear the statement "You're worried you might fall" concretely, as though it meant, "You are going to fall." Crucially, the capacity to encompass one statement at the same time as its opposite is lacking. Anthony's heightened capacity for communicative, symbolic speech might then be understood as a heightened capacity to entertain two meanings at the same time, in parallel with the experience of a mirror that could reflect both him and me.

The sense of abundance which Anne Alvarez has explored theoretically is evident in the many strands of thought which fruitfully come together in her writing, just as it is evident in the enthusiasm and generosity with which she has characteristically responded to the work of students and colleagues. I hope to have conveyed how greatly my experience of working with Anthony has been enriched by her ideas.

References

Alvarez, A. (1980) "Two regenerative situations in autism: reclamation and becoming vertebrate", *Journal of Child Psychotherapy* 6: 91–102.

Alvarez, A. (1992) *Live Company*, London and New York: Tavistock/Routledge.

Alvarez, A. (1997) "Projective identification as a communication: its grammar in borderline psychotic children", *Psychoanalytic Dialogues* 7: 753–68. [Also in J. Symington (ed.) (2000) *Imprisoned Pain and its Transformation: A Festschrift for H. Sydney Klein*, London: Karnac Books.]

Alvarez, A. (1999a) "Addressing the deficit: developmentally informed psychotherapy with passive, 'undrawn' children", in A. Alvarez and S. Reid (eds) *Autism and Personality*, London and New York: Routledge.

Alvarez, A. (1999b) "Disorder, deviance and personality: factors in the persistence and modifiability of autism", in A. Alvarez and S. Reid (eds) *Autism and Personality*, London and New York: Routledge.

Alvarez, A. and Furgiuele, P. (1997) "Speculations on components in the infant's sense of agency: the sense of abundance and the capacity to think in parentheses", in S. Reid (ed.) *Developments in Infant Observation*, London: Routledge.

Bardishevsky, M. (1998) "The compensation of autistic features during a little boy's second year: overcoming pain through the development of attachment", *International Journal of Infant Observation* 2: 40–57.

Baron-Cohen, S. (1995) *Mindblindness*, Cambridge, Mass. and London: MIT Press.

Bion, W.R. ([1950] 1967) "The imaginary twin", in *Second Thoughts*, London: Heinemann.

Britton, R. (1989) "The missing link: parental sexuality in the Oedipus complex", in J. Steiner (ed.) *The Oedipus Complex Today*, London: Karnac Books.

Broucek, F.J. (1979) "Efficacy in infancy: a review of some experimental studies and their possible implications for clinical theory", *International Journal of Psycho-Analysis* 60: 311–16.

Bruner, J. (1968) *Processes of Cognitive Growth: Infancy*, Worcester, Mass.: Clark University Press.

Burhouse, A. (1999) "*Me, you and it: Conversations about the significance of joint attention skills from cognitive psychology, child development research and psychoanalysis*", Unpublished MA Dissertation, Tavistock Clinic/University of East London.

Fonagy, P., Steele, H., Moran, G., Steele, M., and Higgitt, A. (1991). "The capacity for understanding mental states: the reflective self in parent and child and its significance for security of attachment", *Infant Mental Health Journal, 13*: 200–17.

Haag, G. (1991) "Nature de quelques identifications dans l'image du corps", *Journal de la Psychanalyse de l'Enfant* 9: 73–92.

Klein, M. ([1961] 1975) "Narrative of a Child Analysis", in *The Writings of Melanie Klein*, Vol. 4, London: Hogarth.

Leslie, A. (1991) "The theory of mind impairment in autism: evidence for a modular mechanism of development?" in A. Whiten (ed.) *Natural Theories of Mind*, Oxford: Blackwell.

Maiello, S. (1997) "Twinning phantasies in the mother–infant couple and the observer's counterpoint function", *International Journal of Infant Observation* 1: 31–50.

Meltzer, D. (1975) "The psychology of autistic states and of post-autistic mentality", in D. Meltzer, J. Bremner, S. Hoxter, D. Weddell and I. Wittenberg, *Explorations in Autism*, Strath Tay: Clunie Press.

Milner, M. (1955) "The role of illusion in symbol formation", in: M. Klein *et al.* (eds) *New Directions in Psycho-Analysis,* London: Tavistock.

Rhode, M. (1997a) "The voice as autistic object", in T. and J. Mitrani (eds) *Encounters with Autistic States: A Memorial Tribute to Frances Tustin*, Northvale, N.J.: Jason Aronson.

Rhode, M. (1997b) "Going to pieces: autistic and schizoid solutions", in M. Rustin, M. Rhode, A. Dubinsky and H. Dubinsky (eds) *Psychotic States in Children*, London: Duckworth.

Rhode, M. (1999) "Echo or answer? The move towards ordinary speech in three children with autistic spectrum disorder", in A. Alvarez and S. Reid (eds) *Autism and Personality*, London and New York: Routledge.

Rhode, M. (2000) "On using an alphabet: recombining separable components", in J. Symington (ed.) *Imprisoned Pain and its Transformation: A Festschrift for H. Sydney Klein*, London: Karnac Books.

Schacht, L. (1981) "The mirroring function of the child analyst", *Journal of Child Psychotherapy* 7: 79–88.

Steiner, J. ([1987] 1988) "The interplay between pathological organizations and the paranoid–schizoid and depressive positions", in E. B. Spillius (ed.) *Melanie Klein Today*, Vol. 1, London and New York: Routledge.

Stockdale-Wolfe, E. (1993) "Fear of fusion: non-verbal behavior in secondary autism", *Psychoanalytic Inquiry* 13: 9–33.

Trevarthen, C. and Hubley, P. (1978) "Secondary intersubjectivity: confidence, confiding and acts of meaning in the first year", in A. Lock (ed.) *Action, Gesture and Symbol: The Emergence of Language*, London: Academic Press.

Tustin, F. (1972) *Autism and Childhood Psychosis*, London: Hogarth.

Tustin, F. ([1981] 1992) *Autistic States in Children* (2nd revised ed.), London: Routledge.

Winnicott, D.W. ([1967] 1971) "Mirror-role of mother and family in child development", in *Playing and Reality*, London: Tavistock Publications.

Chapter 11

Liking *liking* doing

Elsa First

There has been much work by developmentalists on how the baby's mind grows, how intersubjectivity becomes internalized as intrasubjectivity (Stern 1985). It is a fascinating moment when autistic or other mindless children begin to discover that they like doing something, then that they like *liking* doing it . . . Mothers follow their babies' direction of gaze long before babies begin to follow their mother's . . . Infant observation shows us time and again the way mothers light up as they see what has caught their baby's glance, "Oh it's the movement of the tree!"

(Alvarez, 1997, p. 757)

In a commentary on this essay I wrote:

Notice how Alvarez notices the fascinating moment when autistic or other mindless children begin to discover that they like doing something, then that they like *liking* doing it. She lines this up with how a mother's gaze follows the infant's and lights up "Oh it's the movement of the tree." This sets us thinking about how the precursors for a child's knowing that it likes liking an activity have to do with that early following of an infant's joyful interest. (A wonderfully chosen example because so easy to identify with.) We then start thinking about what in the therapist's awareness and affect and verbal acknowledgments in a session might correspond with a mother following an infant's gaze. We are implicitly encouraged to use these analogies as a guideline in regard to appreciating the depleted borderline child's first claims on potency even if they may sound like defensive omnipotence.

(First, 1997, p. 771)

Alvarez has used work with autism (Alvarez, 1992; Alvarez and Reid, 1999) as a basis for thinking about what ordinary experiences in the development of agency and of relatedness (such as reaching out and grasping) are missing in the most shut down children. She guides us to noticing and articulating small significant increments in the growth of a sense of self, agency, and reparative capacity in a wide range of disturbed children. The complexity and creativity with which she thinks about how "intersubjectivity becomes internalized as intrasubjectivity" is exemplified for me by the wonderful paper on two-tracked thinking, "Speculations on components in the infant's sense of agency: the sense of abundance and the capacity to think in parentheses" (Alvarez and Furgiuele, 1997) which convincingly suggests how qualities of the mother's mental life, her capacity to bear the infant in mind, while going on with other parts of her life, come to be registered in the richness or concreteness of the infant's or toddler's mind.

We might also reflect in the other direction, about how a child using autistic defenses, with some weakness or blocking of the capacity to sustain or to project internal experience, makes it harder for a parent or therapist to think about him. This was I think sometimes the case in the material I will present here, although at other times this atypical child did project quite effectively a sense of terror and of a dangerously fragile object.

I hope to show something of how Alvarez's clinical understanding has been an influence by tracing how I felt it accompany me through the first four somewhat stumbling months of an exploratory twice-weekly psychotherapy with a six-year-old boy whose history suggested autistic spectrum features.

Ian's parents were prompted to consult, after years of sometimes despairing accommodation to Ian's differences, because Ian, who was often in tears in school, had confided in a teacher that he wished he were dead. Teachers found him "odd but engaging," and were distressed by his evident suffering.

The mother said Ian as a baby was an enigma to her. In breastfeeding, he would suck avidly and then abruptly pull away, rigid. She found it difficult to elaborate on their relationship, perhaps because it was too painful to think about. (Later in our work she could volunteer astute observations and nuanced concerns if asked about something I had already noticed, as well as acknowledge what she found distressing.) What concerned the father most was that Ian increasingly "deleted" new activities from his repertoire in a peculiarly insistent way that was hard to decode, just as he had "deleted" most foods. Ordinarily varied foods had been eliminated starting at eighteen months and more thoroughly at three years when Ian's brother was born. (There had been anxiety over this baby's survival, though he was now healthy.) Ian's father had taught him chess, to play a musical instrument, and to ride a bicycle, but Ian would insist categorically on "deleting" the activity after reaching a moment of beginning mastery. Father also accurately observed and was troubled by the fact that Ian never took over new activities as something he could enjoy for himself or want to practice without his father doing it with him.

Ian's difficulties with transitions and separations could be profound. Ian shadowed his parents at home. Outings and vacations had been difficult because Ian often couldn't manage a change of scene. For ordinary transitions such as to and from school, Ian's parents adeptly kept him afloat with ritualized "routines" of comic patter and gaiety. Ian had several good friends but playdates had to be at his house, and sleepovers were unthinkable.

Unlike some tyrannical children, Ian expressed genuine remorse when he made an outing impossible. He seemed a compassionate, even oversolicitous child. His mother believed Ian had always turned away from seeking help or comfort from her, but she was also aware of his overattunement to her. He was like her personal weather man, she complained. "He knows I am angry before I do, when I haven't even noticed."

Ian's parents had come to assume Ian was happiest "in his own world." He spent hours at home in absorbed states which he explained as "thinking."

> Without support there seems to be a natural tendency for the human environment to let such children withdraw as loners (Wolf, 1995), or for adults to create an increasingly rigid structure around the child involving a high degree of ingenuity and effort, but with much reduced opportunities for "live company" (Alvarez, 1992).
>
> (Shuttleworth, 1998)

Ian had been diagnosed early as having low muscle tone, for which he received physical therapy; he had also been borderline failure to thrive as an infant. He wore an eyepatch during the school day to correct a moderately handicapping eye condition, and was reported to lack depth perception. In the effort to minimize any sense of handicap, the topic was little mentioned, which left it mysterious for Ian. In an early session with his mother in the room Ian burst out in a passionate tirade against having to wear a patch. He would be satisfied to have just one good eye! Why was one eye not enough?

Ian proved to resemble a group of children Alvarez discusses (Alvarez, 1999, p. 62) who respond to psychotherapy and the concurrent small "change in emotional temperature" with a cascade of rapid changes that Alvarez likens to a glacier melting.

One change, within a few months, was that his weak eye strengthened to a surprising degree and his visual acuity increased beyond doctors' expectations. Evidently Ian began using eye muscles that had been inert, as has been reported in some autistic spectrum children. I had the impression of his moving from a two-dimensional to a three-dimensional world. He also became newly oriented in time, able to experience continuity in sessions, and able to persist in learning physical activities such as swimming. Also new was an ability to confide in his mother some of his everyday anxieties, and make good use of her support; for example, to go on class trips. Usually solemn, he began to show more humor and some sassiness, for example singing at home, "I know how to sing a song that gets on the nerves of everyone!" (Initiating or choosing an activity at home or in sessions remained highly fraught. He would obsessively ask permission for ordinary choices.)

I entered this exploratory assessment of a child who presented at diverse levels of functioning helped by Alvarez's sense that autistic spectrum and borderline phenomena be seen as part of a continuum. In trying to understand Ian, I was helped by allowing myself to assume a continuum between autistic absorptiveness and narcissistic co-opting of the object, or between autistic and obsessional ritual. I was also helped by being able to consider that Ian might have defects or vulnerabilities in the capacity for introjection as well as for (communicative) projection which might seem evident at some times and be evidently overcome at times of less threatened relatedness.

Ian with a parent in the room presented as oddly awkward and dysfluent, but intensely eager to perform at a high level, and to show himself as creative. In his first session he painstakingly drew the trophy he had received for playing chess in school, and seemed doubtful that I would know anything about his world. He played the wonky toy trumpet, and said it reminded him of a Doctor Seuss drawing; he himself had just outgrown this type of reading, but he didn't mean anything bad to anyone who still liked Doctor Seuss. His parents had to translate a bit because of his dysfluency. When he configured the trumpet to blow sound into his own ear, then air into his nose, I said he might be showing me he wished he could make his own air. He took up this suggestion playfully. I said perhaps the idea was that it would be nice to be able to take care of yourself entirely and not need air or help from anyone else. This won a definite glance of assent.

Once Ian with stern resolution walked into the room on his own, he was more collapsed and fearful. (His mother, incidentally, recognized this "little soldier mode," and it saddened her that he needed it to meet new challenges, or to separate from her.) Ian lay on the mat with his back to me in silence. I spoke of his letting me see how he was in his private times, that we both had to get used to being together and find a way of working together, and that I was getting to spend time with him when he was his private self. (States of dreamy withdrawal later became relaxed times which he used after distressed shut downs to reconnect through shared contemplation of visual phenomena, some play of the sunlight and shade he'd point out to me, knowing I liked it too.)

Greed, depletion and terror

Unusual affective states could be sensed almost uncannily in the countertransference in early sessions. One was an infinite greediness as if Ian would have liked to absorb the whole setting, perhaps through inhaling it. But if he wanted to take home something he couldn't have, he could turn off wanting as if he'd thrown a switch which cut out all desire. Underlying terror could be sensed when Ian needed to perform magic gestures on entering the room as if to ward off enemies, and at times seemed hallucinated. Ian also would arrive in states of depletion or utter exhaustion which frightened him. He complained mildly, of "tiredness," and of pains in his legs which made it hard to stand. I had to contain concern for his survival. He seemed unable to think about linking his exhaustion to exertions.

Ian also early confided lucidly about his wanting to be dead. It came in states of "the worst boredom," a boredom he felt he couldn't get out of. I imagined it must cover a nameless dread in which he felt already dead. We could note and talk about his boredoms a little, only intermittently. (After the summer, he identified his empty states as "loneliness.") He also knew he was commonly afflicted with a "boredom" in which "nothing seems good enough to do." (Sometimes I moved towards pulling Ian out of "bored" states, and sometimes I would try to stay with Ian through the withdrawals, hoping an interested tolerance could make him less afraid that his internal life was crazy.)

Discontinuities and glimpses of play

Alvarez's work led me to notice Ian's often extreme difficulties in initiating and odd discontinuities. Discontinuities between sessions were striking, and enigmatic: Ian took possession of a portfolio for his drawings by "decorating" it with complex cartoon characters, but then wouldn't go near it for a long time, as if either he couldn't see it, or it had become persecutory. When it was re-presented later, he still avoided reaching into it with his own hands, silently soliciting help.

It was hard at any given time to know why there was no sustaining of interest. At various times I thought it might have been because of Ian's sense of his own efforts as damaged, or that he became minutely disappointed, or was so fearful of disappointing or harming an internal object, but it seemed we needed first to establish common ground on which affects could remain long enough to be considered.

From the start there were episodic moments of play, along with dramatized affects, that seemed meaningful, could be thought about, and shared. But they continually proved flashes in the pan that would disappear after a single elaboration, as if they had never been. I was left disappointed, though not, I think, teased. There didn't seem to be an intent to tease. I realized that in the treatment I was having an experience of "deletions" which paralleled the experience of Ian's parents.

A telling symbolic theme appeared in a game with cars which Ian briefly elaborated with some pleasure around the eighth week. As the cars fell over the edge of the table/cliff I noted that their "uh ohs" on landing were very faint. Ian's tentative elaborations let me further muse aloud that it seemed that when they endured a big fall their cries were weak but when they bumped gently into small obstacles they screamed in protest. Ian said big hurts were like nothing to them but little hurts felt awful: he later added in a judgmental tone that this was because they were crazy. It seemed we'd hit upon a way to play together where my understanding could encourage him to elaborate a theme. I supposed he was representing an awareness of his own regulatory disorder as well as aspects of his internal parents, and I expected this would get clearer as the game developed. But the "uh oh" game and any car play was soon abandoned, as if interdicted, and I was left concerned that perhaps my interest in itself had stirred alarm. It was hard not to feel that I had done harm. I couldn't be sure if these brief periods of joint interest were creating some safe territory on which thoughts and feelings could be elaborated, or if any indication of interest was driving them away. Was Ian not able to hold onto his ideas or was he internally prohibited from entertaining them? Or was he just painfully anxious about craziness?

Not long after came a session with a spontaneous exuberance I had not witnessed. Animated moods, before this, had seemed to require Ian's being buoyed up by his parents' presence and bantering support. This time it was as if an unsupported natural self had emerged, awkward and wobbly and unused to ordinary conversation or rough and tumble dramatic play, but earnestly trying out both.

Conversation came first. "On the way here I was talking with my mother and what we were talking about was . . ." The story, evidently about the chess tournament in school, was jumbled, concrete, and dysfluent, eager and troubled. It was hard to know why he was telling me about having told his mother, or the point of the story.

I said, "So you were talking with Mom just for the good feeling of letting her know what was going on, or for figuring out some problem?"

"No, just the first one, "Ian said, with understanding. He was telling about having been able to have a conversation! I could hone in on this because I was watchful for any experience Ian could garner of "live company" (Alvarez, 1992). His parents had reported that just that week they had spontaneously invited him to join them at the table "for conversation," even if he couldn't tolerate their food.

Ian retold the story he'd told his mother: of how he and the other finalist, a girl, didn't finish their game, and a teacher had resolved the problem of how to count it in the tournament. It involved a moment in which Ian's heart was beating so fast he thought he couldn't go on and another moment in which the girl champion said she hated chess and knocked over the board. After some clarification, our conversation petered out.

Ian became restless. The gym mat was offered. Rolling around and thrashing as if in battle led to what he called "The Ian Show" and then "The Circus." He would take a running start, leap, kick the wall (covered by a mat panel) while mid-air, jump back and regain balance. I found myself offering comments in a reflectively appreciative but neutral tone. For example, "In that one you are getting bolder," or "This one is kind of about getting more daring and risk taking." Ian liked this very much. He began telling me what tasks he was setting himself as he went along, trying for example to get more mid-air kicks in before regaining balance. The excited competitive feats, as he explained, were fleetingly imagined as skateboarding, or surfing a big wave, or scoring soccer goals.

In my remarks I continued to find myself simply underlining his intentionality, and that I was noticing and figuring out what he was trying to do. I supposed Ian might be putting on stage longings for effortless prowess and triumph that he had harbored silently while feeling himself so confined by handicap. But this was no time for comments in a "grammar of wishing" (Alvarez, 1997) The new thing seemed to be that he could let himself move independently and assertively in space, and I felt moved and quietly thrilled.

My notes record "There is something about being accompanied in his intentionality that I feel is or may be new to him in this session." The experience of knowing himself to be accompanied by a reliably unambivalent recognition of his intentionality seemed to be a key missing nourishment. I was now on the lookout for shared continuities amid Ian's discontinuities.

Another new feature arose collaboratively, partly out of his wish to know whether I could tell what he was enacting. He ran through a synopsis. "First it was a fight and then it was skateboarding and then the big wave..." This capacity to construct and share a historical sequence also seemed new. I said it was a good feeling to be able to make things up and then to go back and remember together all the things he had done. This led to our reconstructing a list of what he'd done in treatment so far.

Ian asked for the mat setup to continue the circus in the following session, and remarked, as if pleased and astonished at it himself, that he was doing the same thing two sessions in a row. It was as if a prohibition had been lifted, although before it had seemed an automatic oblivion. Now he particularly reminded me of Alvarez's child who discovers first that he likes doing something and then that he *likes* liking it (Alvarez, 1997).

The second time Ian's exuberance seemed more unbridled, and the feats of leaping and kicking at our makeshift padded wall seemed so too, as Ian was heedless of possible hurt. What had seemed Ian's natural self had elided so swiftly into an omnipotent invulnerable self! I felt concern and dismay, and I think subtly drew back. I tacitly accepted the role of safekeeper, and did it by management. It might have been good if I could have found a way then to speak of how it helped him to practice being brave if he could leave the safety to me. At the time Ian's heedlessness struck me more as deficit, and this made it harder to find a way to speak about it.

(Sometime after the summer break Ian confided his idea of "paradise": "A beach with sunshine, where you could play and swim as much as you wanted, and there would be no lifeguard on the beach because on Paradise Beach you wouldn't need a lifeguard because you could have accidents but the accidents wouldn't hurt you." Unexpectedly, he added, "Unless you wanted to hurt yourself.") This suggested an intuitive awareness that he very much needed lifeguards because he hadn't yet internalized that function, as well as evoking how much he had lived in terror of "accidents." I also remarked that he was letting me know he understood the feeling of wanting to hurt yourself.

The week following the circus Ian thought he might want to do the same thing "for three times in a row!" Once the mat was set up, he found he couldn't continue, and broke off, adamant. The circus vanished from our repertoire, another puzzling deletion. Had it felt out of control to him? Was he over-responsive to my caution? (Perhaps also it was hard to warm up from scratch to that level of intensity and this made him feel hopeless.)

In an effort to keep a sleepy session afloat I tinkered idly with a makeshift paper airplane, which led to more glimpses of narrative commentary by Ian, about crashes and safe landings. An earlier theme emerged as a plane crashed badly but barely complained, while another landed fairly well but cried. Ian gave me one of his rare looks of mutual recognition and exclaimed, "That's like what I did when I used to play with the cars!" (He said it as if it felt like remembering something from years ago.) We were taken by surprise, and both amazed. Ian then shut down and said he didn't want to play anymore. I said something had bothered or frightened him. Did he know what? I said I had remembered the car story too, and I wondered if there was something about our having the same idea in our minds at the same time that felt uncomfortable or not safe to him. He could not respond. I thought to myself it might have been unnerving to discover he had an unconscious mind with its own continuity.

Depletions and "having to take a nap," followed. I tried to link it to finding it hard to be in the session. "Sometimes I get sad or mad for no reason," Ian confided.

"Is that what just happened? Is that when you feel like going to sleep?"

"Yes, and there's something more. I get a mixture of sad and mad and bored."

A joint venture

I often longed to provide Ian with some engaging activity. Although this was arguably an evasion of his painful states of boredom or terror, it might serve as "reclaiming." Eventually (Ian never asked for anything) I provided a book of glorious printed paper airplanes that could be constructed simply by folding according to simple instructions, an age-appropriate challenge, more challenging because Ian was unaccustomed to using his fingers. This proved very gratifying. Ian liked finding that instructions could be friendly and helpful, skills learned, mistakes and faulty flying patterns corrected. A notable moment of joint attention and spontaneous joint enthusiasm occurred when our first model, in which we had little faith, soared.

Now there was no lack of continuity because in each session Ian wanted to make another plane. He would affectionately reminisce about the ones we had already made, how they had surprised us ("good surprises" as opposed to "nasty surprises"), and consider which to try next. He looked forward to sessions, and asked on weekends when he'd see me again. Paper airplanes also served to bridge the awkward gap between being in the session and rejoining a parent, as he flew a plane ahead of him into the waiting room.

As the summer approached, the joint adventure of making planes devolved into a routine, almost a ritual, evidently kept to by Ian because it was safe. Alvarez's reflections on deadening in the clinical situation, and especially on autistic rituals, were helpful in noticing this. Again it was difficult to be sure when and why the decline. Disillusion may have begun when a model proved too complex to do well.

The passing of time

Meanwhile, Ian was becoming more aware of, and pained by, the passing of time. Along with this he began to show some capacity to tolerate transience and time's limitations. I had usually managed things so Ian would success-fully complete a paper plane within a session. He now took more responsi-bility by asking whether we had enough time to complete this or that model, especially if we had spent time talking or noodling about. But he earnestly insisted I not give him five-minute warnings of the session's end. He couldn't yet bear to spend time anticipating an end. Ian showed renewed interest in the clock, and revealed, with giggly embarrassment, where he was still unclear about telling time. His confusions cleared up quickly. (Indeed he soon was so oriented in regard to days of the week, he could participate in re-scheduling sessions or afterschool activities, to the surprise of his parents, who had taken for granted that he didn't understand anything about time.) New anxieties were voiced in terms of the clock. What if a second hand went faster and faster, he worried. I wondered if he was telling me about times he felt too speedy. I also speculated that if he accepted time, he was afraid of feeling subject to its arbitrary whims and speedups. Ian talked competently of how seconds nested in minutes and minutes in hours, and so on, then he grandiosely sped through centuries to millennia. "Beyond millennia is for-ever," he said. I said, thinking of Alvarez, that you can have a nice forever feeling in a minute sometimes.[1]

I spoke of how Ian was now learning about time, and starting to feel comfortable letting himself spread out in time, and linked his concern over speedy time with knowing that day camp was ending soon and perhaps wondering how long our working together would continue. He jumped at this opening, relieved, and was able to specify, when I asked, how much information he could take in at that time: just that treatment wouldn't end when camp did, not yet about how long we would continue. In the last week of day camp he became dramatically stuck for most of a session, obsessively repeating a bit of finger play and rhyme from a trick he had learned from an adored male counsellor. Though I noted the stuckness and tried to make links with his wanting to hold on to the counsellor, Ian maintained gallantly that he was just repeating the routine because he liked doing it. Indeed he seemed uncannily unaware of being stuck, as if time for him had really stood still.

In the last session before the summer break, I felt a pull to provide a bridge over the break, or to convey a belief in continuity, in an over-the-summer and an after-the-summer. I asked if I might remark on something about him I had noticed. Ian agreed. I said I had noticed that he had grown a little taller recently. (He looked very pleased, somewhat to my surprise.) I found myself adding that I imagined that when I saw him again after the summer he would be even taller, because children usually grew over the summer. This quickly devolved, as was typical between us, into an abstract scientific conversation about why children grow in summer, as though the pleasure in being pleasurably thought of couldn't be sustained. I wondered why I had abandoned my ordinary exploratory analytic stance around a child's experience of a break. I think my countertransference arose from some sense that Ian couldn't anticipate the break as a break. I felt Ian needed more of a sense of continuity to be established before he could begin to experience separations. I was following Alvarez on the need for a sense of continuity and agency as a foundation for facing depressive anxieties. Yet I questioned myself. Was I supplying ingredients Ian lacked, helping him make continuity thinkable? Or was I in the countertransference only resonating with his unconscious conviction that recognition of separation and the attendant rage would be shattering?

I went further in following the prompting to affirm continuity. Ian wanted me to teach him how to make something new out of paper. By way also of giving a goodbye-for-the-summer present I demonstrated how to make a Moebius strip out of paper. A Moebius strip is in a way an endless loop. So I suppose I was carrying out the theme that you could have a forever feeling within time.

I introduced the Moebius strip by saying I could show him the trick of how to make a piece of paper that had only one side. As I'd just laid a sheet of paper down flat on the rug, Ian thought this was the trick in itself, and from a sophisticated seven-year-old point of view he considered it a hilarious joke. He said he could show me a trick too: how to make one piece of paper into two. With the scissors he cut it in two and laid the pieces apart. I said I thought he was showing me that he was thinking about how we would be apart from each other over the vacation. He looked at me with understanding and seemed relieved to have this acknowledged. I then showed him the Moebius "trick" and he was quite intrigued. He disagreed with the idea that the twisted loop had only one side. It had two sides, Ian said, an outside and an inside, "but the outside turns into the inside, and the inside turns into the outside." I thought this showed courage in developing his own idea based on his own perceptions. (He was able to show where he thought the transitions were from outside to inside and vice versa.) I also thought it showed that while operating with an age-appropriate concreteness, he was developing some capacity for sustaining paradox.

In the waiting room, his mother exclaimed, "Oh I remember that from when I was a kid! It's weird. You look at it and look at it and it goes on and on forever and it makes you crazy!" Ian glanced at me frankly puzzled as to why his mother could think the Moebius strip makes you crazy when to us it had been a subject of wonder.

Infants who use autistic defenses may not have been helped or been able to be helped by mothers' containment of states of rapture or beauty as well as of acute distress. Ian's mother might have found it hard to tolerate (and filter) good states prolonged beyond a certain interval, just as his endowment would have made it hard to feel reciprocal goodness at the start.

Postlude

Resuming after the first break precipitated transient disorganized states in which Ian seemed to try to reconnect with me by absorption and magic stares and gestures, but the developments of this exploratory period and what we could talk about continued to grow. I continue to think about my counter-transference anxieties over traumatizing Ian as reflecting in part primitive anxieties in his internal object world, his struggles, and those of his parents.

Note

1 "I treated the insistence on foreverness as a defense against sadness instead of seeing it as a rightful need for continuity ... I could have said something ... like you like the feeling that this treatment is going to go on for a long time. A nice forever feeling. An infant needs an experience of duration and durability of good experience before he or she can learn to tolerate interruptions or endings" (Alvarez, 1997, p. 761)

References

Alvarez, A. (1992) *Live Company*. London: Routledge.

Alvarez, A. (1997) "Projective Identification as a Communication: Its Grammar in Borderline Psychotic Children," *Psychoanalytic Dialogues*, 7/6, 753–768.

Alvarez, A. (1999) "Disorder Deviance and Personality: Factors in the Persistence and Modificability of Autism," in A. Alvarez and S. Reid, *Autism and Personality*. New York and London: Routledge, pp. 62–98.

Alvarez, A. and Furgiuele, P. (1997) "Speculations on Components in the Infant's Sense of Agency: The Sense of Abundance and the Capacity to Think in Parentheses," in S. Reid (ed.) *Developments in Infant Observation*. London and New York: Routledge, pp. 123–129.

Alvarez, A. and Reid, S. (1999) *Autism and Personality*. New York and London: Routledge.

First, E. (1997) "Irreparable Objects – When There's Nothing To Mend: Commentary on Paper by Anne Alvarez," *Psychoanalytic Dialogues*, 7/6, 769–780.
Stern, D. (1985) *The Interpersonal World of the Infant*. New York: Basic Books.
Shuttleworth, J. (1998) "Theories of Mental Development," *Journal of Infant Observation*, 1/2 (Feb.), 29–50.

Chapter 12

First love unfolding

Developmental and psychoanalytic perspectives on first relationships and their significance in clinical work

Judith Edwards

The title for this chapter had a twofold genesis: I had read Turgenev's powerful short story, *First Love* (1860) in which he tells of a boy's first love for a young girl who comes to live next door. It is only gradually that he discovers that this same girl is actually sexually involved with his father, with whom he has always had a painful and difficult relationship. It is a story told with passion and energy, and this twist of the classical Oedipal situation made me think of the Oedipal struggles which prefigure our adult relationships, and then to think how these struggles themselves are preceded by the passionate drama of the first relationship between a mother and her baby which forms the bedrock for future development, becoming, as Racker (1968) so lucidly put it, "the characteristic way of living our love".

Taking as my starting point intensive psychoanalytic work with a sixteen-year-old post-autistic adolescent boy and drawing also briefly on other case material, I want to illustrate how the "characteristic ways" of relating which are the stuff of the dynamic relationship recreated in the transference can be thought about and worked through over time, with reference both to developmental and psychoanalytic ideas. This process has been greatly illuminated by the bridges which have been built over the last twenty years between the findings of child developmentalists and those of psychoanalytic workers. For those working in the clinical field, theoretical concepts have been expanded and technique has evolved, and Alvarez has been at the forefront of those developments both in thinking and in day-to-day practice in the consulting room. (She was one of the first child psychoanalytic workers, for instance, to allow the video camera into the consulting room in order to further research with the most profoundly ill of her young patients.) She has also inspired generations of child psychotherapy trainees with her energetic connections between texts and thinking from child development research and psychoanalytic techniques that can be modified in order to reach previously unreachable patients and previously uncharted states of mind. For the developmentalists too there has been a gradual shift away from the laboratory into areas where intersubjectively shared experience, what Alvarez has called "a two-person psychology", is accorded significance.

Gradually, a previously pervasive split between cognitive and emotional processes is being healed, and the way we feel is seen as being crucial to the development of the way we come to know about ourselves and others. By the use of developmental research to cross-validate observations of where clinical change is observed to be affected by technical change, further thinking is stimulated and openness of debate continues. As any reader of this book will have become aware, Alvarez has been a significant force for change and development among colleagues and students around the world. Indeed these developments and linkages are now becoming the accepted currency of clinical work and thinking across training schools.

This chapter is not an attempt to encompass the historical developments or the full implications of increasing cross-fertilisation between the different fields. It is rather an idiosyncratic bringing together of research findings and clinical connections, underpinned by what Bion ([1962] 1967) called the K link: the struggle for understanding for its own sake, rather than simply for knowing about knowing. As Winnicott (1965: 19) said: "What we do in therapy is to attempt to imitate the natural process that characterises any mother with her own infant. If I am right, it is the mother–infant couple that can teach us the basic principles on which we may base our therapeutic work when we are treating children whose early mothering was not 'good enough' or was 'interrupted'." The micro-analysis possible through technological advances in the field of film and video, for example, has enabled researchers to trace moment-by-moment fluctuations in this first relationship (which had previously only been closely observed by psychoanalytically trained students with infant observation). Thus in the ordinary good-enough relationship can be seen factors which *in extremis* can generate pathology.

John Bowlby, father of Attachment Theory, recalled how when he qualified as an analyst in 1937, analysts "were occupied in exploring the fantasy world of adults and children. It was regarded as almost outside the proper interest of an analyst to give systematic attention to a person's real experiences" (Bowlby, 1979: 43). It was Bowlby's ethological approach and his work on the need of young children for an emotionally close and secure relationship that made the first substantial contribution to bringing closer the worlds of psychoanalysis and developmental psychology. While some of Bowlby's formulations about monotropism and a critical period for bonding have been modified, attachment theory came to have a powerful impact on psychoanalytic thinking as well as on childcare practice. "It is just as necessary for analysts to study the way a child is really treated as it is to study the internal representations he has ... the principal focus of our studies should be the interaction of the one with the other' (Bowlby, 1979: 43).

Freud, too, had earlier acknowledged the importance of the external world: "We are obliged to pay as much attention in our case histories to the purely human and social circumstances of our patients as to the somatic data ... Above all, our interest will be directed towards the family circumstances"

(Freud, 1916). In his later work he elaborated the relationship between instinctual life and the capacity for contact with reality and the development of rational thought. Although it has been popularly supposed that Klein tended to ignore external factors, she did actually refer to the impact of the environment as being of major importance, underlining that it was indeed the loving and understanding impulses of the mother which could help mitigate internal states of persecution which would otherwise overwhelm the baby (Klein, 1952). And it was Winnicott who underlined the interactional nature of early development in his now enshrined dictum "There is no such thing as a baby, only a baby with someone" (Winnicott, 1965: 5).

Knots: tied, retied and untied

I want to continue this chapter by illustrating under a series of headings themes where psychoanalysis and child development research have been mutually illuminating, beginning by a quotation from *The Shipping News* (Proulx, 1993). The author heads each chapter of the book, which describes a man's rediscovery of his sense of self and place by returning both actually and metaphorically to "Newfoundland", with a quotation from *The Ashley Book of Knots*. There is a description of one such knot which I think illustrates most aptly the complexity and profundity of personality development, rooted as it is in the framework of interpersonal relatedness. "In a knot of eight crossings, which is about the average size knot, there are 256 different 'over and under' arrangements possible. Make only one change in this 'over and under' sequence and either an entirely different knot is made or no knot at all may result" (Proulx, 1993: frontispiece). What I will be thinking about in this chapter are just some of the ways in which a sense of self develops, and some of the ways in which different patterns of 'over and under' may produce different results, or, in more extreme circumstances, may result in an absence of binding knots to integrate the personality.

Primary autism: a revision in thinking

Developmental pioneers such as Piaget and Spitz in the 1940s drew up an unfolding picture of what they called "norms of development". One of their now disproved claims was that infants looked at nothing in particular until they were at least six weeks old. Subsequent researchers such as Bower (1974), Papousek and Papousek (1975), Trevarthen (1979) and Brazelton and Nugent (1989) discovered that things were actually not so barren in the perceptual world of the newborn baby: that babies are in fact born with capacities to relate, reach out, imitate and search from the beginning. In short, Klein's statement (Klein, 1952: 2) that the infant is "a human object related from birth" has been completely and fully validated. Babies look more often at moving faces than at still ones, more often at still faces than random patterns, can nevertheless amazingly enough from a pattern of lights attached to the limbs of baby boys and girls deduce their sex. The list of their competencies is endless and extraordinary, far way from that earlier notion of the young baby as a sort of mindless blob, existing in a world of internal vacancy, in a sense not yet fully born.

One of the notions which persisted was that of a phase of primary autism into which each newborn entered, and out of which he naturally emerged in a good-enough environment at a later stage. However, developmental straight lines have given way to the notion of states, not stages, developmental loops where mental states are more variable, flexible and diverse. Indeed Meltzer (1988) made the radical suggestion that a baby following a good-enough birth experience enters into the depressive position from the beginning, only to retreat in the face of his mother's now unknowable and irretrievable "inside" into a more paranoid frame of mind. Researchers working with neonates discovered that from the beginning they are drawn to imitate their caretakers, to reach out in what Proner (2000) suggested could be called "protomental synchrony" as a precursor to projective identification and thus to a building-up through introjection of an internal world.

In one of her last public presentations, given at the Association of Child Psychotherapy conference and subsequently published in their journal (Tustin, 1994), Frances Tustin described "The Perpetuation of an Error" about primary autism, tracing it back to Freud's formulation of a narcis-sistically enclosed bird's egg feeding itself as being a phase of normal development. She notes Mahler's elaboration of this idea when she talked of the infant's "inborn unresponsiveness" and of a normal symbiotic phase. Tustin thought that the chief benefits in terms of treatment which would be brought about by this revision of thinking would be that therapists would be firmer and less indulgent in their approach, more active to correct deviant tendencies and more aware that an important part of early learning is the gradually coming to terms with the frustration and disillusion involved in separating from a pathological symbiosis designed to deny "two-ness", rather than from a regressive but normal state. When I worked intensively with a post-autistic adolescent boy it was Alvarez who pointed me in the direction of child development texts to indicate how normal mothers of normal children claim and reclaim the attention of their babies in order to build up an ongoing sense of relationship, safety and meaning. While these texts had indeed been a part of my pre-clinical studies, the idea that they could be drawn upon to modify technique when thinking about profound disturbance was a revelation to me. Alvarez went on to expound these ideas fully (Alvarez 1992), and the notion of "reclamation" has now become respectable when previously it had sometimes been felt to be suspiciously like the analyst's acting out.

My patient, whom I shall call Joe, had been prematurely born, one of twins. While his healthy sister had gone home with their mother, Joe had remained for three weeks, unheld, in an incubator. (For a fuller description of this treatment see Edwards, 1994, 1999.) When he arrived home he was, as his mother said, "stiff with terror"; he refused the bottle, and could only be fed facing away from her. This could indeed be what Tustin (1994: 12) described as "the stress associated with a traumatic disruption" felt by an infant who perhaps constitutionally had been striving to perpetuate the "dual unity" of the womb, and who felt catastrophically separated from both his mother and his twin sister by premature birth. The turning away developed from a pathological manoeuvre in the face of unbearable trauma into a chronic state, which included autistic rituals, obsessive behaviour, inappropriate social boundaries and fear of change. While Ogden (1997: 179) sees what he calls "auto-sensuous isolation" as being "an ongoing facet of all human experience that serves as a form of buffer against the continual strain of being alive in the world of human beings", pathological autism represents a more radical withdrawal where, as he says, "the infant moves beyond the 'gravitational pull' of human relatedness and 'floats' off into a realm of impenetrable, uninterrupted non-being". In his first assessment session, Joe told me of his tendency to "sort of go off into distance", a strategy which denuded him of ego strength. I have written elsewhere about Joe's gradual journey towards solid ground (he feared black holes and imagined there was a hole in the cupboard under the sink in the consulting room). What I want to do here is to think about what Tustin called the "firm love" needed when autism is not considered a normal if regressive state, and where the ordinary claiming behaviour of the mothering aspect of the therapist is vital to bring the autistic infant in the patient into the world of "two-ness", with all its pains as well as its delights. This reclaiming function could be seen, as Houzel (Chapter 4, this volume) has pointed out, as the paternal quality inherent in the capacity for reverie.

At his birth, Joe's preconceptions had not been met with realisations, which Bion maintains are essential for thought to develop, but with what must have seemed to him a dark and incomprehensible void – the black hole. Frances Tustin (1972, 1981) explored the idea of the black hole, the traumatic separation, in her work with children with autism. Joe retreated into narcissism and autistic defences, and it was my task to monitor each tiny change in his mood, go for the bits of feeling that came and went during each session, and to treat his smallest communications as though they had meaning, in the way Brazelton and Nugent (1989) describe ordinary mothers as doing. Racker (1968: 42) talked of "the analytic microscopy" which relates to this ordinary interaction as well as to the analytic relationship when he talks of "our growing capacity to understand and recognise the unconscious process underlying the patient's every phrase and mental movement, each silence, each change of rhythm and voice".

As Joe's therapist my counter-transference was often one of fragmentation, but also of featureless boredom, as Joe "went off into distance". He used his watch to regulate our increasing contact, and it was important for me not to see this simply as a defensive turning away but as a beginning sense of self-regulation where, as the developmentalists have shown, periods of digestion are needed in order to process both helpful and difficult moments in the mother–infant "dance" (Stern, 1984). In sessions where his sense of persecution made him fear the sound of wind outside the window, it was necessary for me to be aware of interpreting his need for safety in our room before I began to talk about his persecutory fears. In this way, slowly and painfully, he was able to take his first steps along the road of relating to me as an object who could respect his need for distance while being firm about helping him to maintain rather than sever contact when he felt claustrophobically overwhelmed, which I took to be a projection of his own powerful ambivalence about wanting to communicate to me something of his enormous desires as well as fears in relation to his object. Gradually he was able to be more self-observant as a result of my almost micro-analytic observations alongside interpretations about the meaning of his "rituals" – meanings which as Alvarez (1992) has observed may change within a session as the patient feels at least partially understood as well as firmly held. At the end of one session where the contact between us had been fleeting, fluctuating and hard to maintain, Joe was able to acknowledge "I do look at my watch a lot, don't I? I must try to control it." Self-containment is the end result of repeated experiences of being firmly held and contained by an object who seeks as far as she is able to contain and process and where necessary de-toxify the baby's pleasures and terrors during the first months of life.

Life inside, and inside life

Bion (1978: 29) wondered "when psychiatrists and psycho-analysts will catch up with the foetus". When would they be able to bear to see and think about life (including psychological life) in the womb as being much more on a continuum pre- and post-birth than as being somehow set in motion by what Freud had called "the impressive caesura of birth"? Has the full-term foetus, Bion asked, no character or personality? And what effect would the trauma of birth have upon this emerging personality?

> The first thing to do is to be aware of its existence. If there can be vestiges of what a surgeon would call "branchial clefts"; if, in our development, we do indeed go through these peculiar stages of fishy ancestry, amphibian ancestry and so on, and it shows signs in our bodies, then why not in our minds? ... what sort of mental life can you observe in a premature infant? Can you assume that you are not dealing with a premature baby, a physiological object, but a premature mind?
>
> (Bion, 1978: 27)

The development and routine use of ultrasound scans in pregnancy opened up the world inside the womb, and obstetric researchers such as Liley (1972) described the world of a "splendidly functioning foetus", existing in a humid microclimate neither stupefied nor comatose, but in a situation of cyclical activity. He yawns, he swallows, he sucks his thumb, he opens his mouth and turns towards the stimulus of an abdominal stroke. His face and mouth are the only parts of his body that the infant can reliably locate in space after birth, and the mouth remains an important early tool of exploration. While earlier, psychoanalytic workers had focused on the primacy of the mouth and orality, child development research in cross-sensory information co-ordination (Bower 1974; Stern 1984) led us to understand that, while not minimising the importance of the mouth, it was vital to recognise the importance that the eyes, ears and nose have too in taking in or shutting out the earliest experiences, even before physical birth.

Piontelli (1992), with a background both in medicine and psychoanalysis, decided to take up the opportunity to observe life within the womb via ultrasound and think about the specific issues which might be involved in terms of possible precocious psychological life for twin foetuses. She followed this up by classic infant observation weekly for a year and more sporadic observations subsequently. She had been drawn into the work when she met up with what she took to be vivid fantasies and representations of life inside the womb and of birth in her adult patients. She documented a remarkable pre- and post-natal continuity in the twins she observed, where foetuses showed characteristic ways of behaving which endured over time in spite of (or perhaps in some cases because of) the nature of their subsequent environment. Yet as she is at pains to point out, the closeness to primitive functioning in the consulting room is only apparent: severe regression will also carry with it something different from the earlier non-pathological stage, which has been the result of experiences, distorted and unmodified, in later life. While there are questions raised by Piontelli's work in terms of the effects of the ultrasound observations on parents and their fantasies, and the attribution of adult meanings to a being not yet in a social environment in the way we would normally conceive of this, her longitudinal study seems to show quite clearly incipient personalities which unfold over time.

My patient Joe had experienced no physical continuity after his traumatic birth, where the idea of a caesura as a temporary stop or pause seems less relevant than the idea of something being dramatically cut off and thus also expelled from his own mind. Suddenly he was separated from the proto-experience of "another" in the womb, to become isolated of necessity in the mechanical "womb" of the incubator. Up to when he was six or seven years old he would stop people in the street and express the fear of things "leaking down". This may have been the remnants of a fantasy around tube-feeding, where the equipment in place intended for his survival might have become in his mind the final persecutory design to rob him of his life-blood as well as of his mother and sister. At the time he came into treatment there was little relationship between them. Joe remained stubbornly in the womb of his home while his sister was engaged in appropriate adolescent exploration. One could hypothesise that at the time of flux and the search for identity which characterise adolescence, Joe was indeed a convenient container or receptacle for the uncomfortable, the odd and the "handicapped" parts of his potential peer group. However, over the time of his treatment his parents observed a narrowing gap between the twins. It was as if being able to recreate a space and go over separations in a less catastrophic way enabled Joe to recapitulate something which had been cut off and made unavailable for thinking, and so move closer to the sister he may have thought unconsciously he had lost. Sorensen (2000) describes what she calls *transition facilitating behaviour*, where the mother offers a bridge in order to integrate splits in the baby's world. These bridges are created in relation to four areas of experience: sensory, temporal/spatial, relational and emotional state. They occur both physically and linguistically, and are built repeatedly in different settings and with different events, before the behaviour can be taken in to become a self-containing internal function. My work with Joe was developmentally informed, and consisted of different ways of building a bridge towards the previously unthinkable – the split-off catastrophe of his birth, as it was enacted in his "mindless" states in the consulting room. However, his therapy with me was ended prematurely by him, as had been some previous work done when he was in primary school. Perhaps, although some thinking and reclamation had provided a measure of integration, the power of the repetition compulsion was too great and was not able to be held and analysed. But while one could think of the primary separation and differentiation as being re-enacted in a similarly dramatic way in the therapy despite my best endeavours, Joe did not in fact become mindless. He made it clear as he said in the last session, "You've got a good mind, you know", that he had indeed found that he could use his own. He continued to develop and now lives independently from his parents, which is an outcome they had not previously been allowing themselves to hope for.

Sound, rhythm and musicality

From the first hour of life infants have been shown to move in synchrony with human speech (Condon and Sander, 1974). Neurophysiological research (Prechtl, 1989) has shown that the capacity to hear has already been completely developed in a four-month old foetus, so that he can discriminate the medium and high sound frequencies present in the mother's voice, whereas the low-frequency sounds such as her breathing and heartbeat can be heard even earlier. There is evidence of the cyclical effect on the foetus of these stimuli: the low-frequency sounds slow down foetal motion whereas the high and medium frequencies (the mother's voice) are enlivening and stimulating. So already in the womb some discrimination is possible, but what might this mean? Maiello (1995) speculates on the possibility that the mother's voice, heard by the foetus as "coming and going" within the intra-uterine environment, provides at least some proto-experience of absence and loss. The voice, like the breast after birth, will be sometimes present and sometimes absent, generating feelings both of well-being and anxiety. She quotes the psychoanalyst Mancia who suggested that this formation of what he called "a proto-mental nucleus" could enable the foetus to create an internal object with sound qualities from the maternal voice, which become the beginnings of preconceptions about the breast. He says "it is in fact only if the foetus has been able to elaborate external stimuli making internal representations of these, that we can explain the newborn's preparation for meeting reality, first of all the maternal breast" (Maiello, 1995). Perhaps this use of sound as a containing object could be the precursor for the later formation of the containing "skin" of the mother's attention for the neonate. One might also speculate too on the voice of the father, which could give the foetus the proto-experience of the couple, possibly the distant precursor of later Oedipal struggles. Proner (2000: 59) quotes an observation of a new-born baby who quivers in expectation when he hears his mother's voice: "His fingers open up like his mouth and the arching and opening of his eyes express an entire bodily wave like the most primitive sea-hydra opening up to plankton. Is this the earliest form of projection?"

Maiello quotes two dreams from adult patients which she feels illustrate the qualities of pre-natal experience: a dream of a dancing couple moving in perfect accord, and of a girl walking in a silent forest, hearing as from afar the dropping of a fir-cone and the sound of her own footsteps. My patient Joe reported only one dream in the course of his treatment with me. It was a dream which he said had been repeated many times: of being on a train, of hearing the noise of the train and then the train slowing down. "Everything's going real slow and I'm really small, I'm well scared." He said he often felt very small in relation to objects in the room. At the time of seeing him and when I first wrote about this subsequently, I was linking this with the infinite slowing down of time which is a constituent in theoretical physics of the black hole, defined as "a gravitationally collapsed object". I wondered later about this dream, so often repeated, and whether it might be related to the pre-cipitation of anxiety around Joe's premature birth, where the "train noises" of his mother's body seemed to slow down in a terrifying way, rather as people describe the slowing-down of events before an accident, before he was ejected into a new and, for him, terrifying world, uncontained and feeling tiny and totally helpless in relation to the huge new artificial space of the incubator, rather than being held in his mother's arms. Later work I was able to do with a six-year-old adopted boy who had been born prematurely to a heroin-addicted mother (Edwards, 2000) enabled me to think further about this, as the boy, after some terms of therapy, began to construct spaceships in which I had to drive from the rear seat. He would be at the front, navigating, and would suddenly be hurled with great force out of the ship, to land shuddering on the therapy room floor. I took this to be an enactment of the devastation he had felt as he was hurled into outer space from his mother's womb, and it made me think again of Joe's terror, and his feeling of being infinitely tiny in an alien world. Maiello ([1997] 1998) also describes work with an autistic girl where miscarriage had been a recurring threat in the womb, who hung onto a table leg in an effort to prevent being thrown out into the world. She, like Joe, had been less constitutionally strong than my six-year-old patient, who had become hyperactive as a defence, and she had retreated into an autistic state, evacuating her capacity to think about the unthinkable trauma which had not been able to be processed by a "premature mind".

As already mentioned, from the first hour of life babies have been shown to move synchronously with their mother's voice. Trevarthen (1979), among others, has demonstrated what he proposed to be an innate capacity for intersubjectivity – in other words the capacity to express rudimentary intentions and feelings, and to expect these to be present in and communicable by the other. In micro-analysis of mothers' speech patterns he has been able to show that music, like speech, can have rhythms which can be defined in terms of affect. A depressed mother, even when she is consciously trying to enliven her child, will have an audiological pattern which is largo rather than andante. Murray (1991) published the results of her work with post-natally depressed mothers and their 18-month-old infants. It was found that these infants were less likely to be securely attached, and to demonstrate mild behavioural difficulties such as sleep disturbance. They showed more distress on separation and were more hesitant to explore than those in a control group. If we think of the "dance" between mother and infant as she elaborates on her infant's signals as being a changing wave of fluctuating intensity and amplitude, it would seem that the depressed largo rhythm of a mother unable to dance in synchrony with her infant has implications for his capacity to develop internal resilience, to communicate and to play. And in Joe's case, he had turned away from his mother when he returned home, so that his determined sabotaging of her efforts to relate had a similar effect.

Linking up these ideas of musicality and sound and silence in relation to separation, I want to end by thinking about Joe's undoubted progress during the work, despite its premature end. As over time he became more contained within the structure of the therapy and able to think about finding the object rather than losing it and himself down a black hole, he became interested himself in music. A particular piece of music by a jazz musician he admired became, as it were, the leitmotif of the treatment: "On Solid Ground". He was able to encounter within himself an increasing sense of something solid as opposed to terrifying liquidity. He talked increasingly about other music too, and became interested in classical musicians, perhaps also in relation to a fantasy about me, linked with a father-musician to form a creative couple who could begin to be internalised as the dance devolved from two to three.

> He asked me "Do you like Beethoven and Mozart?" ... He looked interested but not as if expecting an answer at that point. "You can hear the silence in between and then it comes in, da da da DA"!

Just as the silences between the sessions could now be perceived as part of the pattern, so he could begin to trust in the continuity of himself and me "in between": that we could still exist in the silence between the sessions.

Final remarks

As other chapters in this book also emphasise, Alvarez has been a vivifying and intellectually stimulating influence on my own clinical work and my thinking, particularly with reference to the importance of taking a micro-analytic approach to the patient's material which is often pre-verbal. This approach needs to be sustained for much longer with deprived and borderline individuals. Her conviction has been amply borne out by neuro-biological research in terms of the relation between projective identification, earliest communications and the development of the right brain in both patient and therapist (see Schore, Chapter 5 this volume). Her approach might be compared to Primo Levi's description of chemistry:

> We must distrust the almost-the-same, the practically identical, the approximate ... all surrogates and all patchwork. The differences can be small, but they can lead to radically different consequences ... the chemist's trade consists in good part in being aware of these differences, knowing them close up, and seeing their effects. And not only the chemist's trade.
>
> (Levi, 1986: 60)

Note

A previous version of this chapter was presented to an IPC Scientific Meeting at the Westminster Pastoral Foundation in October 1995.

References

Alvarez, A. (1992) *Live Company*, London, Routledge.
Alvarez, A. and Reid, S. (1999) *Autism and Personality*, London, Routledge.
Bick, E. (1968) "The Experience of Skin in Early Object Relations", *International Journal of Psychoanalysis*, 49: 484–8.

Bion, W. ([1962] 1967) "A Theory of Thinking", in *Second Thoughts*, London, Hogarth.

Bower, T. (1974) *Development in Infancy*, San Francisco, W.H. Freeman.

Bowlby, J. (1979) *The Making and Breaking of Affectional Bonds*. London: Tavistock.

Brazelton, T.B. and Nugent, J.K. (1989) "Preventive Interventions with Infants and Families", *Infant Mental Health Journal*, 10 (2): 84–99.

Broucek, F. (1979) "Efficacy in Infancy", *International Journal of Psychoanalysis*, 60: 311–316.

Condon, W.S. & Sander, L.S. (1974) "Neonate Movement is Synchronised with Adult Speech", *Science*, 183.

Edwards, J. (1994) "Towards Solid Ground", *Journal of Child Psychotherapy*, 20 (1): 57–83.

Edwards, J. (1999) "Joe: An Adolescent's Request for a Second Course of Psychotherapy", in A. Alvarez and S. Reid, *Autism and Personality*, London, Routledge.

Edwards, J. (2000) "On Being Dropped and Picked Up: Adopted Children and their Internal Objects", *Journal of Child Psychotherapy*, 26 (3): 349–367.

Freud, S. (1916) *Introductory Lectures on Psychoanalysis*, (1963), Standard Edition 15, London, Hogarth Press.

Kernberg, O. (1975) *Borderline Conditions and Pathological Narcissism*, New York, Aronson Inc.

Klein, M. (1952) "On Observing the Behaviour of Young Infants", in *The Development of Psychoanalysis*, London, Hogarth.

Klein, M. (1952) "Some Theoretical Conclusions, Regarding the Emotional Life of the Infant", *Envy and Gratitude and Other Works, 1946–63*, London, Hogarth Press.

Levi, P. (1986) *The Periodic Table* (R. Rosenthal, trans.), London, Abacus (first published in 1975).

Liley, A.W. (1972) "The Foetus as a Personality", *Australia and New Zealand Journal of Psychiatry*, no. 6: 99–105.

Maiello, S. (1995) "The Sound-object", *Journal of Child Psychotherapy*, 21 (1): 23–41.

Maiello, S. ([1997] 1998) "Trauma prenatale e autismo", *Richard e Piggle* (Vol. 3: 31–47).

Meltzer, D. (1988) Aesthetic Conflict: Its Place in Development", in D. Meltzer and M.H. Williams, *The Apprehension of Beauty*, Strath Tay, Clunie Press.

Murray, L. (1991) "Intersubjectivity, Object Relations Theory and Empirical Evidence from Mother–Infant Interactions", *Infant Mental Health Journal*, 91 (vol. 12): 219–232.

Ogden, T.H. (1997) "Some Theoretical Comments on Personal Isolation", in T. Mitrani & T.L. Mitrani, *Encounters with Autistic States*, Northvale, N.J., Aronson.

Papousek, H. and Papousek, M. (1975) "Cognitive Aspects of Preverbal Social Interaction between Human Infants and Adults", CIBA Foundation Symposium, *Parent/Infant Interaction*, New York, Associated Scientific Pubs.

Piontelli, A. (1992) *From Foetus to Child*, London, Routledge.

Prechtl, H.F.R. (1989) "Foetal Behaviour", in A. Hill and J. Volpe (eds) *Foetal Neurology*, New York, Raven Press.

Proner, K. (2000) "Protomental Synchrony: Some Thoughts on the Earliest Identification Processes in a Neonate", *Infant Observation*, 3 (2): 55–65.

Proulx, E.A. (1993) *The Shipping News*, London, Fourth Estate.

Racker, H. (1968) *Transference and Countertransference*, London, Karnac.

Sorensen, P. (2000) "Observations of Transition-Facilitating Behaviour: Developmental and Theoretical Implications", *Infant Observation*, 3 (2): 46–54.

Stern, D. (1984) *The Interpersonal World of the Infant*, New York, Basic Books.

Trevarthen, C. (1979) "Communication and Cooperation in Early Infancy: A Description of Primary Intersubjectivity", in M. Bulowa (ed.) *Before Speech: The Beginnings of Communication*, Cambridge, Cambridge University Press.

Turgenev, I. (1860) *First Love* (first published in Great Britain as *Love and Death* 1982), London, Folio Society.

Tustin, F. (1972) *Autism and Childhood Psychosis*, London, Hogarth Press.

Tustin, F. (1981) "Psychological Birth and Psychological Catastrophe", in J. Grotstein (ed.) *Do I Dare Disturb the Universe?*, Beverly Hills, Calif.: Caesura Press.

Tustin, F. (1994) "The Perpetuation of an Error", *Journal of Child Psychotherapy*, 20 (1): 3–21.

Winnicott, D. (1965) "The Relationship of a Mother to her Baby at the Beginning", *The Family and Individual Development*, London, Tavistock Publications.

Chapter 13

Glimpses of what might have been

A traumatised autistic boy's struggle to have a mind

Trudy Klauber

Anne Alvarez (e.g. 1992, 1999) has written much about the deficit in self and object, understood through working with severely developmentally delayed and disordered children, whatever the aetiology of their symptoms. Her discoveries have led her to question the Kleinian technique of going for the deepest anxiety in very disturbed patients, who are often concrete and highly selective in what they are able to hear or take in. These children lack a helpful, vitalising, interested, "good" object. Indeed their internal object may be very distant, very flat or extremely hostile. They mistake their internal situation for the facts of external reality. They can, in Alvarez's view, be driven mad by interpretations which assume a developmental stage they have not yet attained. They do not have "defences" which need to be taken down, they need their defences as protection while something healthier is constructed (op.cit.). She has illustrated over the years that psychoanalytic work with these children requires the greatest care in observing the total situation (Joseph 1985). She writes of the need to build primary experience with patients, in the paranoid–schizoid position, in order to help them develop within it before they can move on. Her detailed explorations, linking research into mother–child interaction with the theories of Klein and Bion, provide a map for exploration of development where there is delay and for work *towards* the stage where psychoanalysis with children began in the 1930s, 1940s and 1950s.

Alvarez has enabled us to borrow from her imagination, her vitality and her dogged pursuit of answers to her own questions. This has included looking back at her own early clinical cases to think about why some patients were *not* always helped. She has pursued the question of using the counter-transference in order, for example, to look cold cruelty in the eye when she saw it in a child patient (Alvarez 1995), without becoming a persecutor or providing confirmation that despair is all (1988). She has encouraged a generation of child psychotherapists whom she has taught or supervised to pay a particular attention to their countertransference, and to the grammar and punctuation of their interpretations, looking again and again for the patient's response to inform what is next said or *not said*. She has used the psychological research into child development to look at earlier and earlier elements of interaction between mothers and babies, to help us to understand what are the primary building blocks of development which promote healthy interaction and healthy projection and introjection.

For myself, her teaching has provoked extremely painful questions about what is really clinically effective and has simultaneously provided a truly supportive framework for work with patients such as the boy whose clinical material illustrates this chapter. She underlines the need for the powerful tools provided by developing skills in infant observation (e.g. Bick 1963; Miller *et al*. 1989; Waddell 1987; Reid 1997) which encourage a recognition of the validity of the observer's subjective experience in understanding the experience of very young infants. Bion's concept of containment (1962) illustrates the importance of a therapist who really takes in what is going on, feels it, and is enabled not to enact something detrimental to growth. Bion's influence on Alvarez is enormous. She feels and names experiences which we all seek to turn from a little. She uses them to help her to identify with her patient, to see and experience the world from his perspective, and to inform the what, the how, the when and the why of her interpretation.

The need for a container with many qualities is alluded to throughout Alvarez's writing and work. In a paper on failures to link (1998), her emphasis is on deficit and its importance, and she suggests that there may be an *absence* of links and not always an attack on already established connections. She writes explicitly or implicitly about the qualities of the object in relation to *step by step building* for internalisation, an object with determination, mental space, a sense of time, liveliness, interest; an object more than reminiscent of Alvarez herself. Hers is a model of the container/therapist working at the highest pitch of alertness, observation and attention to the countertransference. One can feel, in Alvarez's description of her attempts to link with her patient, Samuel, her attunement with his wild and often frenzied state and her willingness to work almost tirelessly for a brief moment of proto play, a hint of interest or a few seconds of interaction.

The willingness to work in such a way allows us further windows into the worlds of autistic, psychotic and traumatised children. The work is sometimes at the developmental level of the newborn or young infant and the mother, while it is also tuned into those areas of the mind which are more advanced in their development.

This is "developmentally informed psychotherapy" (Alvarez 1999). The developments in the patient I am writing about have given me high hopes at times. I have seen evidence, in the consulting room, of an intact imagination, intact ability to talk relatively appropriately, and to communicate feeling. And I have seen the evidence melt like snow in spring. Perhaps Alvarez has forged part of the key to the next step: technical and theoretical developments in psychoanalytic psychotherapy with patients at the earliest stages of the paranoid schizoid position; in Kleinian terms at the very beginning of psychic life. She has also been a key figure in allowing us to bear glimpses of what-might-have-been in order to facilitate steps towards a more human existence both for such tragic children and their suffering families.

Twiddling, smoothing and getting away

Billy began intensive psychotherapy three times a week when he was five. He had a cherubic face, wide eyes, rosy cheeks and a haircut which emphasised a toddler innocence and vulnerability. He could also look extremely odd. He would often grin, apparently cheerful, compulsively shuffling or twiddling similar toys or his own fingers. After years of enforced observation of these "village-idiot moments" flicking, twiddling and grinning, I came to see that he was obliterating bumps, protrusions and texture; he wanted a world smooth and without ripples. There seemed to be an omnipotent delusion that he could make it so and then merge seamlessly with people and things in a bump-free, lump-free, world, free of felt emotion or meaningful experience. There were times when he tried to obliterate the tiny bumps in the carpet, the curls in my hair, or to pull off my nose. In verbal moments years later he began to cry out, "Make the bumps go away", in a high, strangulated voice.

I used many of Alvarez's ideas, including "traffic policing", encouraging forward the more relational, playful hints and discouraging the stereotypies and deadliness. I amplified any tiny signs of life, playfulness and curiosity, and there were developments. In moments of contact, he seemed like an inexperienced baby. The active technique was effective. Often he would sit on my knee, and play with my necklace, looking into my eyes for a few seconds and, very occasionally humming the hint of a tune or uttering what sounded like snatches from songs or stories which often I couldn't quite catch. I sang lots of things to him about himself and what I thought I observed. I also used nursery rhymes. On occasional good days I had the most moving and enjoyable sessions and felt filled with optimism.

I also began to notice how frequently I found myself flooded with anger which was difficult to manage within myself, while Billy had a funny smile on his face. He seemed to be caught up in a perverse, possibly masochistic satisfaction. The look seemed quite cynical, even calculating and mocking of my efforts; I felt he was expecting that I would give up and I had a strong reaction against him, feeling that he preferred his autistic state to any connection with me despite my heroic efforts. I thought of him as a boy who *chose* autism,[1] rejecting the option of a relationship with me. I also felt that if he *could* express some of the anger, and own it, then he could also get a grip on his own life, reaching out towards his object; much of his ego function seemed to be projected outside himself into the world and me, both perceived to be dangerous in our bumpiness. He would flinch when I made a quicker movement or gesture, which I interpreted to myself as his paranoid fear of me, projectively identified with all the anger and aggression.

I felt that I operated inside myself in mental slow motion and it took a very long time to be able to think about what might have been going on. I knew, from my own regular work with his mother (who kept me informed of Billy's life at home and at school), how very angry she too could feel at times and how complex her anger was. She knew it included her anger with Billy because she felt so tantalised and attacked by the unpredictable presence of the glimpses of the able-minded boy. It was exacerbated, as any parent's might be, by the disproportionate effort she invested for so little return (Klauber 1999).

The terror of connection

When Billy was eight years old, his father had to work away on a new venture, so he came home only at weekends, when he could. By this time Billy was less passive in anxiety-provoking situations. He was more restless and sleepless when his father was away, he said, "Daddy" quite a lot to me and at home, and I found it very helpful to know his father's schedule and to talk about it while working with him on his growing understanding of the pattern of his psychotherapy week. He responded with interest to my interpretations that I should not go away to work myself – which I felt he equated with my own and his father's absences in his life. "Don't go to work today", became a rhythmic chant which I heard him whispering to himself very softly, recognising sometimes the tone and rhythm alone.

Around this time, occasionally, to my surprise, he would start to hum a tune or to sing something. For a while it was "Humpty Dumpty" – notably "couldn't put Humpty together again'. If I echoed a whole verse back to him he would sometimes provide the last word of each line. Gradually I came to think that the impossibility of putting Humpty together again described the autistic fear which Tustin ([1981] 1992: 139) writes about – fear of something broken and irreparable, something gone forever. The implication was that separation and separateness are a tragic, unbearably painful wound when two are ripped apart, described by Tustin as the "black hole with the nasty prick" (1986: 36). Billy often looked tragically close to tears after singing, as if he equated feeling only with this tragic state.

Billy's father's work away from home involved travelling by plane. Billy made several plane trips to see him, travelling with his mother. When he saw his father he would turn his back and run away, leaving his father baffled and very hurt.

He seemed, on the plane trips, to be impossibly overexcited and uncontrollable to his understandably anxious, overburdened mother. It was often well-nigh impossible to imagine that Billy *was* actually terrified; he was so difficult. I began to use direct play rather practically to prepare him for his weekend flights. I sat him on my lap as if I were the plane seat and my arms the safety belt to be fastened in flight. I would describe the preparations, make take-off noises, offer imaginary drinks like the flight-attendant and imitate the noises of landing. He became better on the flights. I came to believe that he was really deeply afraid, and that the wild overexcitement was related to an absolute conviction that no supportive object would contain his terror.

I had bought him a toy aeroplane to help. He threw it out of the window. One day he held up his hands, palms flat towards the ceiling and I felt immediately certain that he was holding the sky up, fearing it would fall. I felt a sudden and absolute conviction that flying meant, for Billy, that he, Daddy, the plane and the sky would fall down. I told him what I thought and he calmed down.

I took a part of a Noah's Ark toy, stood Noah on it and flew it gently up, along, and let it land. He watched and listened. Towards the end of the session he picked it up and flew it himself for a minute; I was mesmerised. Then he became wild and giggly, jumping up and down until he stopped himself by suddenly biting deeply into his own hand.

He could then join in when I talked about Daddy-away and Daddy-coming-back-again. He could echo, "Back again" on good days – both about Daddy's return home and about his next session coming – but most of the time I felt his energy was concentrated on getting away, moving away on not being really present, and that I was not sufficiently substantial to make a difference for him.

A breakthrough in understanding more about the projected anger and the psychotic nature of his terror of contact came about a term later. He began to spend a lot of time gazing at the tall, leafy trees outside my window and at their shadows reflected in the afternoon sunshine on the wall. He seemed quiet but I began to know, with conviction, that he was not blank in these moments, but in terror of the shadows and the trees themselves. I talked to him about this, saying that the shadows were only shadows. I touched them on the wall and he came, apparently willingly, with me to touch the place where they were reflected. At times he giggled crazily and could not stop; I needed to offer him a hand or an arm to hold to calm him down again. I used phrases like, "Calm down", and "It's all right", and he listened and later echoed them himself. He would look at the trees with me, and if there was not too much wind or rain he *could* sustain the looking and I could talk about the trees staying outside, not coming in, "Not have a great fall" (Humpty Dumpty).

His mother gave me some hope that the work was having an impact outside. She reported that Billy had stood, apparently relatively calm, beside a tree, during a family walk, looking up at it and saying, to her astonishment, "Tree – boing." He seemed tense and still. She knew about his terror of trees and said, "No Billy, it won't go boing. It's standing; it's strong." They walked on and came back on the same path. She heard him, standing at the foot of the tree using a quite different, lighter, almost playful tone. "Tree,

tree–boing, tree–boing", as he held his arms up like branches and let them drop, looked up again at the real thing and doing it again. For his parents and myself, these rare moments sustained some hope.

History

The waters broke a few days before term in his mother's pregnancy with Billy, her first child. Labour did not follow and she had to stay in hospital waiting. The baby was monitored and seemed fine. *Four and a half days later* Billy was born by emergency caesarean section; his mother had a severe infection. The baby seemed healthy and took well to the breast. Within two weeks his mother developed a breast abscess and he was bottle-fed until the infection cleared up. Breast-feeding was resumed successfully. With hind-sight, and comparing him with his younger brother, the mother recognised that Billy had not been a vigorous feeder, and that he had been easily dis-tressed and was passive. In the early weeks and months there were times when Billy's mother was alone with him while his father worked away from home. She found these times of isolation with Billy very difficult.

Billy was left with a childminder for a couple of days just as he was being weaned, and thereafter he made no further demand for the breast. This kind of withdrawal in the face of loss may well have been characteristic. Billy developed a few single words, some of which disappeared during his second year.

By the time he was two years old autism was suspected. He did not play. He was passive, and tended to move away from adults, often running up and down and "twiddling" two objects together, head down, out of touch. He enjoyed stories and videotapes and could recite chunks of stories; a favourite was Thomas the Tank Engine. He was heard to use the word, "Stuck", when he got into a plastic tunnel at nursery and did not come out. (Henry the Engine got stuck in a tunnel and would not come out; eventually he was bricked in for some time to teach him a lesson.) Billy's borrowings from stories (Rhode 1999: 88) have always seemed to have meaning.

While Billy appeared to be cognitively relatively unimpaired, his passivity meant that, left to himself, he had done very little. The ability to absorb himself in videos, stories and music seem to have been used as the means of withdrawal, although a great deal of content was absorbed in a sponge-like way. It seems as if he has used known and predictable narratives, rhythms and melodies as one way of regulating states of hyperarousal, while he often appeared to be content and quite blank. In such states, when he appeared to outsiders to be good, calm and even contented, his heart was racing and his stomach churning – as I came to know directly and from his parents' reports. He used everything, including the stories, principally as a means of keeping deadly terror out, and with the consequence that the outside world and others were equated with destruction.

Glimpses of what might have been

Billy had lived all his life, I think, in a state of hyperarousal, and hypervigilance. His parents confirmed that most of the time his heart was racing. When he began to be more connected in sessions he began to place the palm of his hand over his heart. From the age of ten he became able to say, "Heart go boom, boom, boom," and "Heart go very fast indeed.' One day, very suddenly, he was making a circular motion with his finger above his stomach and he said, "Washing machine, you're driving me mad. I think you've broken down." The burst into expressive language (using borrowed words) seemed to be a description of feeling broken and mad inside, somatised in his fast heart rate and churning stomach. I gave words to the state I imagined, talking about him feeling very frightened, very scared, upset; he didn't know what it was; he wanted to make it go away. In more than one session he added either "sad" and "bad" to my list of adjectives. (He could not reliably distinguish the two.)

Either I was witnessing the *emergence* of a new capacity to put his somatised feelings into words, or I was being given a glimpse into already-established but only intermittently communicable feeling states. When I talked to him about a feeling in his belly, tickling, going round and round (thinking of butterflies in the stomach), and linked the sensation with feeling frightened and upset, he seemed to listen intently. He seemed to have brushed against the hint of a possibility that he was in communication with an object who might be receptive. The moments of speech came unannounced and equally suddenly disappeared. I was left feeling that I must have imagined he had talked.

More than a year earlier, the compression in his speech had been epitomised by a peculiar expression he used, repeating it very fast and emphasising the sound of the "z" against his lips, "Zzweetroo". After I had heard it many times, in many sessions, I began to repeat it, and ultimately to slow it down, "Zzzzssss … wi … Tru," and finally had the inspiration, "Cross with Trudy." He smiled when I got it.

The image of the breaking-down washing machine suggests a malfunctioning object. Billy's raised heart rate and churning stomach suggest that he could not distinguish between objective and subjective experience. The maddening breakdown in the machine was, in his experience, *inside* him. Perhaps he often experienced my attempts to talk *to* him about his experience as a terrifying invasion. Then the twiddling, the blankness and the idiot-grin could be seen as self-protection against a highly dangerous external world. His own intolerant anger, about separation in particular, seemed further to contribute to the perceived dangers in the world around him.

In the consulting room, at times, sometimes at home with his parents and occasionally at school, with containing teachers and with his music therapist, under *optimum conditions* he seemed integrated and to be functioning under the reality principle. At those times words became a currency for communication, albeit enormously developmentally delayed and in slow motion. For a few moments he was capable of healthy projective identification, and felt contained in Bion's sense (1962). He could even ask questions. He could also freeze in mid-sentence in a most alarming fashion.

When he was eleven I had put a new toy into his toy box: a plastic car with a friction motor. He "vrummed" it. He liked it, he found it could be revved up and go fast across the floor. He got a bit nervous of it in a rather ordinary way as it unpredictably changed direction; he could also recover and play with it again. He revved it and listened to the motor. He looked, revved it again and suddenly, in the perfectly normal voice of an eleven-year-old, he asked: "What makes it make that...?" Silence.

I pursued, "What makes it...?" Silence; grin. "Billy, what makes the car make that...?" No response.

For my own peace of mind I completed the question, "What makes the car make that noise? Where is the noise coming from? You wanted to know. Now you feel too scared; you've forgotten that it's okay." Blank grin; the moment had gone.

Trauma and collapsing space

Just around the time of his twelfth birthday, there were major developments in the clinical material of his sessions. Billy, then pubescent, had been increasingly verbal over time, but he used language more often to shut off communication than to make connections. He was, at the time, remaining at his special school, while his parents searched for suitable secondary provision. He was being bullied in class and was withdrawn from his inexperienced teacher.

In the early sessions of the term, I was filled with frustration and some anger as he moved into a monumental withdrawal, moving his fingers in continuous sequence, and repeating requests for coffee and toilet, "please", to get away from contact or out of the consulting room itself. While I felt some understanding that a series of adverse circumstances felt too much for him to manage, I was aware that the degree of my own frustration was in inverse proportion to his blankness. I was filled with feelings of anger and frustration about his external predicament, and with a stronger sense than I had ever had before of his fear that if he were to experience and to express anger or frustration himself, and not to project it into me, the room and his world would fall down around him.

A sequence of three very different sessions during a stormy autumn produced material linking with very early trauma and Billy's personal fantasies.

First session: Tuesday

After a few minutes of mild blankness, when he sat, hands clasped, staring beyond me to the window and the trees outside, I felt sufficiently confident to ask him what he was looking at. He said, "Trees", very clearly. I expected one of our, by now, sterile conversations, about trees falling down. I asked him what about the trees, and he actually replied, "Dying." My heart leapt. We spent some time together looking at the bare trees through the window (there had been a week of high winds and storms which had stripped the trees and broken off many branches) while I talked about the recent bad weather. I said I thought he had muddled the dead leaves with the trees which were, in fact, still alive, but without leaves; this was autumn. I said new leaves would come back again in ... "Spring", said Billy. I talked to him about the changing seasons. Billy whispered, "Trees", and I said perhaps he had seen leaves and branches blown down and that he thought everything was dead.

Later in the session he said my name and then, "... dead", pointed to himself and repeated "dead". He was suddenly very giggly and agitated, playing with his fingers and bending forward clutching at his genitals. He moved away and I felt sure he was feeling claustrophobic as he stood by the door repeatedly asking, "Cup-of-coffee-toilet-please." I said I thought he had got very scared now. He repeated "Scared. Cup of coffee." I said no, he didn't need coffee or the toilet, he could be brave; he had forgotten he was alive, I was alive, not dead, and that he *could* breathe in here. (In some recent sessions he had been clutching his throat and flattening his nostrils as he breathed in. I had been left wondering about a fear of suffocation.) He got up to find the ball and wanted to play catch, at first tentatively, then increasingly boldly. He became very assertive and threw the ball up so vigorously it actually hit the ceiling and the light fitting, which made me jump. He carried on and I commented that he hit the ceiling and the light and they didn't fall down.

The following session

This took place on a dark Thursday afternoon (Daylight Saving Time had just ended). Billy's escort told me he had wet himself twice that day. I found myself wondering whether he had wet himself partly through fear of coming to his session, and whether he was actually being courageous in coming to his psychotherapy. In the room, he seemed only half blank, staring out of the window, and I talked about the darkness outside. Billy said, "Scared", and, "Heart going very fast", as he moved his hand round and round over his stomach. He looked outside, and when I asked him about it he said, audibly, "Trees breaking down." I said he was very scared coming today, and had to be very brave; he had been so scared he'd wet his trousers. He whispered, "Brave", and clutched his genitals, bent over and giggling, but not cutting off. I felt that he was struggling with enormous terror about the dark, and that the room and the trees would fall down, and crush him at any moment (perhaps after throwing the ball so vigorously at the ceiling during the previous session).

Friday

I was eagerly looking forward to his morning session. When he came into the room, he looked at me, then outside, and suddenly, after some familiar preliminaries, he said, "It was a windy day . . . and it squashed you." While I talked to him about the weather and his fears, my mind was full of images of his traumatic birth experience, and of the fluidless uterus collapsed around him. I interpreted that he felt afraid of being squashed, fearing he couldn't breathe, fearing death. He became agitated, asking for coffee. I thought he had lost his nerve. I said I thought he had forgotten he *could* breathe and that he and I would not fall down here. He giggled, steadied himself and said, "May I blow my tissue?" He got a tissue, and, for the first time, made a passable attempt at blowing his nose (a hitherto almost impossible task), with some terrified giggling in between attempts. With encouragement he blew twice more and smiled. I said, "Yes. You did it!" He blew the tissue out of his hand, then caught it again. I talked about the wind *he* was making; that he was not feeling scared now. Suddenly he covered his nose and mouth with his hand, then reached across and did the same, very gently, to me. I said he was showing me how quickly he could feel squashed and not able to breathe, scared of not being alive. He got very overexcited, crumpled up the tissue, and I needed to work hard to help him to calm down.

Suddenly purposeful again, he asked, "May I have the car please?" fetched it for himself, and spent a truly joyful fifteen minutes playing without needing my orchestration or encouragement. He listened to the car's engine and I felt sufficiently bold to ask him whether he remembered when he asked me what made it make that . . . "Noise", he added, and repeated the entire question unprompted. The car was crashing into walls, turning corners and being turned by Billy as he scampered after it, full of fun. Suddenly he set the car off and then stopped it moving (as he had done many times in the past), then pressed his hand down so the friction motor made a terrible grating noise before pressing his hand over the entire windscreen with his hand.

The squashing action seemed overdetermined. I am grateful to Maria Rhode (personal communication) for her suggestion that he felt there was something (suffused as well with his own hostility) waiting to squash him, his vitality and his ability to play with meaningful symbolic content (I suppose like the original trauma of the collapsing womb, always waiting, in his fantasy, to cover his face and suffocate him). It also seemed, to me, to be linked with his experience of feeling various emotions as he played, which suddenly had to be stopped, as if the mounting excitement of the experience might overwhelm, or indeed *kill* him if he were not pre-emptive in stopping everything himself. Some material later in the same session led me to see that he had a story in mind, along with the experience of being separate from me with only words to connect us.

Near the end of the session, Billy said, "Goodness gracious me. How did the fish get in there? Fish don't suit you, Thomas." This was a story I had learnt after Billy had shouted out broken bits of the narrative in previous sessions. The fish get into Thomas's water tank, only to be fished out and cooked for the driver's tea. Billy's recital of the eating of the fish was accompanied by a satisfied grin.

He seemed, in letting the car be free, then squashing it before liberating it again, to be caught in a dilemma about allowing freedom or suffocating the contents of his own mind. The suffocation, perhaps, was impelled by an idea of the fish as proliferating "death-dealing 'rivals'" (Tustin [1981] 1992), immediately present and multiplying in his scarcely differentiated inside-outside, cruel fantasy-dominated world.

Conclusion

The momentous developments in Billy's communicative language, object-relatedness and his interest in the external world, were, at moments such as those illustrated above, surprising and thrilling. However, they only seemed to occur under optimum conditions, and were strongly related to my levels of energy and optimism. I did not know whether they were achievable only temporarily in a way which left Billy as unbelieving as I when they went again. Were they only glimpses of what-might-have-been given his (probably innate) hypersensitivity and his personal response to the traumatic circum-stances of his birth? He seemed always to be vigilant in looking for the holes and tears, not for support and strength. He had indeed lost years of devel-opmental opportunity, but the glimpses also had substance. Perhaps, as they gained experiential weight, they would lodge within Billy's mind, to connect up with other helpful experiences; to be a counterbalance to his cynical and psychotic perspective.

The sophistication of his development, in moments of contact, has led me to debate further the question of whether the imaginative capacity and the ability to think symbolically are developmental givens, not easily disturbed or disrupted. Meltzer *et al.* (1975: 11–13) has described "dismantling" in autistic children where there is a capacity to suspend the attention: "to allow the senses to wander, each to its most attractive object of the moment", thereby not putting together experience in order to "apprehend objects in a multifaceted way". Meltzer emphasises the passivity of loosening the mental attention which creates "common sense" (Bion, quoted in Meltzer *et al.* 1975) While I can recognise, in Billy's twiddling, that he allowed his senses to wander to something sensually attractive, I do not see it as passive. In him it felt like an imperative. He had to dissipate different sense impressions or he believed their coming together would annihilate him. He was actively preventing "mantling".

It seems convincing that Billy needed to protect himself against the continuing reality, in his mind, of the suffocating trauma of living in a collapsed womb. The weather, traffic jams, separations, all seemed to be equated with the trauma so completely that he had very little space where he was not dealing with terror.

Time might tell whether Billy has been helped by his family, his education and his psychotherapy actively to live more of his life. I feel convinced that the autistic state was never comfortable for him. He always seemed surprised and grateful when we made contact, and reports suggested that he could sustain some of it outside the special conditions of the consulting room.

Alvarez's model of developmentally informed psychotherapy is extraordinarily helpful in making contact with children who are as withdrawn and partially "undrawn" as Billy. Her innovative links between psychoanalysis and the need to be alert for "precursors of social/cognitive development" (1999: 50, 59–60) are part of the current evolution of psychoanalytic child psychotherapy.

While she emphasises appropriate "language" to address the very earliest developmental levels which we encounter at times in children like Billy, she is also eager to underline the need to be psychoanalytically rigorous, and to allow children to have their own experience, which is open to interpretation when the time is right. She has battled against those who would interpret simplistically and without due attention to the countertransference, often bludgeoning some deeply disturbed and deprived children's tentative *first* steps *towards* the idea of a good or helpful object, by seeing them as steps *away* from "healthy" psychic pain.

Alvarez's work leads us to new challenges. Schore's exciting work (1994, and Chapter 5 in this volume) alerts us to the changes psychotherapy makes to the individual's neurology. Research in genetics, and using the MRI scans of traumatised children (Perry *et al.*, 1995) leads us into a fascinating future where there is clearly a place for psychoanalysis. We need to understand more about the impact of the external world and trauma on the development of the psyche. We need to work more on the frontier between brain and mind (and soma), and to develop our thinking and technique to meet the challenge. As Alvarez has demonstrated, this requires a *marriage* of ideas achieved through fierce debate, not potentially destructive polarisations within post-Kleinian psychoanalysis or between psychoanalysis and neurological research.

Note

1 For a further discussion on sub-groups in autism see Alvarez and Reid (1999: 9–10).

References

Alvarez, A. (1992) *Live Company,* London and New York: Tavistock/Routledge.

Alvarez, A. (1998) "Failures to link: attacks or defects? Some questions concerning the thinkability of Oedipal and pre-Oedipal thoughts", *Journal of Child Psychotherapy*, 24 (2): 000–00.

Alvarez, A. and Reid, S. (eds) (1999) *Autism and Personality: Findings from the Tavistock Autism Workshop*, London and New York: Routledge.

Bick, E. (1964) "Infant observation in psychoanalytic training", *International Journal of Psycho-Analysis*, 45: 558–566.

Bion, W.R. 1962) *Learning from Experience,* London: Heinemann.

Joseph, B. (1985) "Transference: the total situation", *International Journal of Psycho-Analysis*, 66: 447–454.

Klauber, T. (1999) "The significance of trauma and other factors in work with the parents of children with autism", in A. Alvarez and S. Reid (eds) *Autism and Personality: Findings from the Tavistock Autism Workshop*, London and New York: Routledge.

Klein, M. ([1935] 1975) "Contribution to the psychogenesis of manic-depressive states", *The Writings of Melanie Klein*, Volume I, London: Hogarth Press.

Meltzer, D. *et al.* (1975) *Explorations in Autism: A Psycho-Analytical Study*, Strath Tay: Clunie.

Miller, L., Rustin, M., Rustin, M.J. and Shuttleworth J. (eds) (1989) *Closely Observed Infants*, London: Duckworth.

Perry, B.D. *et al.* (1995) "Childhood trauma, the neurobiology of adaptation and use-dependent development of the brain: how states become traits", *Infant Mental Health Journal*, 16: 271–291.

Rhode, M. (1999) "Echo or answer? The move towards more ordinary speech in three children with autistic spectrum disorder", in A. Alvarez and S. Reid (eds) *Autism and Personality: Findings from the Tavistock Autism Workshop*, London and New York: Routledge.

Schore, A.N. (1994) *Affect Regulation and the Origin of the Self: The Neurobiology of Emotional Development*, Hillsdale, N.J.: Lawrence Erlbaum.

Tustin, F. ([1981] 1992) *Autistic States in Children* (revised edn), London: Routledge and Kegan Paul.

Waddell, M. (1988) "Infantile development: Kleinian and post-Kleinian theory: infant observational practice", *British Journal of Psychotherapy*, 4 (3): 000–00.

Chapter 14

On temporal shapes

The relation between primary rhythmical experience and the quality of mental links

Suzanne Maiello

Introduction

Clinical experience with severely disturbed children is the ground on which Anne Alvarez's thinking has grown, leading to the formulation of innovative ideas on theoretical and technical aspects of psychotherapeutic work with patients presenting early deficit or precocious distortions of mental development. Alvarez raises her voice for "a meta-theory which is more relational ... and more able to accommodate novelty, growth, change, and the mentalness of the mind" (1999b: 60).

Since Klein's first conceptualization, object-relations theory has been seen increasingly in its twofold dimension of internal *and* external reality, in terms of a more rigorous "two-person psychology" (Alvarez, 1999b), involving both interpersonal and intrapersonal relations.

One of the merits of Alvarez's writing is her openness towards the contributions of infant research and developmental psychology. Whilst recognizing the specificity of the different approaches, she creates thought-provoking links between psychoanalytical formulations and the developmentalists' view of subjectivity as being inherently intersubjective and dialogic (1999b).

When working with very disturbed patients, her interest in the dynamic aspects of external and internal relationships brought about a shift of attention from "contents" and "objects" to the meaning of "movements", "shapes" and "patterns" which develop in space and time. "Where there is a real difficulty or deficit in making links ... the therapist may need to attend to certain *temporal and dynamic features of the link* which can enable sequentiality, ordinality and twoness to be bearable and pleasurable" (Alvarez, 1998: 213; italics added). Alvarez adds that in normal development, internalized objects maintain a dynamic form, a shape in time (1998).

The issue of presence and absence of the primary object in relation to the development of the capacity for thinking is revisited by Alvarez in the dimensions of space and time. She sustains that thought is generated not only by absence, but also by the modulation of presence which is seen as a prerequisite for a gradual acquisition of experiences around the non-catastrophic modifiability of the present object. These experiences seem to form the basis for the capacity to establish flexible and articulated links.

Moving from Alvarez's ideas on the temporal and dynamic qualities of objects and their relations, I shall give further thought to the rhythmical aspects of her notion of temporal shapes on the background of my concept of the sound-object (Maiello, 1995). With this term, I describe an early, possibly prenatal precursor of the later maternal object, whose sound qualities may result from the earliest auditory experiences of the maternal voice. The most basic rhythmical qualities of the sound-object may be rooted in the foetus's perception of the maternal heartbeat, the pulsations of her blood-flow and the respiratory rhythm. In developmental terms, I would place the rhythmical aspects of prenatal reality at the primordial end of auditory, and in part vibratory, experiences. Intertwined with kinaesthetic and tactile levels of experience, they may constitute the foetus's, and later the infant's, most basic awareness of pulsating life, and therefore be at the core of "basic trust" (Erikson, 1950).

Recent formulations, both of psychoanalysts and developmentalists, show a shared need to create new conceptual containers for the primary levels of proto-mental experiences. Sandler and Joffe made a distinction between *structure,* which is not accessible to consciousness, and *experience* (1969). Bollas introduced the concept of the *unthought known* (1987), and Emde *et al.* used the term *procedural knowledge* (1991), which includes the notion of relational knowing, i.e. knowing how to do things with intimate others (Lyons-Ruth, 1998).

I suggest that the temporal shapes described by Alvarez, and their rhythmical qualities, belong to these deep levels of proto-mental inter-personal experience and have a bridging function in the transition from states of non-mental psycho-physical at-oneness on the way to mental activity and symbolic thinking.

Inversely, as suggested by Alvarez, clinical experience shows that severely disturbed patients are invariably affected at these primary levels of temporal experience.

Considerations on rhythm

Rhythm is an ever-present element in all that is living. The embryo begins its existence as a pulsating entity, and the end of life coincides with the last breath and heartbeat. In prenatal life, sensory-motor materno–foetal inter-action is characterized by constancy and rhythmicity (Mancia, 1981). He writes:

> Primary mental activity might consist of a process of "reading" or "decodifying" the rhythmical and constant stimuli that reach the foetus

coming from the maternal container. Furthermore, by virtue of its rhythmicity and constancy, the foetus' object world might constitute the groundplan of a *primitive biological clock* that will permeate the prenatal psychic nucleus.

(Mancia, 1981: 353)

Papousek (1996) underlines the constant rhythmic-dynamic stimulation during prenatal life coming from the maternal heartbeat, breathing and walking, and from the rhythms of maternal speech. The author explores the synchronization of vocal and kinetic patterns in postnatal maternal behaviour with the infant, as well as the infant's sensitivity to rhythmical patterns of behaviour. Her analysis of euphonic cooing sounds produced by a two-month-old infant showed a frequency and rhythmical structure which corresponds to the rhythm of the heartbeat of an adult.

Stern explored the structure and timing of mother–infant interaction and observed that moments of engagement and moments of rest and silence alternate "at a surprisingly regular rate". Not only is there a "temporal patterning of human social behaviour" as a result of experience, but "the infant seems to be equipped ... to deal with the temporal world of his social interactions" (1977: 100). Stern's later concept of *shared attunement* (1985) is considered by Alvarez (1998) as central in the early stages of introjective processes.

Trevarthen observes how mothers and infants "adjust the timing, emotional form and energy of their expression to obtain intersynchrony, harmonious transitions and complementarity of feelings between them in an emotional partnership of confluence" (1993: 57). Nursery rhymes seem to have similar characteristics in all cultures and languages. "They have predictable features of beat, rhythm, melody and rhyme that suggest innate foundations in brain activity for what turn out to be universals in the timing and prosody of music and poetry" (Trevarthen *et al.*, 1996: 81).

Rhythm as structuring element of temporal shapes

Rhythm combines presence and absence in a temporal dimension. A beat and a pause alternate at regular intervals. I suggest that at the earliest stages of awareness, the continuity and regularity of the alternation of beat/pause may represent the structuring element of the experience of rhythmicity, and the prerequisite for the internalization of reliable temporal shapes and the development of basic trust. The experience of continuity may represent the safe starting point for the exploration of discontinuity (beat/pause, presence/absence).

Rhythmical aspects of reality could have a bridging function, leading from the primary state of unstructured fusional unity through the experience of reliable temporal shapes towards the first dawning awareness of difference and the capacity to bear variations. This capacity could correspond to the first fleeting awareness of separateness, without which symbolic mental activity cannot be set in train.

Alvarez suggests that the quality of these early internalized rhythmical experiences may contribute to the quality of the later mental links, in particular to their flexibility or, respectively, their rigidity.

The dream that follows is of a 45-year-old woman. It illustrates both the dreamer's trust in a reliable rhythmical shape or object, and the joyful experience of its flexible variation:

> "I am standing in an undefined inner space. A man whom I don't know comes towards me. He is slim, but there is nothing special about him. We embrace and start dancing. It all happens quite naturally. We have neither sought nor chosen each other. We dance together in perfect harmony to the sound of music that comes from somewhere, our bodies moulded to each other. But there is nothing sexual about our closeness. There is no tension or excitement, just a deep and total sense of well-being. Our legs and feet are in such perfect agreement that they sometimes step out of the beat of the music, without ever losing their harmonious correspondence. The most wonderful of all sensations is to feel our steps moving in syncopation with the rhythm of the music while effortlessly maintaining their movements in perfect accord."
>
> (Maiello, 1995: 28–29)

The dream is about one-ness, two-ness and potential three-ness, experienced at the level of "song-and-dance" (Meltzer, 1986) in the dimension of time. Three stages of experience seem to be represented simultaneously in the dream. On the first and deepest level, the two bodies of the standing "I" and the approaching "He" are "moulded together" and re-experience the blissful primordial state of fusional We-ness. The sense of unity of the bodies is unquestioned. Is this why they can dare to be in movement? Movement in space is movement in time, and both introduce the principle of change. On the second level of experience, the synchrony of the dancers' feet is so unquestioned that the music, with its melody and rhythm, can be perceived by the dancing "We-unit' as coming from somewhere else, as being "other", representing the potential third element in the nascent awareness of the couple's two-ness. The dreamer in fact knows that the couple is formed by an "I" and a "He". On the third level of experience, the dancers discover that they can step out of the regular beat of the music. Movement in space and time having been safely and harmoniously explored, the dancing couple feels sufficiently anchored in its "rhythmical identity" to dare to differentiate itself from the rhythm of the "not-me"-music, in a playfully syncopated dialogue with the "other" recognized in its otherness. Variation, which implies the experience of separation and separateness, is not traumatic, but actively and joyfully sought by the dancers.

The dream seems to suggest that once there is sufficient trust in "going-on-being", oscillations between "at-one-ness" and separateness become possible in the mental modality described by Grotstein as "double track" (1980). Inversely, if the basic "rhythm of safety" (Tustin, 1990), which develops in the interpersonal relationship between the infant and the primary caregiver, has not been established, separation and differentiation are experienced as existential threats.

Rhythmic constancy and variations as precursors of the experience of presence and absence

Meeting the maternal breast is the infant's first experience of active rhythmical interplay with the external world. Alvarez writes: "A sucking movement involves pulling and slackening ... there is huge activity, but hidden in the pulling and drawing is the letting go – the fundamental rhythm of life" (1992: 28). The "hidden letting go" is there, as the element that heralds in the possibility of absence, in the middle of the gratifying experience of presence, containment and nourishment.

It is not only variations in rhythm that are harbingers of change; rhythm itself, in the pulsating alternation of beat and pause, represents the principle of inconstancy within constancy, of absence contained in presence. Alvarez describes the mother's distance-regulating looming games with the baby, and the baby's scanning of the mother's face. Both are seen as reciprocal rhythmical adjustments and explorations in terms of sequentiality of "temporal forms or dynamic shapes in time by which presence and absence are linked" (1998: 229).

I sustain that both aspects of rhythmical experiences have specific functions for psychic growth. Constancy and reliability seem to be indispensable ingredients for the establishment of basic trust, whereas variations and imperfections create the space for interpersonal and intrapsychic links to acquire flexibility and for mental activity to develop. Both aspects are "positions" in the sense of mental ways of functioning, but at the earliest stages of life I suggest that rhythmical inconstancy and discontinuity are bearable only after a congruous experience of constancy and continuity has been internalized, which occurs normally during prenatal life.

The later rhythmical imperfections offer not only minimal spaces for frustration, thanks to which attention is reoriented and thinking is set in train, but at this stage variations and discrepancies in the mother's talk, singing or play can become pleasant experiences (Papousek, 1996; Tronick, 1989).

Alvarez suggests that the caregiver "offers a complex, varied and *constantly changing presence*, full of dynamic flows and temporal shapes' and that "modulation and regulation of presence is a task for the infant ... which is probably prior to maintaining object constancy throughout absence" (1999a: 193–194).

In terms of Bion's theory of thinking (1962), Alvarez shares his idea of the existence of an innate preconception of a living and thinking human object, which needs adequate realizations in experience for mental activity to develop, but she questions Bion's idea that the absence of the external object is the prerequisite for the onset of thinking. She claims that the first forms of thinking do occur in the presence of the object, and that conceptions, which precede concepts in developmental terms, should be considered as the result of primitive forms of thinking (1998, 1999a). In accordance with Meltzer, who asserts that "conflict about the *present* object is prior in significance to the host of anxieties over the *absent* object" (1988: 29), Alvarez sustains that "the present object in its aliveness and mobility may be as thought-provoking and demanding of attention and interest as is the absent object" (1988, 1998: 215).

Although Bion was more interested in the relation between the absence of the object and concept formation, he made one statement which is relevant to temporal shapes and rhythmical structures (i.e. to the mental level at which preconceptions meet with positive realizations). He described this "meeting" in terms of the formation of "articulated links' (1957), whose living, dynamic and imperfect character is underlined by Alvarez (1999b). Bion's term is mobile and unsaturated and leaves space for the dialectic between continuity and discontinuity, constancy and variation. An "articulated link" is formed with a living, pulsating present object and prepares the ground for the infant's later capacity to bear those absences which are no longer embedded in a rhythmical temporal presence.

Premature birth and the breakdown of rhythmical containment

In the event of premature birth, one of the potentially traumatic experiences of the infant can be expected to be in connection with the loss of the temporal and rhythmical continuity of the intrauterine environment at a time when the infant may not be ready yet to deal with the discontinuities imposed by postnatal life. Observational material of two premature babies born at approximately the same gestational age shows their different response to the untimely interruption of the rhythmicity of intrauterine life. The children were observed weekly up to the age of three months, and once a month until one year of age.

David

David was born at thirty one weeks of gestational age with a birth weight of 1,200 grams and was in an incubator for six weeks. Sterility was the first priority in his neonatal intensive care unit. Visits were restricted, and parents had to wear sterilized overalls, headwear and shoes.

The baby needed assisted breathing for the first three days only and was given the first bottle with his mother's expressed milk at one week. He sucked a little, but his initial interest tended to diminish, and more and more often he slept through his parents' visits. The frequency of his heartbeat was higher and more irregular as compared to other premature babies, and the mother felt that he tended to withdraw when she touched him. He did not clutch her finger when she slipped it in his open hand. When kangaroo care[1] was started at two weeks of age, David responded with severe bradycardia and had to be put back into the oxygenated incubator immediately. At the breast, which he met two weeks later, the sucking got worse. He tended to lose the nipple and could not find a regular rhythm.

The difficulties continued at home. David cried when he was hungry, but did not open his mouth actively when put to the breast. He seemed contented with smelling it. The end of the feed was as difficult as the beginning. He was agitated after his meals, seemed to search for the absent breast, but did not take it if it was offered again.

Finding a rhythm of waking and sleeping times was equally problematic. David often slept through his feeding time and woke up only for the subsequent feed. He also had a very particular way of crying. His vocal emissions were monotonously repetitive and had a hopeless quality, as if he could not imagine that relief from distress was possible. Despite his parents' loving dedication, he was difficult to comfort.

At four months, he found his thumb and sucked it eagerly. When he was weaned shortly after, he did not seem to resent the loss of the breast and accepted the bottle and the spoon without difficulties. When he did not cry, he was a quiet and gracefully smiling baby. His vocalizations were melodious and had a high and gentle pitch. On the whole, there was a quality of cautious and fleeting lightness about his being, as if he had not yet made up his mind whether he really wanted to engage with the world around him.

At seven months, he was put prone on the carpet. He did not reach out actively for toys, or threw them away sideways out of sight. In front of a difficulty, he tended to give up and suck his thumb.

At nine months, things gradually improved. David could show his distress when his mother left. He became easier to comfort, babbled in a more articulated way and began to enjoy interactive play. Meaningful interpersonal rhythms developed. His favorite activity was to point to pictures or books and to repeat "ca ... ca ... ca ... ca" with a tone of urgency, so as to induce the caregiver to tell him what the pictures represented. He needed to hear the stories over and over again, but also accepted variations to the theme, as long as no detail was left out.

David now trusted the world sufficiently to express his need for relationships and explored vocal dialogue in all its aspects by "talking", eliciting speech, listening and taking turns in a shared experience.

For a few days, he had a fever and was restless and miserable. The only way in which he would fall asleep was lying prone on his nanny's large breast. The observer wondered whether the prolonged contact with a warm body and a beating heart was a reparative experience in relation to the early trauma – not only of the loss of the maternal heartbeat but also of the breakdown of the rhythm of his own heart at the first encounter with his mother.

As soon as he had recovered, David began to pull himself to his feet and proudly emitted high-pitched little cries of enthusiasm and satisfaction which developed into a personal little song of his. It was a rhythmically oscillating continuous melody, sustained by two alternating vowels: "a" at the highest pitch, and "o" at the lower end. The change of vowels "a–o–a–o–a–o" was fluid and followed the undulating sequence of his song. The temporal shape of the melody was that of a regular sequence of waves, with a time distance of approximately one second between one "a"-pitch and the following.

Discussion

It is difficult to tell to what extent the emotional sterility of the intensive care unit contributed to David's difficult start. He certainly was a particularly sensitive baby who reacted to the trauma of his premature birth and his isolation by taking refuge in the continuity of sleep.

Rhythms were a difficult issue in all areas, beginning with his heartbeat, the extreme and uncontrollable oscillations of which seemed to be related to his emotional states.

The baby's sucking rhythm was irregular, beginnings and endings of the feed were problematic, and no reliable rhythm of waking and sleeping times would develop.

His endless repetitive crying, which was exasperating in its evacuative "meaninglessness", seemed to convey his despair around the loss of the intrauterine constancy, without which it was too difficult for him to accept any kind of rhythm, i.e. of alternation and variation of internal or inter-personal temporal shapes.

However, when David began to relate more to living others, he did so in a cautious but competent way. His "ca … ca … ca" in itself was rhythmical and intermittent, and his voice clearly conveyed his search and need for contact and response.

As to his "a–o–a–o–a–o" melody, it could be seen as a vocal expression of his restored sound-object, including its rhythmical aspect. His song was continuous, but rhythmically undulated, and with softly alternating vowels, as if, after the traumatic beginning of his life, he had been able to introject some form of pleasant togetherness.

Leo

Leo was born at thirty weeks of gestational age with a birth weight of 1,300 grams and spent seven weeks in an incubator. The staff of the neonatal intensive care unit were alert to the emotional needs of the premature babies.

Leo needed assisted breathing for the first eight days and struggled to find a regular breathing rhythm. Three weeks later, a severe respiratory crisis made further assisted breathing necessary. Although he was visibly distressed by the intrusion of numerous tubes, he showed a keen interest in the world. He sucked his mother's finger vigorously and drank his first bottle in the incubator quickly and without hesitation. He made rhythmical sucking movements with his mouth between feeds, and his breathing rhythm became gradually more regular.

At five weeks, Leo had his first kangaroo care experience. As soon as he was in skin-to-skin contact with his mother, he searched frantically for the breast. With her help, he attached to the nipple and sucked immediately.

At home, he continued feeding well. He pulled the nipple deep into his mouth, with his tiny jaws working rhythmically. At the end of the meal, he let go with a satisfied expression on his face. He quickly found his rhythm of waking and sleeping times. At night, however, he cried a lot, was difficult to comfort, and calmed down only if put on his mother's or father's chest.

Leo was an intensely present and active baby. His eyes explored the environment, his smiles were rare and selective, but open and hearty, and his protests vehement.

He was weaned at five months and had a hard time accepting the bottle. A striking change occurred in the use of his hands. At the breast, they had been open and passive, as if the experience had been totally concentrated in his mouth. When the bottle was introduced, he used to join his hands tightly throughout the feed. It was as if he needed to reproduce an active contact between two substitute live body parts.

Leo reached out for toys, held them tightly and explored them with passionate concentration, communicating a feeling of strength. His vocalizations were rather poor, but he was fond of producing a growl deep in his throat.

During an attack of flu at ten months of age, his breathing difficulties threw him into a state of panic. He needed to be put back into his cot, which he had long outgrown, and lay there, passively abandoned to his painfully irregular breath, needing to be walked and rocked continuously.

Discussion

Despite his premature birth and serious breathing problems, Leo had had an intense and gratifying experience of rhythmicity at the breast, which he searched and found with the instinct of a little animal. The active sucking of his parents' fingers in the incubator and the sucking movement of his mouth before he ever met the breast showed his capacity to wait for the realization of its preconception, including the rhythmical interaction with it.

By joining his hands when drinking from the bottle after weaning, he showed his imaginative capacity to create new conjunctions and find an alternative realization for his need for tactile physical closeness.

Leo's most traumatic experiences were in the area of the breakdown of his breathing rhythm, and his first bad cold brought back the terror of suffocation of his early respiratory crises.

However, despite the traumatic beginning of his life, he had been able to keep the preconception of a rhythmical interpersonal relationship alive, to whose realization he contributed with passion and determination.

The satisfied growl deep in his throat may well have been an echo of the depth of his nurturing experience at the breast.

Comment

The two premature babies were born at comparable gestational age, spent a similar amount of time in the incubator, were both breast-fed and grew up in the care of loving parents. The difference in the two children's reactions to early trauma, however, is striking from the point of view of temporal shapes and the early rhythmical aspects of mother–infant interaction.

Leo had managed to maintain hope and a basic trust in the alive rhythmical quality of the relationship, despite the serious respiratory crisis at one month of age and the intrusive manipulations he had had to undergo. The material from his follow-up observations is readable and interpretable in terms of fantasies, defences and conflicts from the very beginning of his life.

David, on the other hand, seemed to have been tempted to give up in the sterile environment of his intensive care unit and to have come close to a breakdown of the capacity to wait for the realization of the preconception of rhythmical interpersonal interaction. At the same time, the realization itself had been emotionally too overwhelming for him.

Where Leo's mental "skin" had strengthened in his struggle for life, David's "skin" had been too fragile initially to bear the impact of premature birth. His observational material was more difficult to read in terms of symbolic meanings, but over time it showed his silent struggle and finally his capacity to find ways to restore, months later, the rhythmical aspects of his internal maternal object in the relationships with his sensitive and caring parents.

The scene of both children's reparative experience was the "theatre of the mouth" (Meltzer 1986). Leo had a satisfying emotional experience of rhythmical cooperation at the breast. David had missed the experience at this primary level, but when he was emotionally ready, his dialogue-seeking rhythmical vocalizations and the narrative response of the adults seemed to represent a delayed form of realization of interpersonal temporal shapes. And the undulating melody and alternation of vowels of his personal little song appear as the testimony of the internalization of a harmonious rhythmical object.

The absence of rhythmicity in autistic states

In autistic states, the experience of time is avoided. There is no awareness of a past, or a future, and therefore there is no present in terms of the perception of one's own and others' presence. If there is no time, there are no temporal shapes in Alvarez's sense. Primary interactive rhythmical patterns seem to have broken down. In terms of the sound-object, this means that its rhythmical qualities, which are the result of the internalization of an experience developing in time, are lost as well.

When Kanner (1944) referred to rhythmical actions and movements of autistic children, he used the term in a purely descriptive sense. With a view to psychotherapy with these children, it is important to distinguish between *rhythmical* and *stereotyped* activities. Formally, they may appear similar, but stereotypies stir countertransference sensations of boredom, exclusion or irritation, whereas the initial rhythmical expressions of a formerly autistic child are among the initial promising signs of relational awareness.

Alvarez describes autistic activities as "the replacement of imagination with repetitive or stereotyped rituals" (1999b: 68). Stereotypies are in fact the desolate solipsistic caricature of and protection against the exploration of interpersonal dynamic temporal shapes.

Psychotherapists who work with autistic patients often report material which is linked to basic physiological rhythms such as the heartbeat (Tustin, 1990; Maiello, 1997; Alvarez, 1999b) and breathing (Rhode, 1994), which can be either the expression of the child's omnipotent protection against interpersonal relationships, or the first signs of their awareness of temporal shapes. It seems that these children have to make primary rhythmical interactive experiences once they become capable of abandoning the omnipotent control over their self-generated autistic stereotypies.

Frances Tustin refers to rhythmical aspects of the experience when she describes her "heartbroken" patients.

> Their "heartbreak" goes beyond what we usually mean by the term. The feeling of brokenness goes into the very fabric of their being ... Since the sucking rhythm had become associated with the beating of the heart, it was the "teat–tongue–heart" that was felt to be broken ... For these patients bodily awareness of their separateness had been experienced as an interruption to the pulsing rhythm of their "going-on-being".
>
> (Tustin, 1990: 156)

Clinical material of a little girl with autistic features will be used to show both the manifestations of the breakdown of rhythmical temporal shapes and the first interpersonal experiences of rhythmicity during psychotherapy.

The dawn of rhythmical experience: a clinical case

Rosetta was a little girl with autistic features whom I saw from the age of five. Her speech was mostly echolalic.

Years later, she could talk in a less adhesive way, but the absence of interpersonal rhythmical patterns continued to make verbal exchange difficult. Rosetta seemed to know nothing about the sequentiality of talking and listening and the spontaneous rhythmical alternation which develops in the dialogue between a mother and her baby and becomes part of primary "relational knowing".

During the session, it could happen that when we had been silent for a while, she would start speaking at exactly the same moment as I did. I would stop immediately, in order to hear what she was saying, but she would stop at the same time as I did. I would then wait for her to speak again and listen. If she remained silent, at some point I would try to say something about my wanting to hear what she was telling me, but she would start speaking again the very moment I did, and again I could not hear what she said.

The absence of rhythmical alternation had the effect of non-communication. It was as if we were both deaf, and in a way also mute. In echolalic speech, differences and separateness are obliterated by the adhesive sameness of verbal utterings. Here, the potential dialogue broke down, and our words merged and became an indistinct cluster because the rhythmical pattern of reciprocity that develops in time had collapsed. Two voices coincided and annihilated each other, and two pairs of ears were made useless (Maiello, 1998).

On one occasion, Rosetta came to the session with a toy parrot, which contained a battery, a microphone and a loudspeaker:

> Rosetta switched the parrot on and said something. The parrot repeated her words. The articulation was blurred, but the intonation was imitated with irritating perfection. This went on for some time, with the parrot repeating everything she said. She was completely absorbed in her mock-dialogue, and I was totally excluded. At some point, I started talking about what I thought was happening and what Rosetta was doing. The parrot readily produced an indistinct melodious parody of my comment. Rosetta continued talking to her toy without taking any notice of me, and I had the choice between trying to make another comment, knowing that the parrot was there to caricature any attempt of verbal interaction, and withdrawing into silence allowing the autistic "sound-shapes" to continue.
>
> (Maiello, 1997: 17)

Tustin (1986) and Alvarez (1992, 1999b) write about the strenuous resistance of these children against unpredictable "shapes", and their unflinching efforts to reproduce endlessly those which are familiar to them. With the parrot, Rosetta took the need for sameness and omnipotent control to its extreme.

In terms of temporal shapes and rhythmical aspects of reality, this means that in autistic states constancy and continuity are the only ruling principles, with the consequence of eliminating every possible manifestation of "otherness". Variation and discontinuity – that is, of the aspects of reality which open the experience to change, growth, transformation and surprise, and to meeting the living "other" – are banned from these children's world.

In her third year of therapy, Rosetta started showing the first signs of a nascent awareness of the passing of time, of separations and of rhythmical aspects of the relationship:

> The first thing Rosetta did when she entered the room for the last session before a brief holiday, was to look at my wrist watch and ask me at what time her mother would pick her up. She then put her ear to my watch and listened. After some time, I asked her what she heard. She got up, looked at me and said: "toc – toc – toc". She then bent her head and leaned lightly with her ear against my chest, listened for another while and said: "the heart".

> (Maiello, 1997: 14)

Rosetta seemed to be able to re-enact and represent early experiences, which at the time had been mentally heartbreaking for her, and to meet and acknowledge temporal and rhythmical aspects of reality for the first time. The rhythm of our sessions was about to be interrupted, but now she could check that there was a beating heart in my body, that I was alive, and maybe that we would both remain alive during the separation. In fact, she seemed able to bear the idea that the sound of my heart was *there*, inside me, and out of her control. She seemed to have internalized some rhythmical aspects of our relationship.

At a later stage, Rosetta began to sing nursery rhymes in the session and needed me to sing them with her in unison. However, she no longer used this to obliterate separateness, but to reinforce her capacity to bear it. She particularly liked a play-song about the names of the weekdays. The singing was accompanied by fairly complex sequences of mutual hand-clapping. Our vocal "togetherness" seemed to give her sufficient confidence in a shared temporal experience to enable her to explore variations in the accompanying rhythmical interaction of our hands. Furthermore, through this rhyme, she became interested in the days of the week and in the alternation of the "yes-days", in which she came to therapy, and "no-days" when she had no session. The calendar became meaningful.

This is how Rosetta learnt to count. The learning process was imbued with emotions about presence and absence, meeting and parting. She had known the names of numbers for some time, but so far these had been without a true meaning in her experience of reality. The first difficulty had been related to the fact that the rhythm of her counting voice did not correspond to the rhythm of her rising fingers, as if the "interpersonal" communication between voice and hand had been missing. When Rosetta noticed the discrepancy, she used to give up. The second difficulty had been due to the fact that once she started counting, she could not get herself to stop and went on until she lost herself in the higher ranges of senseless numbers once the connection with the object of her counting had broken down. Stopping represents a boundary, an ending, including the end of the illusion of infinite continuity and sameness. For Rosetta, learning to stop counting did not mean only maintaining the relation with a finite object, but put her in touch with the anxieties around the acknowledgement of the finitude of time.

Her capacity to count started developing once she had dared to expose herself to interpersonal rhythmical experiences. It seemed that their reliable constancy allowed her to internalize sufficient basic trust to begin to explore discontinuity, variations and endings on her way towards acknowledging differentiation and separateness.

Concluding remarks

From the point of view of psychotherapeutic technique, Alvarez claims that autistic states may require adaptations of the setting, if we want to meet these patients' special needs (1992, 1999b). In terms of temporal shapes and rhythmical patterns, one of the therapist's tasks in his function of "live company" could be seen in a special attention for a balance between elements of continuity and discontinuity. The patient's perception of two-ness can be sustained by sharing unthreatening temporal experiences through a cautious, sensitive and timely attention to rhythmical aspects of the interactive reality and to minimal forms of discontinuity, with the aim of facilitating a gradual creation or restoration of the dynamic aspects of broken mental links. Then, and only then, mental contents begin to become emotionally meaningful.

The experience gained through infant observation and clinical work with severely disturbed children puts us in touch with the development or, respectively, the breakdown of the earliest stages of mental life. At these levels of experience, Alvarez's notion of temporal shapes gives access to a deeper understanding of the way in which the dynamic qualities of internal links are formed.

Temporal shapes and their rhythmical aspects are part of primary experience, and their internalization seems to represent the basis on which relational knowing and basic trust develop. The exploration of the levels of experience, where preconceptions meet with the first positive realizations, opens the way to illuminating insights into proto-mental activity and the gradual transition from a state of fusional unity towards the awareness of separateness.

I suggest that primary temporal shapes and rhythmical patterns are not abandoned with mental maturity and that the basic "rhythms of safety" continue to sustain the activity of the mind throughout life.

Pathology appears only when temporal shapes and rhythmical patterns are used as omnipotent protections against the unbearable awareness of loneliness and mortality. In normal development, aesthetic experience, creativity, flexibility, tolerance and joyfulness maintain a deep connection with the rhythmical aspects of temporal experience. The emotional links of symbolic thinking rest on these deep levels of relational knowing. Creative thinking is not the result of overcoming the temporal and rhythmical aspects of internalized experience, but of its integration in the mature awareness of the finite reality of life-time.

Note

1 Kangaroo care provides skin-to-skin contact between the mother and the pre-term infant, who is placed between the breasts or on one breast.

References

Alvarez, A. (1988) "Beyond the unpleasure principle: some preconditions for thinking through play", *J. Child Psychotherapy*, 14: 2.
—— (1992) *Live Company*, London: Routledge.
—— (1998) "Failures to link: attacks or defects?", *J. Child Psychotherapy*, 24, 2.
—— (1999a) "Frustrations and separateness, delight and connectedness: reflections on the conditions under which bad and good surprises are conducive to learning", *J. Child Psychotherapy*, 25, 2.
—— (1999b) *Autism and Personality*, London: Routledge.
Bion, W.R. (1957) "Differentiation of the psychotic from the non-psychotic personalities", *Intl. J. Psycho-Analysis*, 38.
—— (1962) "A theory of thinking', *Intl. J. Psycho-Analysis*, 53.
Bollas, C. (1987) *The Shadow of the Object: Psychoanalysis of the Unthought Known*, London: Free Association Books.
Emde, R., Biringen, Z., Clyman, R. and Oppenheim, D. (1991) "The moral self in infancy: affective core and procedural knowledge", *Developmental Review*, 11.
Erikson, E.H. (1950) *Childhood and Society*, New York: W.W. Norton.
Grotstein, J.S. (1980) "Primitive mental states", *Contemporary Psychoanalysis*, 16.
Kanner (1944) "Early infantile autism'. *J. Paediatrics*. 25, 3.
Lyons-Ruth, K. (1998) "Implicit relational knowing: its role in development and psychoanalytic treatment", *Infant Mental Health J.* 19, 3.
Maiello, S. (1995) "The sound-object: a hypothesis about prenatal auditory experience and memory", *J. Child Psychotherapy* 21, 1.
—— (1997) "Going beyond: notes on the beginning of object relations in the light of

'The perpetuation of an error' ", in J. Mitrani and T. Mitrani (eds) *Encounters with Autistic States*, New York: Jason Aronson Inc.

—— (1998) "Trauma prenatale e autismo", *Richard e Piggle*, 3/98.

Mancia, M. (1981) "On the beginning of mental life in the foetus", *Intl. J. Psycho-Analysis*, 62.

Meltzer, D. (1975) *Explorations in Autism*, London: The Roland Harris Educational Trust.

—— (1986) *Studies in Extended Metapsychology*, Strath Tay: Clunie Press.

Papousek, M. (1996) "Intuitive parenting: a hidden source of musical stimulation in infancy", in I. Deliege and J. Sloboda (eds) *Musical Beginnings*, Oxford: Oxford University Press.

Rhode, M. (1994) "Autistic breathing", *J. Child Psychotherapy*, 20, 1.

Sandler, J. and Joffe, W. (1969) "Towards a basic psychoanalytic model", *Intl. J. Psycho-Analysis*, 50.

Stern, D.N. (1977) *The First Relationship: Infant and Mother*, London: Open Books.

—— (1985) *The Interpersonal World of the Infant*, New York: Basic Books.

Trevarthen, C. (1993) "The functions of emotions in early infant communication and development", in J. Nadel and L. Camaioni (eds) *New Perspectives in Early Communicative Development*, London: Routledge.

Trevarthen, C., Aitken, K., Papoudi, D. and Robarts, J. (1996) *Children with Autism*, London: Jessica Kingsley.

Tronick, E. (1989) "Emotions and emotional communication in infants", *American Psychologist* 44.

Tustin, F. (1986) *Autistic Barriers in Neurotic Patients*, London: Karnac.

—— (1990) *The Protective Shell in Children and Adults*, London: Karnac.

Anne Alvarez's published work

Books

Live Company: Psychotherapy with Autistic, Borderline, Deprived and Abused Children, Routledge, London, July 1992 (4th printing 1998). Published in Italy by Astrolabio-Ubaldini, Rome, 1993; in Brazil by Arte Medica, Porto Allegre, 1994; in Sweden and in France, 1997; in Germany, Japan and Spain, in press.

Edited with Susan Reid, *Autism and Personality: Findings from the Tavistock Autism Workshop*, Routledge, London, May 1999. To be published in France and China, in press.

Anne Alvarez in Sao Paulo: Clinical Seminars, Acervo Psicanalitico (Brazilian Psychoanalytical Society of São Paolo), São Paolo, 1999.

Other publications (originally under maiden name of Adams)

Adams, A. and Foulds, G.A. (1962) Personality and Depressive Illness. *J. Ment. Sci.* 108, 474.

Adams, A., Mallinson, T.J. and Greenland, C. (1962) Measuring Remotivation. *Psychiatry: J. for the Study of Interpersonal Processes* 25, 2.

Adams, A. and Foulds, G.A. (1963) Personality and the Paranoid and Depressive Psychoses. *Brit. J. Psychiatry* 109, 459.

Heath, E.S., Adams, A. and Wakeling, P.L.G. (1964) Short Courses of E.C.T. and Simulated E.C.T. in Chronic Schizophrenia. *Brit. J. Psychiatry* 110, 469.

Foulds, G.A., with collab. of T.M. Caines and assistance of A. Adams and A. Owen (1965) *Personality and Personal Illness*, Tavistock, London.

Alvarez, A. (1977) Problems of Dependence and Development in an Excessively Passive Autistic Boy. *J. Child Psychotherapy* 4.

Alvarez, A. (1980) Two Regenerative Situations in Autism. *J. Child Psychotherapy* 6.

Alvrez, A. (1983) Problems in the Use of the Counter-transference: Getting it Across. *J. Child Psychotherapy* 9.

Alvarez, A. (1985) The Problem of Neutrality: Some Reflections on the Psychoanalytic Attitude in the Treatment of Borderline and Psychotic Children. *J. of Child Psychotherapy* 11. (Also published in Italian in *Il Setting*, Borla, Rome, 1985.)

Alvarez, A. (1986) Identificazione Proiettiva- Meccanismo o Processo? Problemi nell'uso del controtransfert, in M. Pontecorvo, *Il Modello Tavistock*, Psycho, Florence.

Alvarez, A. (1987) Moderni sviluppi nell psicoterapia psicoanlitica coi bambini. *Giorn. Neuropsic. Eta Evol.* 7, 3: 247–254 (Turin).

Alvarez, A. (1988) Beyond the Unpleasure Principle: Some Preconditions for Thinking Through Play. *J. Child Psychotherapy* 14, 2.

Alvarez, A. (1989) Ways of Seeing. *J. Child Psychotherapy* 15, 2.

Alvarez, A. (1989) Development Toward the Latency Period: Splitting and the Need to Forget in Borderline Children. *J. Child Psychotherapy* 15, 2.

Alvarez, A. (1989) Child Sexual Abuse – the Need to Remember and the Need to Forget, in *The Consequences of Child Sexual Abuse*, ACPP Occasional Papers No. 3.

Alvarez, A. (1990) Play: Denial of Depression or Expression of Hope? *Bambini 90*, Maggio, Bergamo.

Alvarez, A. (1990) Reparation: Some Precursors. *J. of Group Processes*, Rome.

Alvarez, A. (1991) Wildest Dreams: Aspiration, Identification, and Symbol-formation in Depressed Children. *Psychoanal. Psychother.* 5, 3: 177–188.

Alvarez, A. (1993) An Interactional Approach to the Psychotherapy of Autism, in *Richard & Piggle*, Il Pensiero Scientifio Editore, Rome.

Alvarez, A. (1995) Motiveless Malignity: problems in the Psychotherapy of Psychopathic Patients. *J. of Child Psychotherapy* 21, 2.

Alvarez, A. (1995) Fantasia inconscia, pensare e camminare: alcune riflessioni preliminare, in *Richard e Piggle* 2, Il Pensiero Scientifico, Rome.

Alvarez, A. (1996) Different Uses of the Counter-transference with Neurotic Borderline and Psychotic Patients, in J. Tsiantis, A.-M. Sandler, D. Anastasopoulos and B. Martindale (eds) *Countertransference in Psychoanalytic Psychotherapy with Children and Adolescents*, EFPP Clinical Monograph Series, Karnac, London.

Alvarez, A. (1996) Addressing the Element of Deficit in Children with Autism: Psychotherapy which is both Psychoanalytically and Developmentally Informed. *Clinical Child Psychology and Psychiatry* 1, 4.

Alvarez, A. (1996) Projektive Identifizierung als Kommunikation: Ihre Grammatik bei Borderline-psychotischen Kindern, in *PsA-Info* Nr. 47, Berlin.

Alvarez, A. (1997) Speculations on Components in the Infant's Sense of Agency: The Sense of Abundance and the Capacity to Think in Parentheses, in S. Reid (ed.) *New Developments in Infant Observation*, Routledge, London.

Alvarez, A. (1996) The Clinician's Debt to Winnicott. *J. of Child Psychotherapy* 22, 3: 373–401.

Alvarez, A. (1997) Projective Identification as a Communication: Its Grammar in Borderline Psychotic Children. *Psychoanalytic Dialogues* 7, 6 (Symposium on Child Analysis, Part I).

Alvarez, A. (1998) Failures to Link: Attacks or Defects? Some Questions Concerning the Thinkability of Oedipal and Pre-Oedipal Thoughts. *J. of Child Psychotherapy* 24, 2.

Alvarez, A. (1998) Response to Blake Morrison's Lecture on Childhood and Violence at BJP Annual Lecture. *British J. of Psychotherapy* 14, 4.

Alvarez, A. (1998) Form in Unconscious Phantasy, Thinking and Walking, in Junqeira Filho, L.C.U., *Silencios e luzes: sobre a experiencia do vazio e da forma* (Silences and lights: concerning the experience of emptiness and form), Sao Paolo, Publisher.

Alvarez, A. and Phillips, A. (1998) The Importance of Play: A Child Psychotherapist's View. *Journal of Child Psychology and Psychiatry*, Forum on Play.

Alvarez, A. (1999) Motiveless Malignity: Problems in the Psychotherapy of Psychopathic Patients. In Tavistock issue of *Psychoanalytic Inquiry*.

Alvarez, A. (1999) Widening the Bridge: Commentary on Paper by Stephen Seligman and Paper by Robin C. Silverman and Alicia F. Lieberman. *Psychoanalytic Dialogues* 92.

Alvarez, A., Hodges, S. and Reid, S. (1999) Autism and Play. *Child Language Teaching and Therapy* 15, 1.

Alvarez, A. (1999) Frustration and Separateness, Delight and Connectedness: Reflections on the Conditions Under which Bad and Good Surprises are Conducive to Learning. *J. of Child Psychotherapy*, 25: No. 2.

Alvarez, A. (2000) La prise en compte de la deficience de chez l'enfant autiste: une psychotherapie d'inspiration psychanalitique de developpmentale. *Journal de la Psychanalyse de l'Enfant* 26: 263–290.

Alvarez, A. (2000) Discussion Il, in J. Sandler, A.M. Sandler and R. Davies (eds) *Clinical and Observational Psychoanalytic Research: Roots of a Controversy*. Psychoanalytic Monograph No. 5, Karnac, London.

Alvarez, A. (2000) Moral Imperatives in Work with Borderline Children: The Grammar of Wishes and the Grammar of Needs, in J. Symington (ed.) *Imprisoned Pain and its Transformation: A Festschrift for H. Sydney Klein*, Karnac, London.

Author Index

Subject Index

abandonment: trauma of, clinical illustration 111, *see also* loss; separation

absence: and presence, experience of 183–4; and presence, thought generated by 179–80; sound in the womb 161, *see also* loss; separation

abundance, developing a sense of 128–38

adaptation, and construction of the object 116

adhesive identification 90, 91; separation anxiety 100, *see also* identification

adolescence: autistic child thawing-out, clinical illustration 96, 98–100; as critical period for autistic children 90, 91, *see also* children

affect regulation 65–6

affects: mother-infant relationship 58; as psychobiological phenomena 67, *see also* projective identification

aggression 11

alexithymia 24

alone: ability to tolerate 103, 104, *see also* separateness

amygdala 18

analyst-analysand relationship: and mother-infant relationship 23; space 78, *see also* countertransference; transference

anxieties: adolescence 90; and hearability of interpretations 77–8; holding and giving interpretations 79; as motivation 39; separation anxiety 100, *see also* terror

assimilation, and construction of the object 116

at-one-ness 183

attachment: attachment theory 154; disorganized/disoriented attachment 64; insecure attachment and projective identification 70; and learning xvi; neuroscience view of 67–8, 69; post-natal depression, impact 162; and projective identification 62

attention: joint attention 132, 136–7; mother's capacity for 128–9; suspension of 176

attunement 62; overattunement in autistic children 143; shared attunement 181

Autism and Personality (Alvarez and Reid) 4, 57

autobiographical memory 26–7n

autonomic hyperarousal 65

autonomic nervous system (ANS) 63, 67

autoregulation 65

avoidant strategy 64

basin of attraction 51

Belief and Imagination (Britton) 84

'Beyond the Pleasure Principle' (Freud) 48, 50, 78

binocular vision 135

birth: as caesura 158; premature birth, breakdown of rhythmical containment 184–92; premature birth, clinical illustrations 156–8, 159–60, 161–3,